Artificial Intelligence and Architecture

From Research to Practice

Second Edition
Updated & Expanded

Stanislas Chaillou

Birkhäuser
Basel

Stanislas Chaillou

On behalf of the publisher
Acquisitions Editor: David Marold
Content Editor: Bettina R. Algieri
Production Editor: Heike Strempel-Bevacqua

Proofreading: Alisa Kotmair
Layout, cover design, and typography: Stanislas Chaillou
Image editing: Stanislas Chaillou
Printing: Beltz Grafische Betriebe GmbH, Bad Langensalza, Germany
Paper: Magno Natural 120 g/m²
Typeface: Geist, Geist Mono, Neue Haas Grotesk

Library of Congress Control Number: 2025936962

Bibliographic information published by the German National Library
The German National Library lists this publication in the Deutsche Nationalbibliografie; detailed bibliographic data are available at http://dnb.dnb.de.

1st edition, Birkhäuser 2022
2nd, expanded edition 2025:
ISBN 978-3-0356-2941-5
e-ISBN (PDF) 978-3-0356-2942-2

Im Westfeld 8, 4055 Basel, Switzerland
Part of Walter de Gruyter GmbH, Berlin/Boston

Questions about General Product Safety Regulation:
productsafety@degruyterbrill.com

9 8 7 6 5 4 3 2 www.birkhauser.com

ACKNOWLEDGEMENTS

Before anything else, I would like to take the opportunity to thank the people who made this new edition possible — our contributors — for their time and effort: Foster + Partners' Applied R+D team, Immanuel Koh, Mario Carpo, Anastasis Germanidis, Andrew Witt, Carlo Ratti, the team at Coop Himmelb(l)au, Aaron Hertzmann, and Phillip Bernstein. I am also grateful to David Marold at Birkhäuser for his continued support of this project. Last but not least, I would like to dedicate this book once again to Reinier.

ABOUT THE AUTHOR

Stanislas Chaillou is a Paris-based architect and machine learning engineer. He is the co-founder of Rayon, a software company building a new generation of software for the AEC industry. He holds a Bachelor of Science in Architecture from the École polytechnique fédérale de Lausanne (2015) and a Master of Architecture from Harvard University's Graduate School of Design (2019). Since 2018, his work has focused on the theoretical and experimental aspects of artificial intelligence in architecture. Stanislas was the curator of the exhibition "Artificial Intelligence & Architecture," held at the Arsenal Pavilion in Paris in 2020. He is also the author of several books, including "The Architect's Sourcebook" (Birkhäuser, 2024), "Artificial Intelligence and Architecture: From Research to Practice" (Birkhäuser, 2022), and "L'Intelligence Artificielle au service de l'Architecture" (Moniteur Editions, 2021).

Table of contents

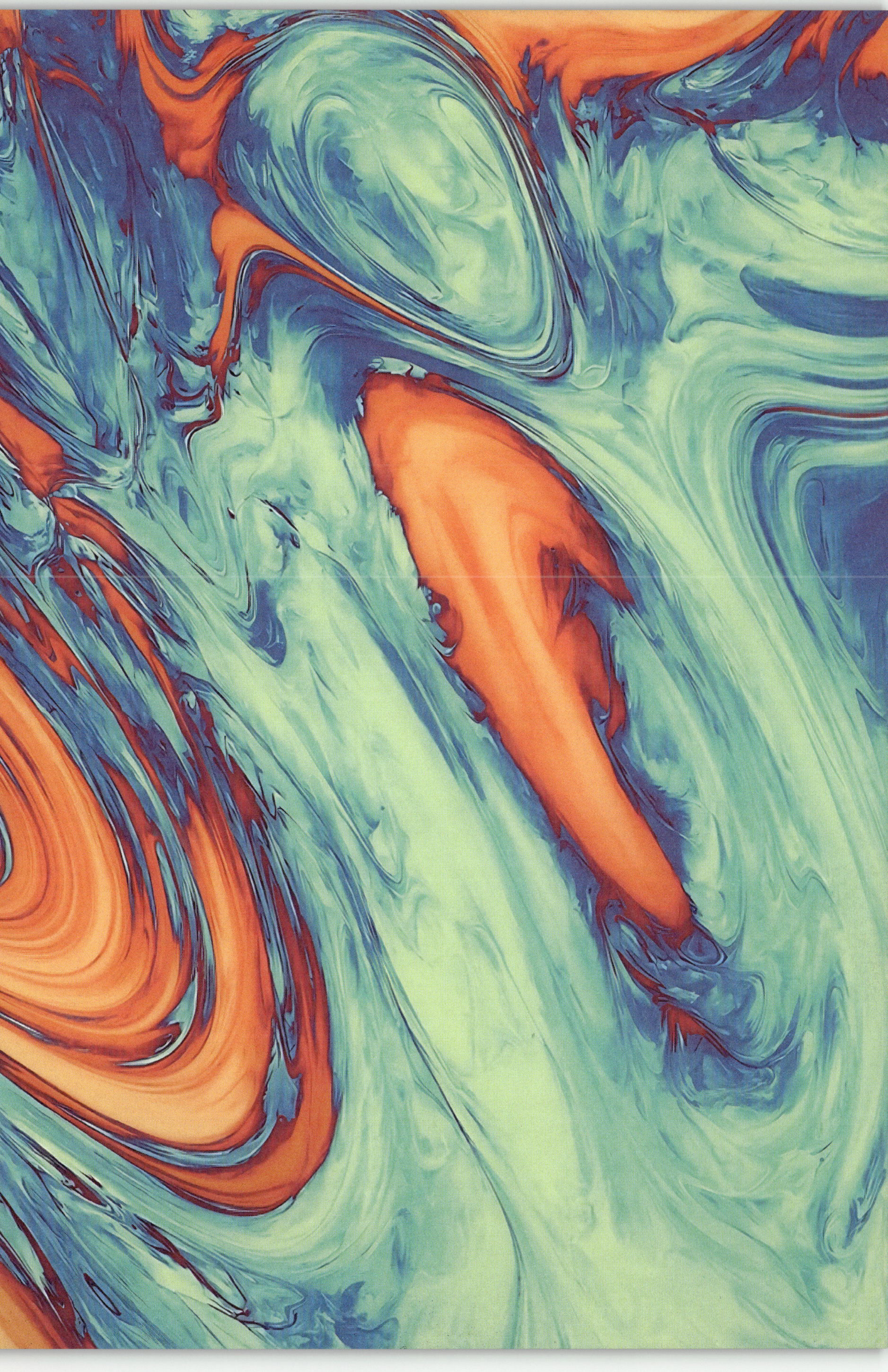

Foreword

Three years: that is the span of time it took for the rapid pace of advancements in artificial intelligence (AI) to render the first edition of this book nearly obsolete. In that brief period, AI has not only gained unprecedented recognition beyond our discipline but has also earned a place in the highest echelons of scientific achievement.

Just last year, Geoffrey E. Hinton and John J. Hopfield were awarded the Nobel Prize in Physics for their contributions to machine learning. Within the architectural sphere, the 2025 Venice Architecture Biennale explicitly embraced the notion of intelligence, placing AI at the center of its discourse. The convergence of these events underscores the seismic shift witnessed in merely 36 months — an evolution that has transformed AI from an emergent technology into an indispensable force shaping the trajectory of architectural thought and practice.

This second edition, therefore, emerges in direct response to a fundamental reality: AI's presence, initially external to architecture, has now become deeply woven into the discipline itself. Since our last exhibit, "Artificial Intelligence and Architecture," at the Arsenal Pavillion (Fig. 1, Paris, 2019), AI has left its infancy behind and entered a phase of accelerated deployment, transitioning from isolated experimental applications to large-scale integration within architectural design, theory, and practice. Consequently, the imperative to frame the discussion around its assimilation into our field has grown exponentially. Yet this phenomenon is not confined to architecture alone. The discipline's encounter with AI is but one manifestation of a broader technological shift — an inflection point that is redefining creative fields at large. Architecture stands as

1

Interior view of the virtual exhibit "Artificial Intelligence and Architecture," Arsenal Pavilion, Paris, 2019.

We invite readers to explore the virtual exhibit, accessible online through the QR code below.

one of many disciplines being reshaped by the proliferation of AI, as artistic, engineering, and scientific domains all grapple with its disruptive potential.

At its core, the transformation of the past three years is not merely the result of isolated breakthroughs but rather the culmination of longer-term trends that have now reached maturity. Several key developments have catalyzed this new era: the rise of foundation models, which have recalibrated the scope and scale of AI applications; the restructuring of AI's value chain, which has altered how expertise, tools, and computational power are distributed; and the increasing democratization of access to AI, allowing a far broader range of practitioners to experiment with and deploy these technologies. Against this backdrop, a quorum of researchers, theorists, and practitioners — spanning entrepreneurs, designers, and academics — has emerged to shepherd AI's integration into architecture, ensuring that this technological turn is accompanied by rigorous discourse and critical reflection.

This book aims to contribute to our discipline's understanding of the full magnitude of this transformation. To that end, it adopts three complementary perspectives, each offering a pedagogical lens through which to examine AI's architectural implications. By exploring the historical, experimental, and theoretical dimensions of AI's introduction into architecture, this volume invites readers to engage with both the tangible and speculative aspects of this encounter.

The first section takes a historical approach, situating AI within a broader conversation that has long shaped the intersection of technology and architecture. By tracing its conceptual lineage, this segment contextualizes contemporary developments within the technological discourses that have animated architectural thought over the past century.

The second section transitions into an exploration of experimental applications, grounding the discussion in recent advances in AI research as they pertain to architecture. Here, the emphasis shifts to concrete outcomes — research papers, computational workflows, and existing software — that illustrate the ways in which AI is materially and operationally transforming architectural practice. Finally, the third section provides a platform for leading theorists, researchers, and designers currently at the vanguard of this revolution. From esteemed academic institutions such as Harvard and University College London to pioneering technology firms like Runway and Adobe, as well as leading architectural practices including Coop Himmelb(l)au and Foster + Partners, this segment presents a diverse array of perspectives that together offer a telling sample of the evolving discourse surrounding AI's role in architecture.

Beyond merely documenting AI's emergence within the field, this book seeks to engage with its broader theoretical and speculative dimensions. Five years into AI's integration into architecture, we are now in a position to discern the deeper tendencies that define this moment — its underlying logics, its philosophical undercurrents, and its implications for the discipline's future. While the initial years were marked by fascination with AI's technical capabilities, we have now reached a point where more critical, nuanced, and reflective discussions can take shape. This book, therefore, does not merely catalogue the present state of AI in architecture; it aims to interrogate its direction and significance within a larger historical arc of technological change.

In doing so, it aspires to equip architects, scholars, and students with the intellectual tools necessary to navigate this evolving landscape — one in which AI is not merely an external instrument but a force that is actively redefining the very parameters of architectural imagination and practice.

CHAPTER I

Artificial Intelligence

ANOTHER FIELD

"Stories about the creation of machines having human qualities have long been a fascinating province in the realm of science fiction; yet we are about to witness the birth of such a machine — a machine capable of perceiving, recognizing, and identifying its surroundings without any human training or control."

1 Rosenblatt, "The Design of an Intelligent Automaton," 1958.

These words by Frank Rosenblatt in 1958 capture the bold optimism of early AI pioneers. Yet nearly 70 years later, his vision remains a work in progress. The trajectory of AI has been anything but linear (Fig. 1), shaped by cycles of breakthroughs and setbacks. From its theoretical foundations in the 1940s and 1950s to the deep learning revolution, AI has evolved through a gradual accumulation of knowledge and technological advancements.

Far from the isolated research efforts of its early years, AI today intersects with a wide range of disciplines — architecture among them. Understanding its role in this field requires a look at its foundational principles, the challenges it has faced over time, and the ways in which it has transformed industries beyond computer science.

1

AI timeline, from the postwar period to the generative AI boom of the 2020s.

Postwar Period
1950s

First AI Winter
1970s

Expert Systems
1980s

Artificial Neuron
W. McCulloch & W. Pitts ('43)

Transistor
Bell Labs ('47)

Dartmouth Workshop
('56)

Perceptron
F. Rosenblatt ('57)

ELIZA
J. Weizenbaum ('66)

"Perceptrons"
M. Minsky, S. Pappert ('69)

Lighthill Report
J. Lighhill ('73)

R1 Program
J. McDermott ('78)

SID Program
DEC ('82)

Second AI Winter
1990s

Deep Learning Revolution
2010s

Generative AI
2020s

CYC Program
D. Lenat ('84)

"Some Expert Systems Need Common Sense"
J. McCarthy ('84)

DeepBlue vs Kasparov
('97)

Stanley at DARPA Challenge
('05)

AlexNET
A. Krizhevsky
('12)

Generative Adversarial Net
I. Goodfellow
('14)

AlphaGO vs Sedol
('16)

Transformers
Vaswani et al.
('17)

Diffusers
Ho et al.
('20)

Notion of Foundation Model
Stanford CRFM
('21)

Postwar Period

The 1940s represent a pivotal juncture in the history of artificial intelligence, marked by a confluence of breakthroughs that would establish the foundational principles of the field. During this decade, multiple scientific disciplines — ranging from neuroscience to electrical engineering — contributed to the nascent conceptualization of machine intelligence. In 1943, American scientists **Warren McCulloch and Walter Pitts formulated the first mathematical model of the biological neuron**. Although largely theoretical, their work provided the scientific community with an early framework for understanding the computational principles underlying neural activity. Their model described the logical operations a neuron could perform to process and transmit information, effectively introducing the rudimentary concept of an artificial neural network. This early theoretical insight laid the groundwork for later developments in machine learning and computational neuroscience.

2 McCulloch and Pitts, "A Logical Calculus of the Ideas Immanent in Nervous Activity," 1943.

The significance of McCulloch and Pitts's model was soon amplified by an equally transformative invention emerging from Bell Laboratories, a research institution operated by the US telecommunications company AT&T. In 1947, physicists **John Bardeen, Walter Houser Brattain, and William Bradford Shockley developed the transistor**, a new type of semiconductor device that could amplify or regulate electrical signals (Fig. 2). This invention proved instrumental in translating theoretical models of artificial networks into tangible computing systems. The transistor's ability to enable efficient signal processing meant that complex neural models, previously confined to mathematical abstraction, could now be implemented in physical circuits. As a result, the confluence of computational theory and hardware innovation set the stage for future advancements in AI.

3 Bell Labs, "The 1956 Nobel Prize in Physics," 1956.

A decade later, this synergy of theoretical and hardware advancements culminated in a landmark experiment conducted by American psychologist Frank

Rosenblatt at the Cornell Aeronautical Laboratory. In 1957, Rosenblatt successfully built and tested the Perceptron (Fig. 3), an early machine learning model designed to classify visual images. Unlike earlier algorithmic approaches, the Perceptron introduced a self-adjusting mechanism that enabled it to refine its predictive accuracy over time (Fig. 4). This process — now known as training — allowed the model to modify its internal parameters through a feedback-driven learning cycle. The novelty of Rosenblatt's approach attracted widespread attention, with The New York Times lauding it as a "New Navy Device [that] Learns by Doing." The Perceptron's ability to adapt autonomously represented a radical departure from rigid, rule-based computation, offering a glimpse into the potential of machines capable of learning from experience. This development marked a significant leap forward and laid the foundation for future research in machine learning.

5 McCarthy et al., "A Proposal for the Dartmouth Summer Research Project on Artificial Intelligence," 1955.

In parallel, another critical milestone was achieved in 1956 at **the Dartmouth Summer Research Project**, where a group of pioneering scientists formally introduced the term "artificial intelligence." Organized at Dartmouth College, this seminal workshop convened key figures in the field, including Marvin Minsky, John McCarthy, Ray Solomonoff, and Oliver Selfridge. The participants sought to define AI in explicit terms, proposing that intelligence could be replicated in machines by emulating the fundamental cognitive processes of the human brain. Their discussions provided an initial blueprint for AI research, framing it as an interdisciplinary pursuit that would integrate insights from logic, probability, and neuroscience. The Dartmouth workshop is widely recognized as the official birth of AI as a distinct scientific discipline, setting a long-term research agenda that would influence subsequent decades.

6 Weizenbaum, "ELIZA, A Computer Program for the Study of Natural Language Communication Between Man and Machine," 1966.

The period following these early theoretical and conceptual breakthroughs saw the practical application of AI expand into various domains. One particularly promising area was natural language processing (NLP), which sought to enable computers to engage in human-like textual interactions. A notable example from this era was **ELIZA, a chatbot developed in 1966 by German-American scientist Joseph Weizenbaum** (Fig. 5). Designed to simulate human conversation, ELIZA relied on pattern-matching techniques to generate responses that mimicked natural dialogue. Though relatively simplistic by today's standards, the program demonstrated that machines could convincingly engage in structured exchanges, offering an early glimpse into the potential of AI-driven communication systems.

At the same time, robotics engineering began leveraging AI to grant machines a degree of autonomy. Industrial applications of AI-powered automation emerged as early as the 1950s, exemplified by the development of Unimate, the first industrial robot. Created by American engineers George Devol and Joseph Engelberger, Unimate

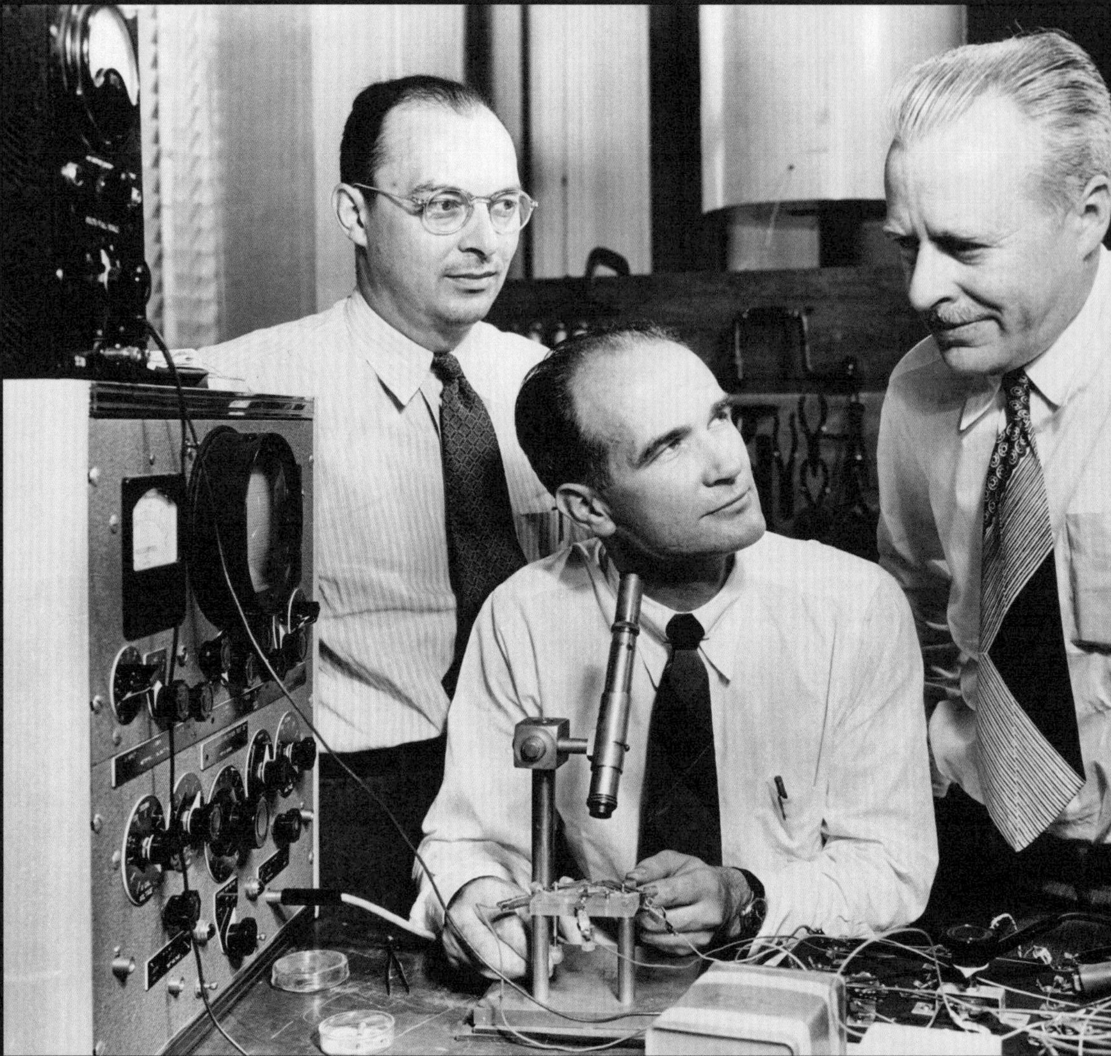

2

J. Bardeen, W. B. Shockley, W. Brattain and the transistor at Bell Labs in 1948.

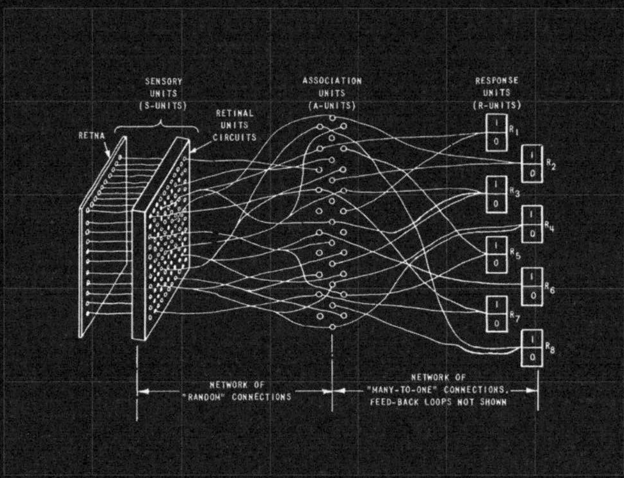

4

Diagram of the functional logic of the Mark I Perceptron computer, by Frank Rosenblatt.

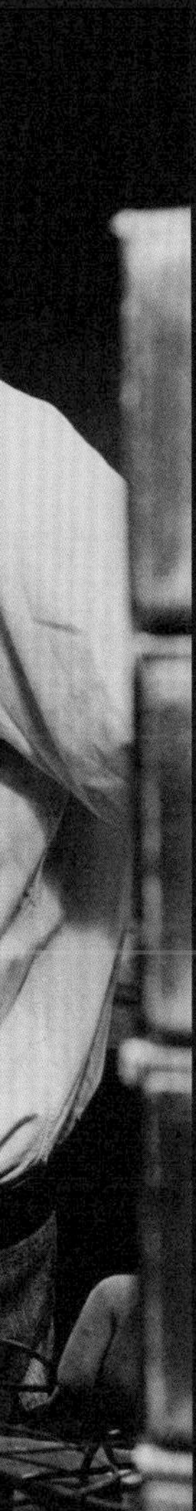

5

A conversation
with the ELIZA
chatbot.

```
Welcome to
                    EEEEEE  LL      IIII   ZZZZZZ   AAAAA
                    EE      LL       II       ZZ   AA   AA
                    EEEEE   LL       II     ZZZ    AAAAAAA
                    EE      LL       II    ZZ      AA   AA
                    EEEEEE  LLLLLL  IIII ZZZZZZ    AA   AA

Eliza is a mock Rogerian psychotherapist.
The original program was described by Joseph Weizenbaum in 1966.
This implementation by Norbert Landsteiner 2005.

ELIZA: Is something troubling you ?
YOU:   Men are all alike.
ELIZA: What is the connection, do you suppose ?
YOU:   They're always bugging us about something or other.
ELIZA: Can you think of a specific example ?
YOU:   Well, my boyfriend made me come here.
ELIZA: Is it important to you that your boyfriend made you come here ?
YOU:   He says I'm depressed much of the time.
ELIZA: I am sorry to hear that you are depressed.
YOU:   It's true. I am unhappy.
ELIZA: Can you explain what made you unhappy ?
YOU:
```

3

Frank Rosenblatt
and the Perceptron.

Bridgeport

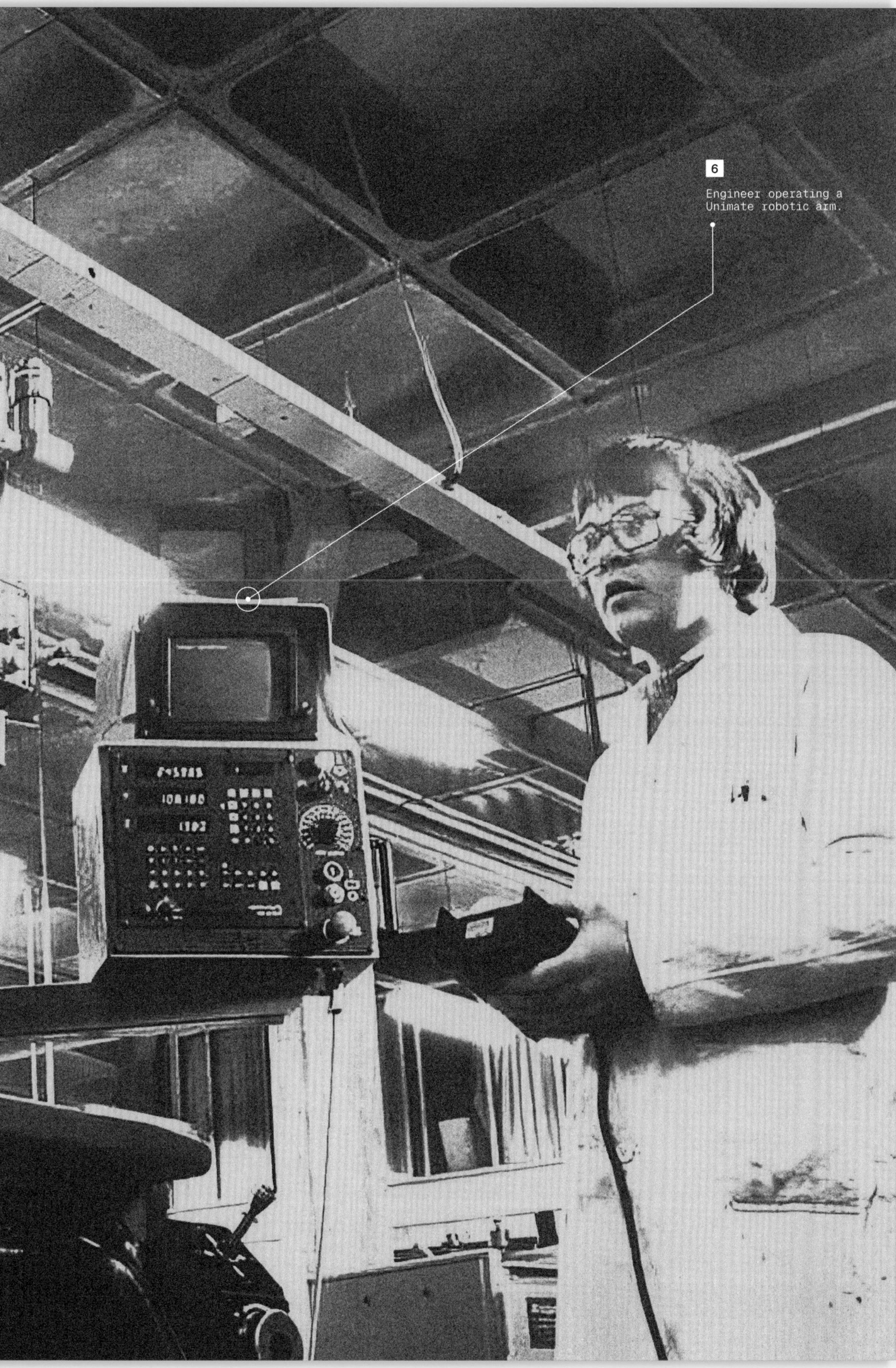

6

Engineer operating a Unimate robotic arm.

was deployed in 1961 on General Motors' assembly lines (Fig. 6). Its robotic arm could transport manufactured parts and perform welding tasks, significantly enhancing production efficiency. Unimate's successful implementation in a real-world setting demonstrated AI's transformative potential in industrial automation and laid the foundation for modern robotics.

ELIZA and Unimate exemplify the broad enthusiasm that characterized AI research during this formative period. As the field continued to yield tangible results, confidence in its future prospects grew. The American cognitive psychologist Herbert Simon aptly captured the prevailing optimism, asserting: **"The simplest way I can summarize is to say that there are now in the world machines that think, that learn, and that create. Moreover, their ability to do these things is going to increase rapidly until [...] the range of problems they can handle will be coextensive with the range to which the human mind has been applied."** Simon's statement reflected the prevailing belief that AI would soon achieve significant milestones across multiple disciplines. However, this optimism would soon be tempered by the onset of significant technical and conceptual challenges, leading to a prolonged period of stagnation in AI research. The initial momentum of the 1960s would soon give way to an era marked by skepticism and funding constraints, challenging the field's trajectory for the decades to come.

7 Simon, "Heuristic Problem Solving: The Next Advance," 1958.

REFERENCES

A Proposal for the Dartmouth Summer Research Project on Artificial Intelligence
[Article]
McCarthy, Minsky, Rochester, Shannon, 1955

The Perceptron, a Paper by F. Rosenblatt
[Article]
Psychological Review 65.6, 1958

Demonstration of ELIZA
[Video]
Interview, Joseph Weizenbaum

The Transistor
[Video]
Documentary, AT&T, 1953

The Perceptron
[Video]
The Machine That Changed the World, Documentary, 1992

What Is AI? Basic Questions With John McCarthy
[Article]
Stanford University

A Robot for Industry
[Video]
Unimate Demonstration, AP, 1967

Interview, Warren S. McCulloch
[Video]
Canadian Broadcasting Co., 1969

Expert Systems & AI Winters

Throughout the 1960s and 1970s, and again in the 1990s, the field of artificial intelligence endured two significant periods of stagnation and disillusionment, now commonly referred to as the "AI winters." These episodes were marked by a stark contrast between the initial enthusiasm surrounding AI research and the subsequent downturn in confidence, both within the private sector and among academic institutions. Funding dried up, public interest waned, and the once-promising advancements in AI were met with widespread skepticism.

The first AI winter arose in the wake of Frank Rosenblatt's pioneering experiments with the Perceptron. While early successes had generated excitement, a confluence of factors contributed to growing disenchantment with neural networks and AI in general. Two publications from this period became emblematic of the deepening doubts surrounding the field. The first, **"Perceptrons" (1969)**, was co-authored by Marvin Minsky and Seymour Papert. Their critical analysis underscored what they perceived as fundamental limitations in Rosenblatt's Perceptron model, particularly its inability to solve complex problems beyond linear classification. The book cast a shadow over the feasibility of neural networks, discouraging further research in the area.

8 Minsky and Papert, Perceptrons: An Introduction to Computational Geometry, 1969.

The growing skepticism was compounded by the "Lighthill Report" (Fig. 7) in 1973, commissioned by the British government and authored by mathematician James Lighthill. Originally titled **"Artificial Intelligence: A General Survey,"** the report provided a comprehensive assessment of AI's progress and shortcomings. Lighthill's conclusions were notably pessimistic, as he asserted: **"Most workers in AI research and in related fields confess to a pronounced feeling of disappointment in what has been achieved in the past twenty-five years. Workers entered the field around 1950, and even around 1960, with high hopes that are very far from having been realized**

9 Lighthill, "Artificial Intelligence: A General Survey," 1973.

10 Lighthill, "Artificial Intelligence: A General Survey," 1973, p. 8, 1973.

in 1972. In no part of the field have the discoveries made so far produced the major impact that was then promised." These assertions reinforced the notion that AI research had failed to deliver on its early promises, leading to a sudden, sharp decline in funding. Both public and private investments were either frozen or redirected to more traditionally scientific endeavors, forcing AI research into a prolonged period of dormancy.

Despite these setbacks, the 1980s ushered in a revival of AI, fueled in part by the emergence of expert systems. These models, leveraging rule-based reasoning and knowledge representation, gained traction due to their ability to operate reliably within well-defined domains. The increased availability of computational power further facilitated the resurgence of AI research, attracting renewed interest and investment from both governmental agencies and private enterprises. As a result, funding flowed back into the field, enabling researchers to develop sophisticated AI applications.

Among the most influential expert systems of this era was DENDRAL, developed beginning in 1965 at Stanford University by computer scientist Edward Feigenbaum — often referred to as the "father of expert systems" (Fig. 8) — and geneticist Joshua Lederberg. Considered one of the first expert systems ever built, DENDRAL used a basic inference engine to apply a structured set of facts stored in a knowledge base to answer user queries about chemical-analysis (Fig. 9). The functioning logic of DENDRAL served as a model for many expert system-based projects that followed, including the MYCIN project, launched at Stanford in 1972 (Fig. 10). Designed to assist medical professionals in diagnosing bacterial infections, **MYCIN employed a knowledge base of approximately 600 rules** to infer potential diagnoses and recommend appropriate treatments. While the system was never implemented in clinical practice, it served as a compelling demonstration of expert systems' potential within specialized fields.

11 Buchanan and Shortliffe, Rule-Based Expert Systems: The MYCIN Experiments, 1984.

Another landmark achievement was R1, also known as XCON, developed by John P. McDermott in 1978. Unlike MYCIN, R1 was actively deployed in a commercial setting, assisting the US computer manufacturer Digital Equipment Corporation (DEC) in automating the configuration of computer systems based on customer requirements. By efficiently processing complex orders, R1 significantly improved the reliability and accuracy of DEC's manufacturing processes, showcasing the tangible benefits of expert systems in industrial applications.

12 Matuszek et al., "An Introduction to the Syntax and Content of Cyc," 2006.

Perhaps the most ambitious expert system of this period was **Cyc, a project launched in 1984 by AI researcher Douglas Lenat**. Cyc sought to model common-sense knowledge by encoding a vast array of facts and rules about the world.

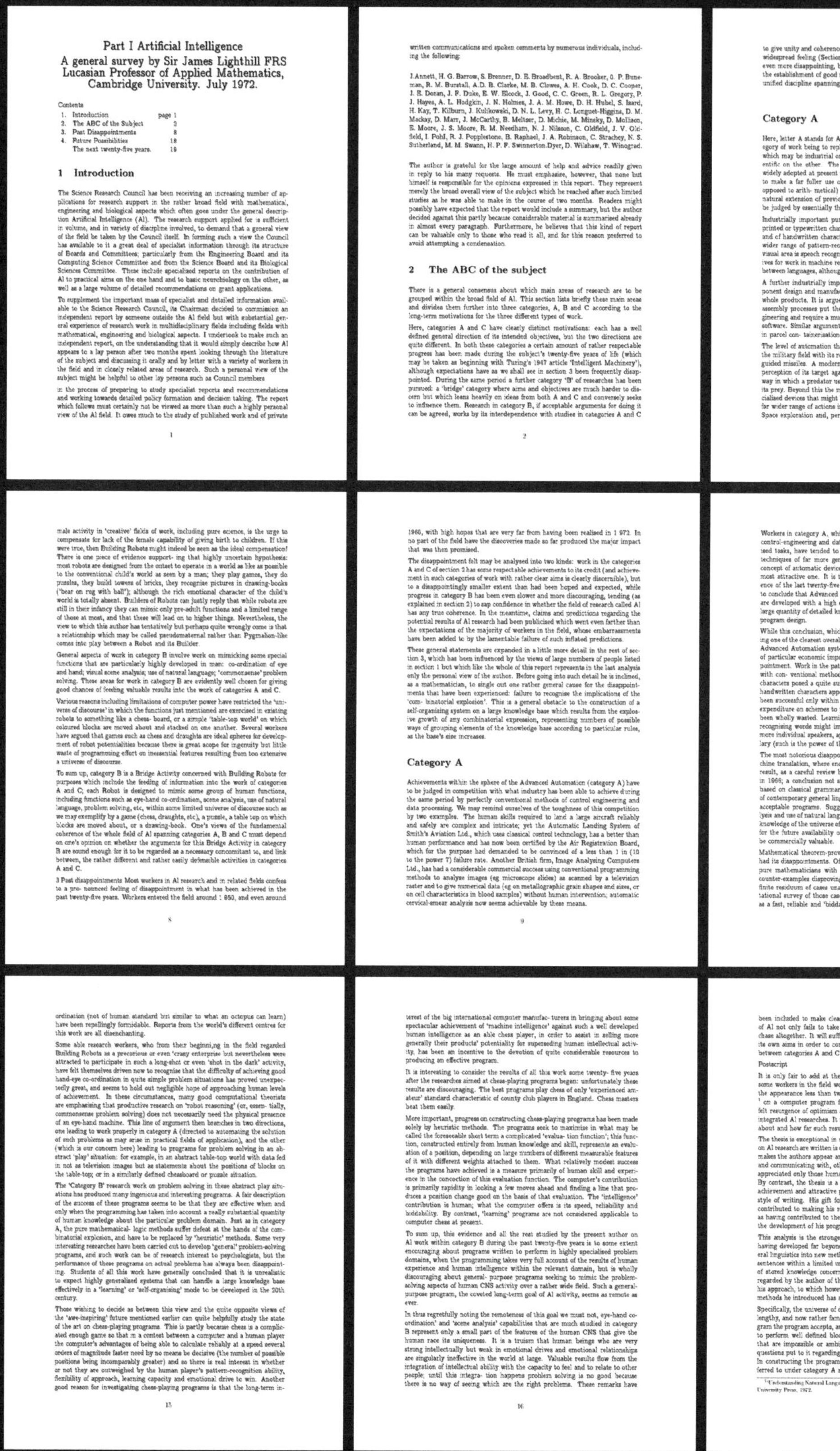

7

"Artificial Intelligence: A General Survey," also known as the Lighthill Report, a 22-page document that triggered the first AI winter, 1973.

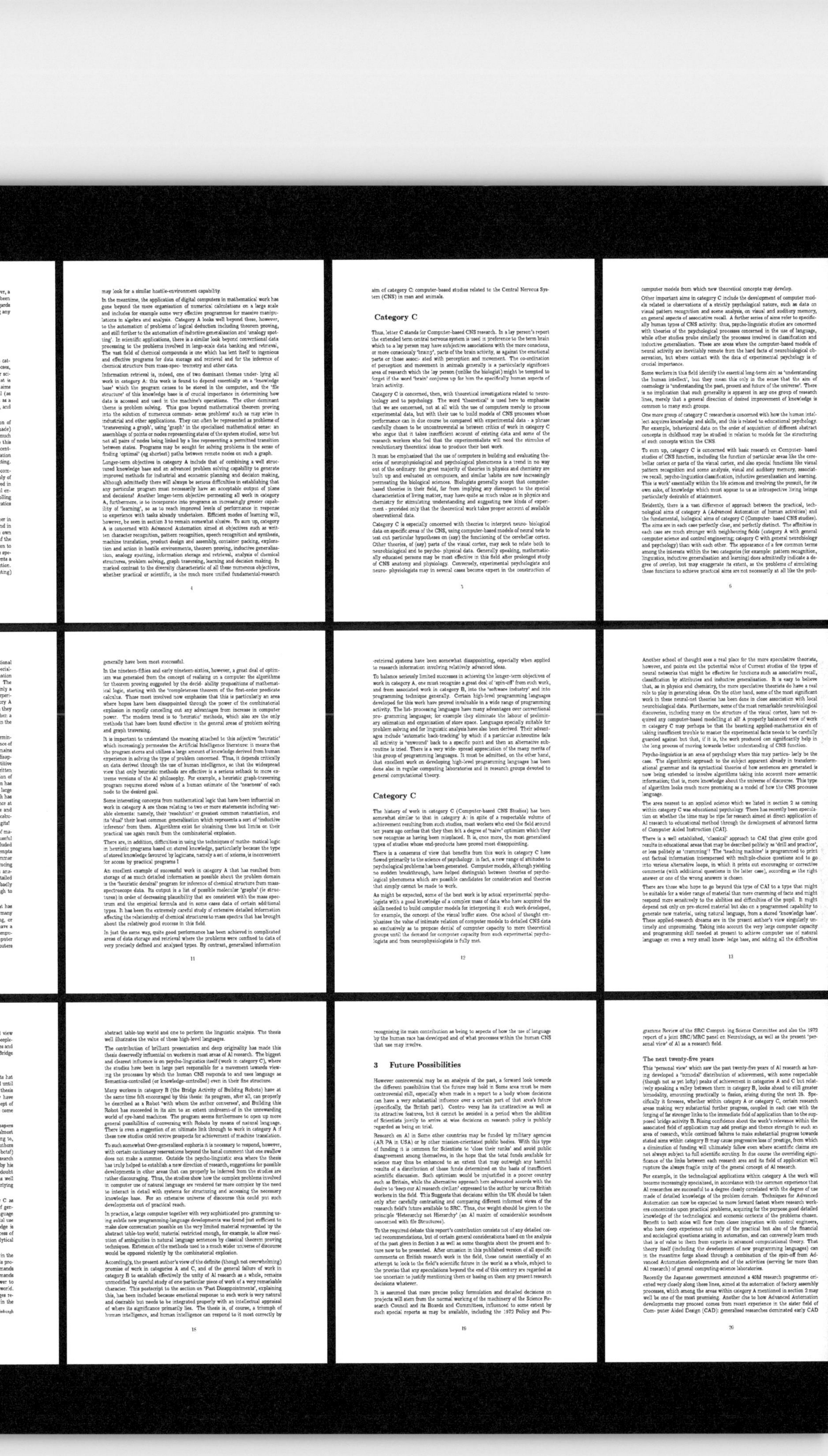
Category C
Category C
3 Future Possibilities
The next twenty-five years

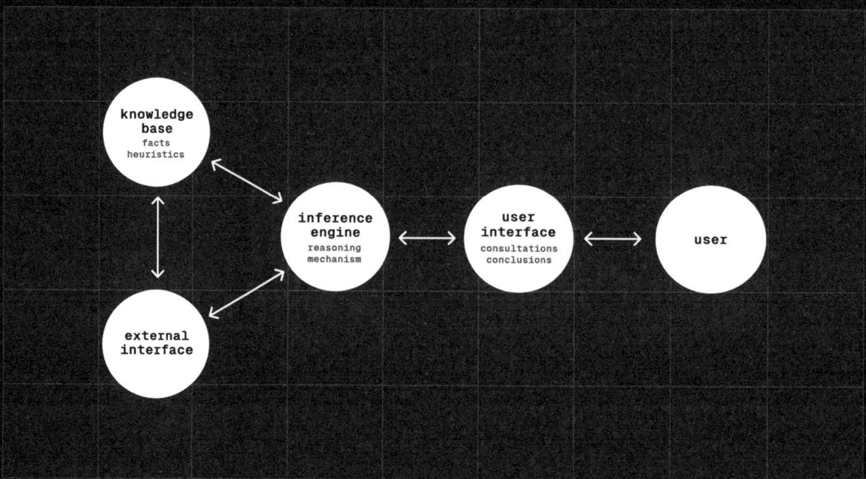

9

Functional logic of the DENDRAL expert system.

8

Edward Feigenbaum, director of the Stanford Computation Center, with members of its board of directors, 1966.

10

Cover of the MCYIN expert system research publication, 1972.

This extensive knowledge base was intended to enable AI systems to perform reasoning tasks that require an understanding of everyday concepts. The project remains ongoing under the stewardship of Cycorp — a testament to the enduring interest in knowledge-based AI models.

Despite these advancements, expert systems eventually encountered significant limitations, leading to another period of stagnation. By the late 1980s, researchers began to recognize that expert systems struggled to adapt beyond their predefined rule sets. These models lacked the ability to generalize knowledge beyond the narrow domains for which they had been programmed, making them inflexible in the face of novel or ambiguous scenarios. John McCarthy articulated this critique in his essay **"Some Expert Systems Need Common Sense,"** in which he highlighted the systems' inability to recognize their own limitations or extend their reasoning beyond their initial design parameters.

13 McCarthy, "Some Expert Systems Need Common Sense," 1984.

Simultaneously, institutional support for AI research began to wane. Jacob T. Schwartz, then director of the Information Science & Technology Office (ISTO) at DARPA, echoed similar concerns regarding the constraints of expert systems. In response, DARPA significantly reduced its funding for AI projects, further exacerbating the challenges facing the field. As investment declined and skepticism mounted, AI research once again entered a prolonged period of stagnation, marking the onset of the second AI winter.

This second downturn persisted throughout the 1990s, mirroring the earlier decline of the 1970s. With diminished financial support and growing disillusionment, AI was once again relegated to the periphery of technological research. However, as history would later demonstrate, these periods of stagnation were not the end of AI but rather temporary setbacks in a long and cyclical journey. In time, the limitations of expert systems would pave the way for a paradigm shift, ultimately leading to the resurgence of AI through the advent of machine learning and deep learning techniques in the 21st century.

REFERENCES

Some Expert Systems Need Common Sense
[Article]
John McCarthy, Stanford University, 1984

The Society of Mind
[Book]
Marvin Minsky, Touchstone, 1986

Perceptrons: Intro to Computational Geometry
[Book]
M. Minsky, S. Papert, MIT Press, 1988

Why Did Expert Systems Fail?
[Video]
Interview, D. Korkin by L. Fridman, 2021

Artificial Intelligence: A General Survey
[Article]
James Lighthill, 1973

The General-Purpose Robot Is a Mirage
[Video]
Lighthill Debate on Artificial Intelligence, 1973

Interview, John McCarthy
[Video]
Thinking Allowed, by Jeffrey Mishlove

AI History: Expert Systems
[Video]
AAAI Panel Discussion, 2017

Deep Learning Revolution

During the 1990s and early 2000s, artificial intelligence research underwent a significant transformation, shifting from the rule-based expert systems of previous decades toward more adaptive, learning-oriented methodologies. The rigid nature of expert systems, which prioritized explicitly programmed rules over autonomous learning, revealed critical limitations that encouraged researchers to explore alternative paradigms. In response, various machine learning-based approaches gained traction, including neural networks, Bayesian networks, and evolutionary algorithms. These methods shared a common foundation: the gradual acquisition of knowledge through iterative learning and feedback mechanisms. Though AI research initially progressed quietly in the background, interest in these emerging models steadily grew. A few pivotal events would soon galvanize the scientific community, revitalizing a field that had, for a time, appeared to be stalling.

One of the first major milestones in this revival came in 1997, when **IBM's Deep Blue**, an AI-powered chess-playing computer, defeated reigning world champion Garry Kasparov. This landmark event was an initial wake-up call, demonstrating AI's potential beyond theoretical applications. The significance of Deep Blue's win was not limited to chess; it illustrated AI's ability to process vast quantities of information and execute strategic decision-making at levels that seemed to rival human expertise. However, Deep Blue's approach was primarily based on brute-force computation rather than true learning. A more profound demonstration of machine learning's potential came in 2005 with the DARPA Grand Challenge, a competition that tested the capabilities of autonomous vehicles. The event was won by **Stanley**, a self-driving car developed by a collaboration between Stanford University and the Volkswagen Electronics Research Lab (Fig. 11). Using a feedback loop between onboard sensors and a machine learning model, Stanley successfully navigated a desert course and

14 Newborn, Deep Blue: An Artificial Intelligence Milestone, 2002.

15 Stanford AI Lab, "Stanley: The Robot that Won the DARPA Grand Challenge," 2006.

secured first place. This achievement underscored AI's growing ability to interact with and adapt to complex real-world environments.

These two events reignited interest in AI and helped restore funding streams that had dwindled during the previous AI winter. However, this resurgence did not occur in isolation. Several concurrent technological advancements provided fertile ground for AI's expansion. The rapid growth of the internet facilitated the collection and curation of massive datasets, significantly improving the quality and variety of information available for AI training. Meanwhile, hardware capabilities were evolving in parallel. The increasing availability of graphical processing units (GPUs) played a crucial role in AI's acceleration. Originally designed for rendering graphics, GPUs were repurposed for AI research due to their ability to perform parallel computations — executing multiple operations simultaneously rather than sequentially. This development drastically reduced the computational time required for training machine learning models, rendering previously infeasible AI applications suddenly viable. By the mid-2000s, GPUs had become widely accessible, both locally on personal computers and remotely via cloud computing services, democratizing AI experimentation.

Building upon these technological foundations, a new term emerged at the start of the 2010s: "deep learning." This term signaled a paradigm shift within AI research, as artificial neural networks increasingly took center stage, supplanting earlier approaches like expert systems. The "deep" in deep learning referred to the growing complexity of these networks, characterized by multiple layers of artificial neurons that enabled the modeling of intricate patterns and relationships within data. While these deeper architectures expanded AI's problem-solving capabilities, they also introduced new challenges, particularly in terms of computational expense and training complexity. Despite these hurdles, the potential of deep learning became increasingly evident, leading to a series of groundbreaking achievements that cemented its place at the forefront of AI research.

A defining moment in this deep learning revolution occurred in 2009 with the launch of the ImageNet project at Stanford University. This initiative sought to compile the largest and most precisely labeled image dataset to date (Fig. 12), ultimately amassing over 14 million annotated images. In an effort to benchmark AI performance, the project introduced an annual classification competition, challenging participants to develop models capable of categorizing images with high accuracy. The competition's importance became clear in 2012, when a deep learning model known as **AlexNet** outperformed all previous benchmarks by a substantial margin (Fig. 13). This breakthrough demonstrated the superiority of deep architectures in complex pattern recognition tasks and set a new standard for the field. The impact

16 Krizhevsky et al., "ImageNet Classification with Deep Convolutional Neural Networks," 2012.

13

AlexNet's performance on the ImageNet benchmark, 2012.

11

Stanley, the autonomous vehicle developed by the Volkswagen Electronics Research Lab, 2005.

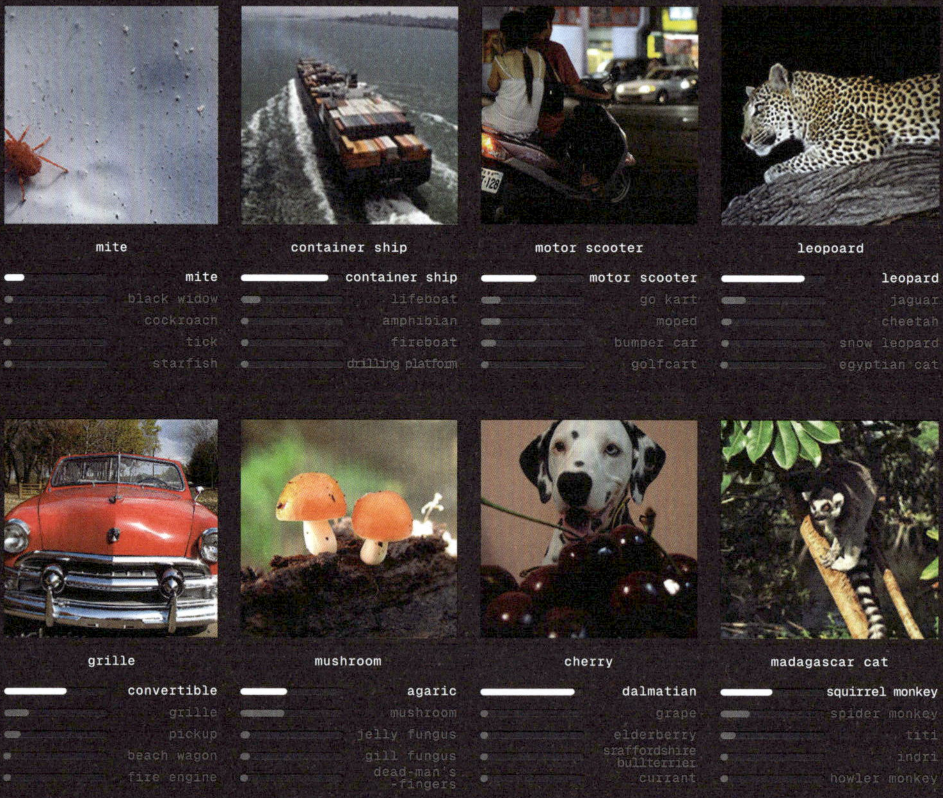

14

Pattern image generated by DeepDream.

12

Example images from an ImageNet classification model, 2012

extended beyond academia, drawing widespread attention to deep learning's capabilities and inspiring a wave of research and investment. Another landmark achievement came in 2016, when **AlphaGo, an AI system developed by DeepMind**, defeated world champion Lee Sedol in the ancient board game Go. Unlike chess, Go involves an immense number of possible moves and strategic nuances that had long been considered beyond the reach of AI. Until this event, many experts doubted that an AI system could rival human intuition in such a complex domain. AlphaGo's victory shattered this assumption, demonstrating that deep reinforcement learning — a technique that combines deep learning with self-improving algorithms — seemed able to achieve much higher performance than expected. This milestone was not only a technological triumph but also a pivotal moment in public perception, signaling that AI had reached an entirely new level of capability.

17 Silver et al., "Mastering the Game of Go with Deep Neural Networks and Tree Search," 2016.

Following the breakthroughs of ImageNet and AlphaGo, the deep learning era entered a period of rapid expansion, producing transformative applications across numerous disciplines. In bioengineering, deep learning revolutionized drug discovery by enabling the rapid generation and evaluation of molecular structures, dramatically **accelerating the drug development process** while broadening the scope of viable chemical compounds. In mechanical engineering, deep learning played a crucial role in **optimizing structural design**. Traditional engineering methods had long struggled with complex load distribution problems, relying on computationally intensive simulations and heuristic-based adjustments. AI's ability to analyze vast datasets and identify optimal material distributions introduced unprecedented efficiencies, leading to the creation of lighter, stronger, and more efficient components. In computer vision, early results began to demonstrate how deep learning models might soon be able to open new creative avenues for the visual arts. Projects like DeepDream (Fig. 14), developed by Google Research, presented the world with models capable of generating dream-like patterns from canonical images. This research and a handful of similarly visionary projects stand as seminal demonstrations of the generative AI scene we are witnessing today.

18 Hwang et al., "Comprehensive Study on Molecular Supervised Learning with Graph Neural Networks," 2020.

19 Rawat et al., "A Novel Topology Optimization Approach Using Conditional Deep Learning," 2019.

By the late 2010s, deep learning had not only revitalized AI research but had also entered mainstream public consciousness. The technology that had once been sidelined in the 1980s was now a focal point of innovation, investment, and debate. As deep learning laid the foundation for increasingly sophisticated AI models, a new chapter began to emerge — characterized by the rise of generative AI. The rapid progression from early machine learning experiments to today's generative systems traces AI's trajectory, transforming fields as diverse as medicine, engineering, and the creative industries. The legacy of deep learning continues to shape the technological landscape, forming the bedrock upon which the current generative AI wave is built.

REFERENCES

Marvin Minsky: Artificial Intelligence
[Article]
Edge Interview, 2002

Deep Blue vs. Kasparov
[Video]
Documentary, BBC, 2017

DARPA Grand Challenge
[Video]
Presentation, Gary Bradski, 2020

AlexNet: The Moment We Stopped Understanding AI
[Video]
Documentary, Welch Labs, 2024

AlphaGo - A Movie
[Video]
Documentary, DeepMind, 2016

Where Did ImageNet Come From
[Video]
Lecture, Fei-Fei Li, 2019

Deep Learning
[Article]
Y. LeCun, Y. Bengio, G. Hinton, 2015

Nvidia's Rise in the Age of AI
[Video]
Documentary, FT Film, 2005

Generative AI

The notion of generative AI marks a new turn for this technology; one that builds upon the strides made during the deep learning era, but signals a significant enough leap to warrant recognition as a distinct moment of this chronology. This period marks a new stage where an entirely different breed of model architectures suddenly offers AI much higher performance while expanding the range of mediums it can address, eventually propelling its adoption and market penetration. Behind the term "generative" lies a simple observation: in the past decade, AI has evolved into a technology capable of synthesizing images, sound, videos, 3D content, and more at ever higher levels of realism. This shift is unfolding rapidly before our eyes, and a few key elements help explain its trajectory.

Rewinding just a few years, a first wave of innovations shaped the initial rise in both model architecture complexity and output quality. Variational Autoencoders (VAEs) and, soon after, generative adversarial networks (GANs) formed the core of this early breed of models, setting the stage for the decade's generative AI boom. **VAEs, first introduced by Diederik P. Kingma and Max Welling** in their seminal 2013 paper, proposed combining two distinct models — an encoder and a decoder — to generate high-fidelity visuals (Fig. 15, 16). The experimental success of this new type of architecture quickly won over the research community, as VAEs became essential to numerous academic projects.

20 Kingma and Welling, "Auto-Encoding Variational Bayes," 2013.

Just a year later, Ian Goodfellow, then a researcher at the University of Montreal, introduced **the GAN architecture**, which, while pursuing the same goal as VAEs, employed a very different approach. Based on a novel framework, GANs leverage competition between two models — a generator and a discriminator — to produce data that resemble the features of an observed dataset. GANs sparked an entirely new wave of research, leading to models such as pix2pix (Fig. 17, Isola et

21 Goodfellow et al., "Generative Adversarial Networks," 2014.

22 Karras et al., "A Style-Based Generator Architecture for Generative Adversarial Networks," 2018.

23 Brock et al., "Large Scale GAN Training for High Fidelity Natural Image Synthesis," 2019.

al., 2018), which can generate an image based on a dataset and a conditioning input image **StyleGAN by Nvidia Research** (Fig. 18, Karras et al., 2018), capable of emulating image styles from a given dataset; and **BigGAN** (Brock et al., 2019), which extended GANs to produce much higher-resolution images. While VAEs and GANs made their most immediate and visible contributions in image synthesis, their generative potential was also applied in fields such as biology, natural language processing, and engineering. However, this first wave of generative models came with technical limitations, and their output quality remained constrained. Despite their success in academic settings, early generative models faced challenges when it came to industrial applications.

24 Ho et al., "Denoising Diffusion Probabilistic Models," 2020.

A second generation of models soon followed and set the stage for the period we are witnessing today. New architectures such as transformers and diffusion models are pushing the boundaries of existing benchmarks, while also broadening the scope of input and output formats, giving users greater control over the generation process. Diffusion models — a class of generative models based on the thermodynamic concept of diffusion — marked a turning point in the reliable synthesis of images. A landmark paper, **"Denoising Diffusion Probabilistic Models"** (Ho et al., 2020), demonstrated how this new type of architecture could iteratively denoise random noise to produce high-quality outputs (Fig. 19). This work laid the foundation for a new family of generative models — diffusers — which are now widely deployed in tools such as OpenAI's DALL·E (Fig. 20) and Stability AI's Stable Diffusion models are also being applied to audio and video generation, demonstrating their versatility across creative and scientific domains.

25 Vaswani et al., "Attention Is All You Need," 2017.

Transformers represent another key innovation shaping the current period. Introduced by Vaswani et al. in their 2017 paper **"Attention is All You Need,"** transformer architectures excel at processing sequential data in parallel using self-attention mechanisms. This approach has profoundly reshaped natural language processing (NLP) and is now widely applied in tasks such as machine translation, text summarization, and question answering. The commercial success of models like ChatGPT and the widespread adoption of large language models (LLMs) are rooted in the progress made in transformer architectures over the past seven years. Both transformers and diffusion models have not only improved the quality of generative outputs but also expanded user control over the generation process, allowing outputs to be conditioned on a range of inputs: text prompts, reference images, audio, and more. This capability has enabled context-driven customization in AI-generated content.

One additional concept is central to understanding the current generative AI moment: the notion of the foundation model. Introduced in 2021 by the Stanford Center

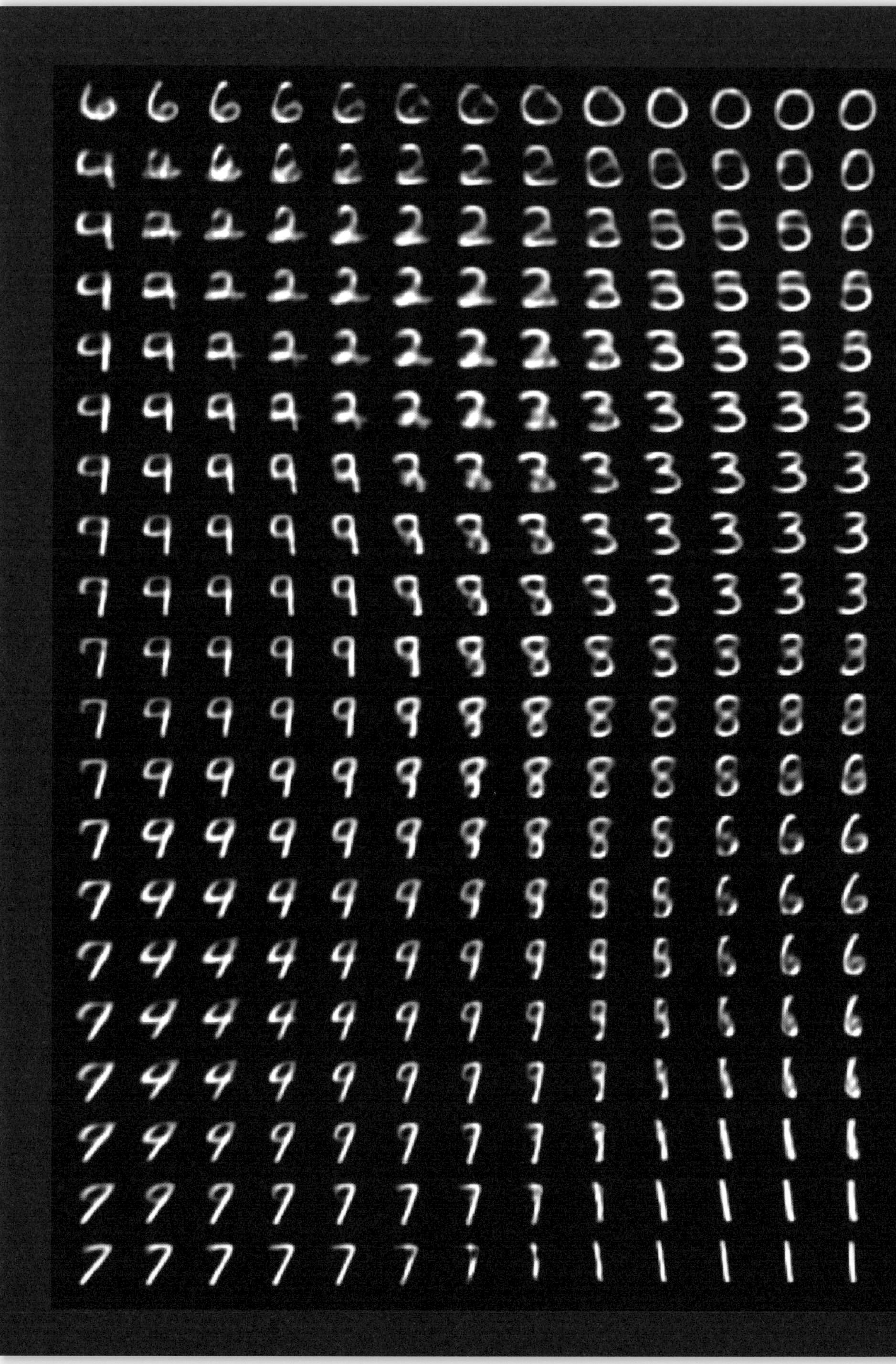

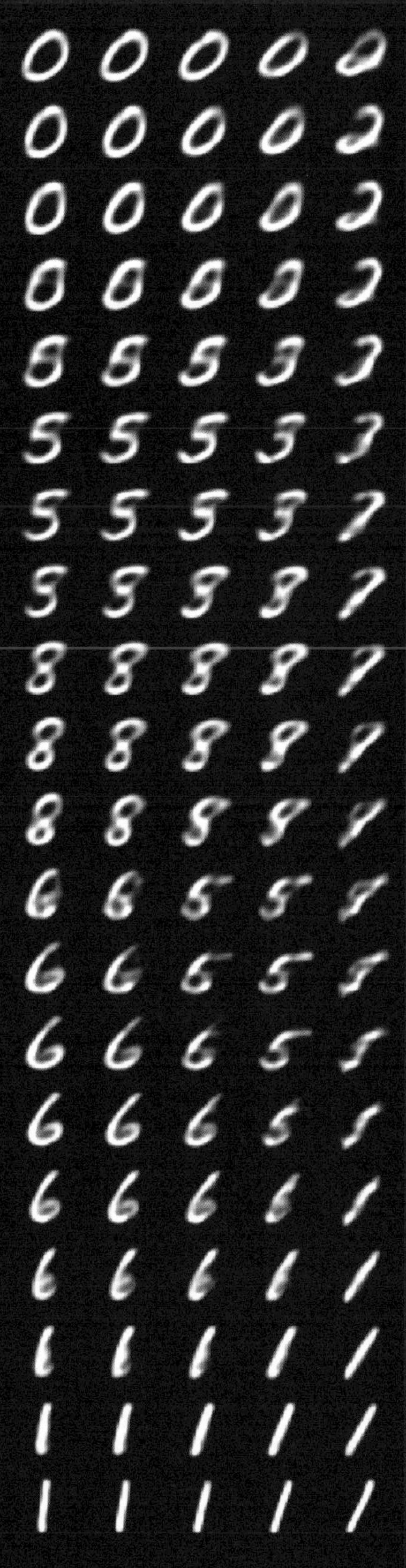

15

Result from Kingma et al., showing VAE-generated handwritten digits trained on the MNIST dataset.

16

A sample from the MNIST dataset, a well-known benchmark for generative AI.

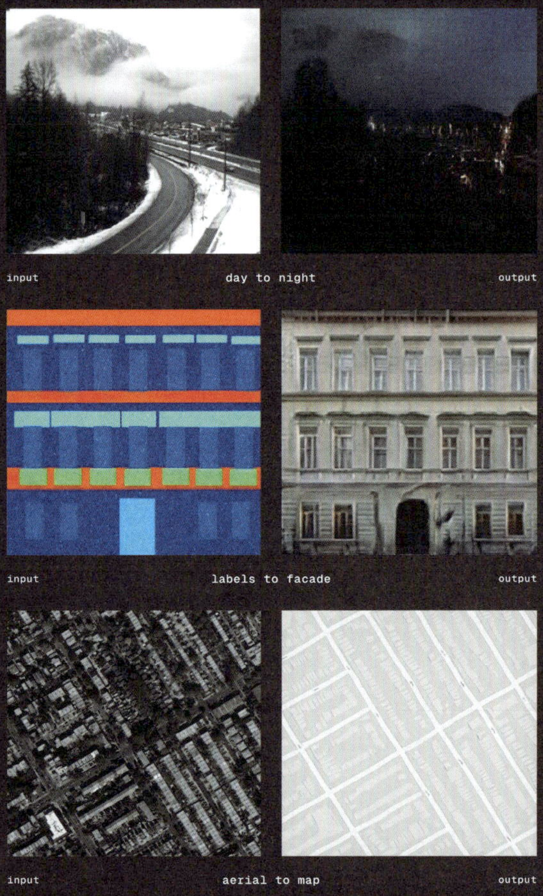

17

Input-output pairs from pix2pix. Isola et al., 2018

18

Results of StyleGAN, Nvidia, 2018.

20

DALL·E 3 output for the prompt: "An illustration of an avocado sitting in a therapist's chair, saying 'I just feel so empty inside' with a pit-sized hole in its center. The therapist, a spoon, scribbles notes."

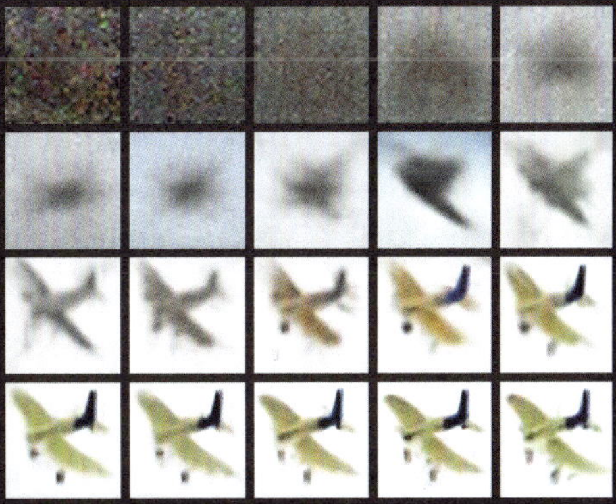

19

Step-by-step denoising sequence generating an image of a plane. Ho et al., 2020.

for Research on **Foundation Models**, the term describes "models (e.g., BERT, DALL·E, GPT-3) trained on broad data (generally using self-supervision at scale) that can be adapted to a wide range of downstream tasks." Since this initial definition, the concept of foundation models has become widespread in AI discourse, especially as companies like OpenAI, Mistral, and Stability AI have built and released large-scale models based on this paradigm. One key tendency associated with foundation models — especially in contrast to models of the early 2020's — is their increasing convergence toward multimodality. From "text-to-image" to "text+image-to-image," multimodality refers to the ability of foundation models to map between multiple types of input and output. This capability is exemplified by models such as Mistral's Pixtral or OpenAI's GPT-4.

General in purpose and massive in scale, foundation models are now produced by a handful of leading tech companies, and in a few cases, academic research labs. Their deployment in real-world contexts typically takes place downstream, as applied researchers, businesses, and end users adapt them to domain-specific tasks. While this value chain is beginning to stabilize, supported by broad market adoption, certain limitations remain. The scarcity of clean, publicly available training data and the technical shortcomings of current architectures (including those of diffusers and transformers) represent potential ceilings for future development.

Yet for now, the momentum continues. AI has entered an industrialization phase, in which mature model architectures are leaving research labs — both corporate and academic — and are being packaged and deployed across a growing array of industries.

This is where we conclude our chronology. It sets the stage for a deeper understanding of the current dialogue between architecture and AI. While the following chapters offer a more detailed introduction to the technology and its technical underpinnings, this genealogy serves as a concise reminder of how a field once entirely foreign to architecture came into being.

[26] Bommasani et al., "On the Opportunities and Risks of Foundation Models," 2021.

REFERENCES

StyleGAN
[Video]
Presentation, NVIDIA Research, 2019

Generative Adversarial Networks
[Video]
Presentation, Ian Goodfellow, NIPS 2016

Transformers & BERT models
[Video]
Presentation, Google Cloud Tech, 2023

Exploring Foundation Models
[Video]
The Alan Turing Institute, 2023

The Physics Principle That Inspired Modern AI Art
[Article]
Anil Ananthaswamy, 2023

Will Transformers Take Over Artificial Intelligence?
[Article]
Stephen Ornes, Quanta Magazine, 2022

The Future of AI Is Here
[Video]
Interview, World Labs by a16z, 2024

Introducing General World Models
[Article]
Anastasis Germanidis, 2023

CHAPTER II

The Advent of Architectural AI

A HISTORICAL PERSPECTIVE

The ties between architecture and technology are neither recent nor stable. Despite having quite distinct agendas, their respective histories display moments of alignment and mutual enrichment. Whether through simple inspiration or the sharing of entire frameworks, their exchange has brought significant contributions to both domains.

This back-and-forth has roots deep in the history of architecture. From the systematization brought by the modular grid at the turn of the century to the advent of computer-aided design (CAD), and later, parametric modeling, the discipline has benefited from the progressive refinement of its technological means and methods over the past century (Fig. 1). Today, AI appears as a potential fourth stage in this chronology. As architecture's relationship to technology has matured in parallel with AI's development, understanding how AI might eventually be integrated into the discipline's technological landscape is essential. This chapter intends to tie both histories together, while setting the stage for AI's presence in architecture.

1

Timeline of technological developments in architecture since the 1920s.

Modularity
1940s

Computer-Aided Design
1960s

PRONTO
P. Hanratty
('57)

UNISURF
P. Bézier
('66)

Dymaxion House
B. Fuller
('30)

Unité d'habitation in Marseille
Le Corbusier
('52)

Urban 5
N. Negroponte
('73)

Generat
C. Price
('76)

Baukasten
W. Gropius
('23)

Modulor
Le Corbusier
('48)

SketchPad
I. Sutherland
('63)

AI History

Artificial Neuron ('43)

Dartmouth Workshop ('56)

Perceptron ('57)

ELIZA ('66)

Lighthill Re ('73)

Parametricism
2000s

Artificial Intelligence
2010s

Vectorworks First Release
Le Corbusier
('85)

Revit First Release
RTC
('00)

CATIA First Release
Dassault Systèmes
('82)

Rhinoceros Version 1.0
McNeel
('98)

Grasshopper
D. Rutten
('07)

Intelligens. Natural. Artificial. Collective. Venice Biennale '25
C. Ratti
('25)

AutoCAD First Release
Autodesk
('82)

Pro/ENGINEER
S. Geisberg
('88)

Manifesto on Parametricism
P. Schumacher
('09)

"Some Expert Systems Need Common Sense"
('84)

Deep Blue vs Kasparov
('97)

Stanley at DARPA Challenge
('05)

AlexNET
('12)

Generative Adversarial Network
('14)

AlphaGO vs Sedol
('16)

Modularity

Reflecting on the architectural transformations of the last century, modularity emerges as both a pivotal milestone and a catalyst for the increasing systematization of architectural processes. As a salient starting point in this chronology, modularity marked a significant shift in architectural discourse, prompting both theorists and practitioners to reconsider some of architecture's core constructive principles and methodologies. As the 20th century unfolded, the pursuit of efficiency and rationalization propelled modularity from a conceptual framework into a practical methodology that reshaped a large part of the discipline.

The theoretical underpinnings of modularity were first articulated within the Bauhaus movement by German architect Walter Gropius. His ambition was twofold: to simplify the technical complexities inherent in construction while simultaneously reducing financial expenditures. To that end, Gropius introduced **the concept of "Baukasten"** (literally "building kit") as early as 1923. This methodology advocated the use of standardized components, assembled according to predefined structural and spatial rules, effectively mitigating the intricacies of detail resolution through the rigor of modular logic. The Baukasten principles established a foundational approach to modular design, wherein architectural elements were conceived as interlocking components of a larger, systematized whole.

1 Seelow, "The Construction Kit and the Assembly Line, Walter Gropius' Concepts for Rationalizing Architecture," 2018.

Building upon these early explorations, American architect and visionary Buckminster Fuller advanced modularity toward a more integrated and systemic definition. His **Dymaxion House**, conceptualized in 1930, exemplified an unprecedented degree of modular integration by embedding systems — such as water supply, HVAC, and electrical networks — directly within prefabricated modules. Through this project, and others such as his work on modular geodesic construction, Fuller sought to push the log-

2 Cohen and Prosina, "Buckminster Fuller's Dymaxion House as a Paradigm for a Space Habitat," 2020.

ic of modularity to an extreme, wherein the decomposition of architectural functions into discrete, manufacturable units heralded a new paradigm in architectural production (Fig. 2, 3). These projects served as early demonstrations of the feasibility of industrialized modular construction, laying the groundwork for subsequent advancements in prefabricated architecture.

That same year, the Winslow Ames House, designed by American architect Robert W. McLaughlin, emerged as another seminal experiment in modular construction. McLaughlin sought to test the economic viability of modular dwellings by applying an even more stringent approach to cost reduction and production efficiency. Through rigorous streamlining of the manufacturing process, he succeeded in bringing the construction cost of a single dwelling down to an unprecedented 7,500 dollars — a compelling demonstration of modularity's potential to democratize housing. The success of this experiment established a lasting precedent, demonstrating the financial and logistical upsides inherent to the modular methodologies.

As the rationalization of architecture into systematic frameworks gained momentum, the influence of modularity extended beyond economic imperatives to inspire theoretical discourse across the field. Perhaps the most emblematic manifestation of this development was **Le Corbusier's "Modulor,"** (Fig. 4) developed in 1946. Unlike purely technical approaches, Le Corbusier's Modulor sought to harmonize architectural dimensions with the human scale, integrating modularity into a broader theoretical framework. This system of proportional relationships dictated the spatial and structural organization of his architectural oeuvre, from the Unité d'Habitation in Marseille (Fig. 5, 1952) to the Convent of La Tourette (1960). By aligning building dimensions with standardized metrics derived from human anatomy, Le Corbusier's work underscored the capacity of modularity to function as both a rationalizing tool and a conceptual driver of architectural form.

3 Le Corbusier, Le Modulor, 1950.

These early experiments signaled a broader shift in architectural practice, as designers increasingly adapted their methodologies to the exigencies of modular construction. By transferring a significant portion of technical complexity to the systematic logic of grids and assembly frameworks, architects discovered a means of achieving affordability and scalability without sacrificing formal coherence. Two primary advantages of modularity propelled its rapid adoption: first, it significantly reduced both the design and construction complexities, offering a more cost-effective approach to building production. Second, it enhanced reliability by introducing greater precision and consistency into the construction process. The enduring legacy of modular principles is evident in a number of iconic postwar projects, such as Moshe Safdie's Habitat 67 and Archigram's visionary "Plug-In City".

2

United States Pavilion at Expo '67 in Montreal, Buckminster Fuller.

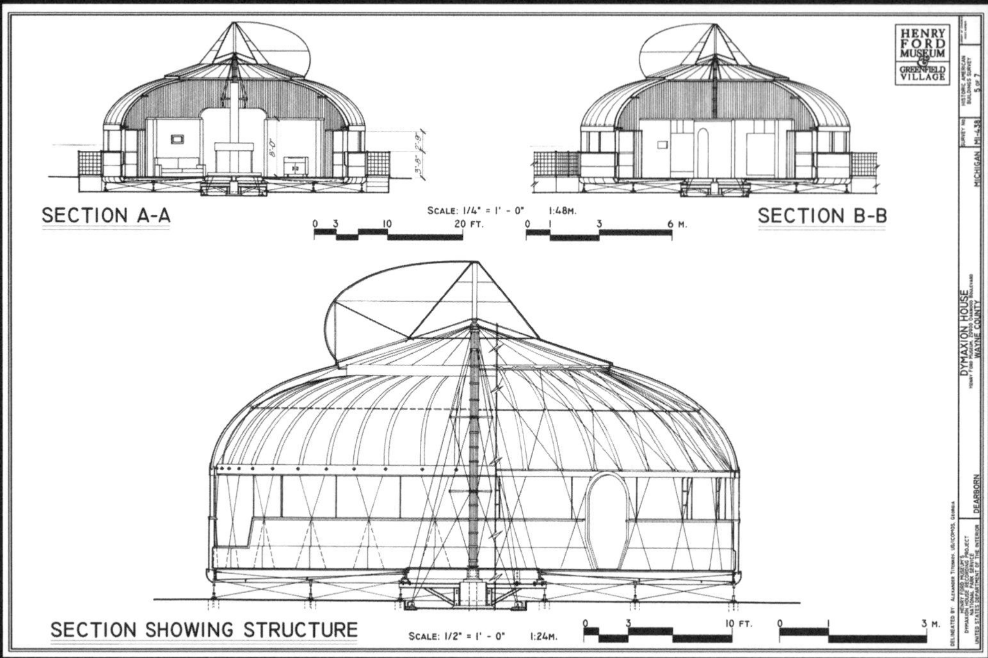

3

Section drawings of Buckminster Fuller's Dymaxion House, 1933.

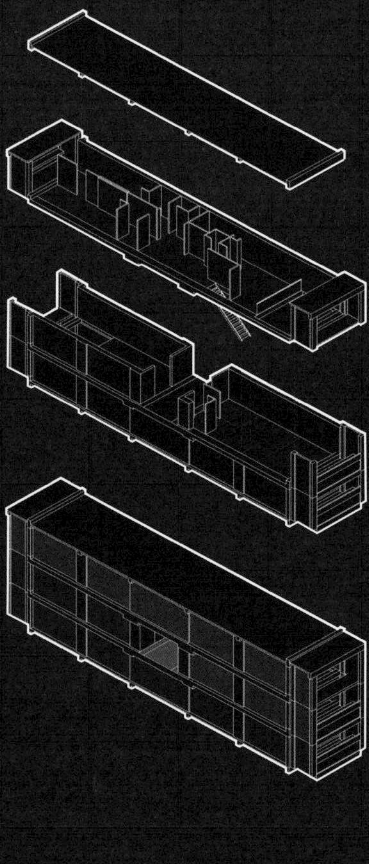

5

Unité d'habitation, Marseille, Le Corbusier.

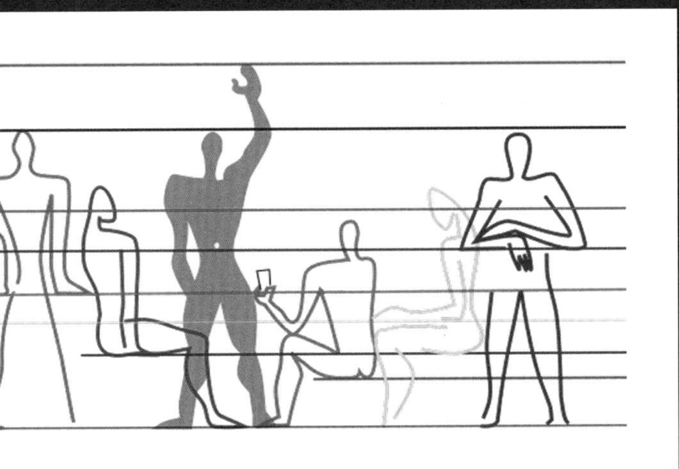

6

Assembly of Habitat 67, Moshe Safdie, 1967.

4

Le Corbusier's Modulor, a proportional system based on the human scale.

In 1967, Israeli-Canadian architect and urban theorist **Moshe Safdie completed Habitat 67**, a radical modular housing complex that remains a landmark in prefabricated architecture (Fig. 6). Safdie's approach synthesized the economic efficiencies of prefabrication with a novel compositional strategy, wherein standardized housing units were craned into place on site, forming an intricate yet adaptable spatial arrangement. Unlike earlier modular experiments that often yielded uniform and repetitive configurations, Habitat 67 demonstrated the capacity of modular systems to generate spatial diversity while maintaining systemic rigor. Through the interplay of standardization and variation, Safdie's project reaffirmed modularity's potential to reconcile mass production with architectural richness. Simultaneously, theoretical explorations of modularity reached new heights with Archigram's speculative urban proposals, most notably the **"Plug-In City."** Conceived in the 1960s, this vision for a modular metropolis proposed a dynamic framework in which prefabricated living units could be plugged into a vast infrastructural superstructure. This radical reimagining of urban growth suggested a city capable of continuous transformation, wherein modular components could be added, removed, or reconfigured in response to changing needs. Though never realized, Archigram's work underscored the conceptual elasticity of modularity, extending its implications beyond individual buildings to the scale of entire cities.

4 Safdie, For Everyone a Garden, 1974.

5 Sadler, Architecture Without Architecture, 2005.

Despite these advancements, the limitations of early modular approaches soon became apparent. The rigid adherence to predefined module sizes and grid-based assembly processes often resulted in a reductive architectural expression, constraining design possibilities and stifling formal innovation. Many architects resisted the notion of serving merely as assemblers of standardized components, seeking instead to preserve a degree of creative autonomy within the constraints of modular logic. Additionally, the monotonous aesthetic character of early modular buildings, coupled with technical challenges such as durability and adaptability, ultimately tempered the initial enthusiasm surrounding modular construction. Consequently, as the 20th century progressed, architectural interest in modularity, at least in its most rigidly systematized form, began to wane.

Nevertheless, the impact of modularity on architectural thought and practice remains profound. Modularity introduced a new intellectual framework — one that encouraged architects to conceive buildings as dynamic systems rather than static objects. This systemic perspective continues to shape contemporary architectural discourse, informing ongoing explorations. As a testament to its enduring influence, the principles of grid-based organization, modular assembly, and prefabrication remain deeply embedded within the architectural lexicon, ensuring that modularity's legacy persists as a cornerstone of architectural innovation.

REFERENCES

The Modulor I & II
[Book]
Le Corbusier, Harvard Univ. Press, 1954

Le Corbusier's Modulor System
[Video]
Interview, Richard Meier, 2017

Towards A New Architecture
[Book]
Le Corbusier, J. Rodker Publisher, 1931

The New Architecture and the Bauhaus
[Book]
Walter Gropius, MIT Press, 1965

Archigram's Plug-In City
[Video]
VDF, Dezeen, 2020

Buckminster Fuller's Dymaxion House
[Video]
1940s Futuristic Architecture, 1946

The Dymaxion World of Buckminster Fuller
[Book]
Robert W. Marks, SIU Press, 1960

The Dessau Bauhaus
[Video]
Architecture Collection, ARTE, 2000

Computer-Aided Design

At the turn of the 1980s, the rapid expansion of computing power, coupled with the increasing availability of new hardware — such as microprocessors, memory storage, and computer networks — ushered in a transformative era for architectural design. This technological shift facilitated the emergence of multiple design software programs that would redefine the methodologies employed by architects. The advent of what would later be termed "computer-aided design" (CAD) profoundly influenced architectural practice, introducing new tools that not only accelerated drafting processes but also restructured the underlying principles of design representation and production.

Although the widespread adoption of CAD occurred in the late 20th century, conceptual reflections on its potential applications date back as early as the mid-1950s within certain engineering circles. In 1957, American computer scientist and entrepreneur **Patrick Hanratty developed PRONTO**, a precursor to CAD designed for engineering applications. The capabilities of PRONTO underscored the revolutionary potential of computer-based drafting, sparking a wave of research initiatives aimed at refining the role of digital tools in design workflows.

6

Carlson, "A Critical History of Computer Graphics and Animation," 2005.

In 1963, American computer scientist **Ivan Sutherland introduced Sketchpad** (Fig. 7), one of the earliest CAD programs to feature an accessible and intuitive interface. Developed at the Lincoln Laboratory of the Massachusetts Institute of Technology (MIT), Sketchpad allowed users to draft technical elements in precise 2D representations while incorporating a more approachable, pen-based input system. Using a light pen and streamlined controls, the software provided drafters with an unprecedented degree of precision and flexibility, laying the groundwork for the development of more advanced CAD systems.

7

Sutherland, "Sketchpad: A Man-Machine Graphical Communication System," 1964.

8 Bézier, Essai de Définition Numérique des Courbes et des Surfaces Expérimentales, 1977.

9 Bézier, "Example of an Existing System in the Motor Industry: The Unisurf System," 1971.

The evolution of CAD from 2D drafting to 3D modeling marked another critical leap forward, facilitated by the pioneering work of French mathematician and computer scientist Pierre Bézier. **His research on complex curvatures** enabled designers to manipulate intricate 3D forms with greater ease, thereby expanding the possibilities of digital modeling (Fig. 8). In 1966, Bézier's Unisurf software, initially developed for the automotive industry, **allowed Renault to model car prototypes** with new levels of accuracy (Fig. 9). This technological advancement, however, was not confined to automotive applications; it catalyzed the development of CAD tools across multiple design disciplines, including architecture.

The collective contributions of Sutherland, Hanratty, Bézier, and other pioneers positioned CAD as a distinct field of research, fostering its rapid dissemination across various industries. Architecture, in particular, embraced CAD as a means of streamlining design processes. At its core, this new generation of software enabled users to create and manipulate basic geometric primitives, organize elements into hierarchical structures using concepts such as blocks, groups, and layers, and output final designs in both digital and printed formats. Beyond merely expediting drafting tasks, CAD introduced a new level of structural organization to design workflows. Layers facilitated systematic organization, blocks allowed for the replication of modular components, and geometric entities were endowed with consistent properties. Through these conventions, CAD not only rationalized the drafting process but also established a new paradigm for architectural representation.

10 Negroponte, The Architecture Machine, 1970.

11 Negroponte, "Toward a Theory of Architecture Machines," 1969.

As CAD systems became increasingly integrated into architectural practice, their influence extended beyond conventional drafting applications to inspire speculative and experimental research directions. The Architecture Machine Group (AMG) at MIT, led by Greek-American computer scientist and professor Nicholas Negroponte, played a pivotal role in this intellectual expansion. Negroponte's seminal book, **"The Architecture Machine"** (1970), encapsulated the AMG's vision of leveraging computation to enhance architectural design methodologies. His research initiatives, including the **Urban 2 and Urban 5 projects**, sought to explore the interface between human designers and computational tools, anticipating the eventual integration of CAD into mainstream architectural workflows even before the industry fully embraced it.

By the late 20th century, architects and industrialists alike increasingly adopted CAD software, often contributing to its advancement through their own innovations. Among the most notable figures in this transition was American-Canadian architect Frank Gehry, whose pioneering use of computational design tools set a precedent for future generations. Recognizing the potential of digital technologies to transcend

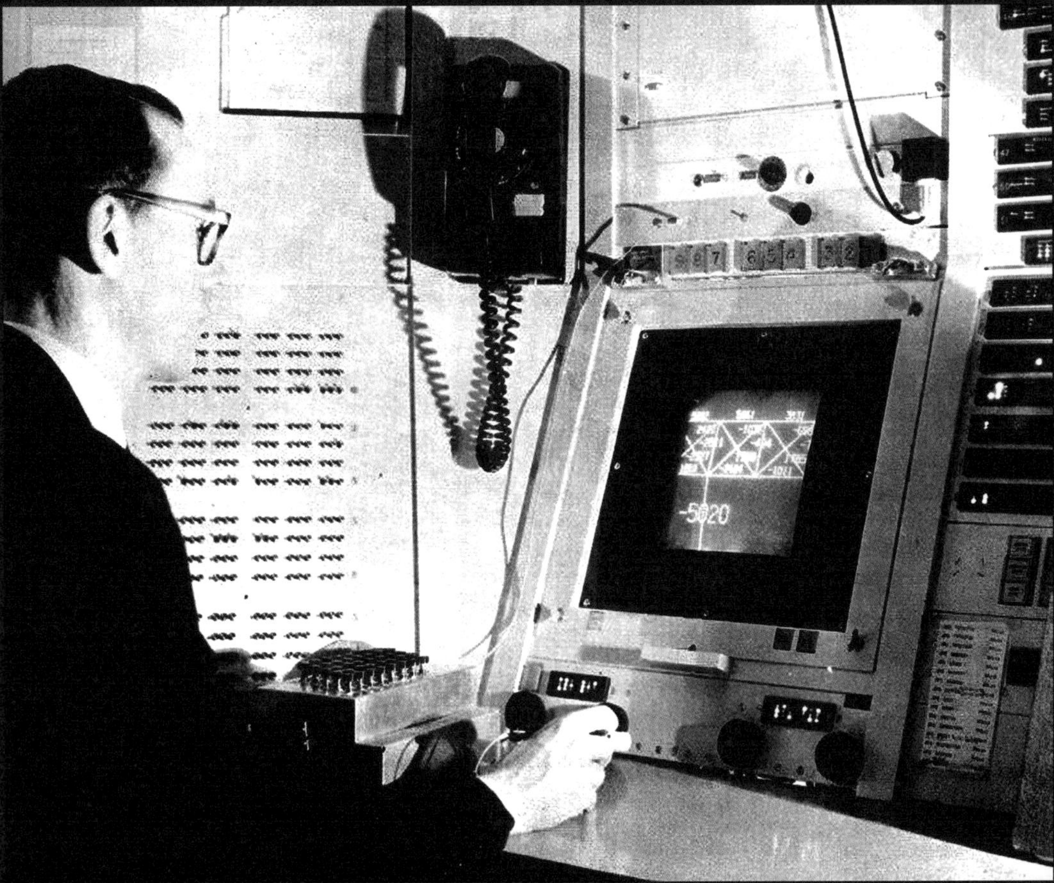

7

Ivan
Sutherland and
Sketchpad,1963.

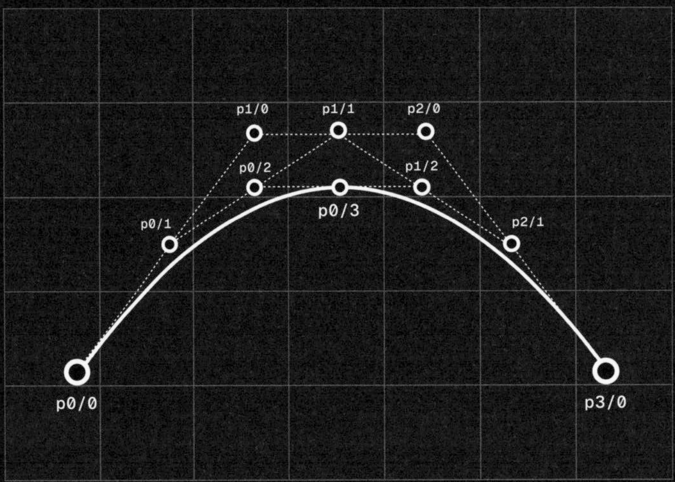

8

Formulation of
cubic Bézier curve,
equation and geometric
representation.

11

Commercial for Puget Sound Computer User, an authorized AutoCAD dealer, featuring AutoCAD 2.6, 1987.

9

Wireframe model of a Renault 14 car, created with Unisurf CAD system, 1978.

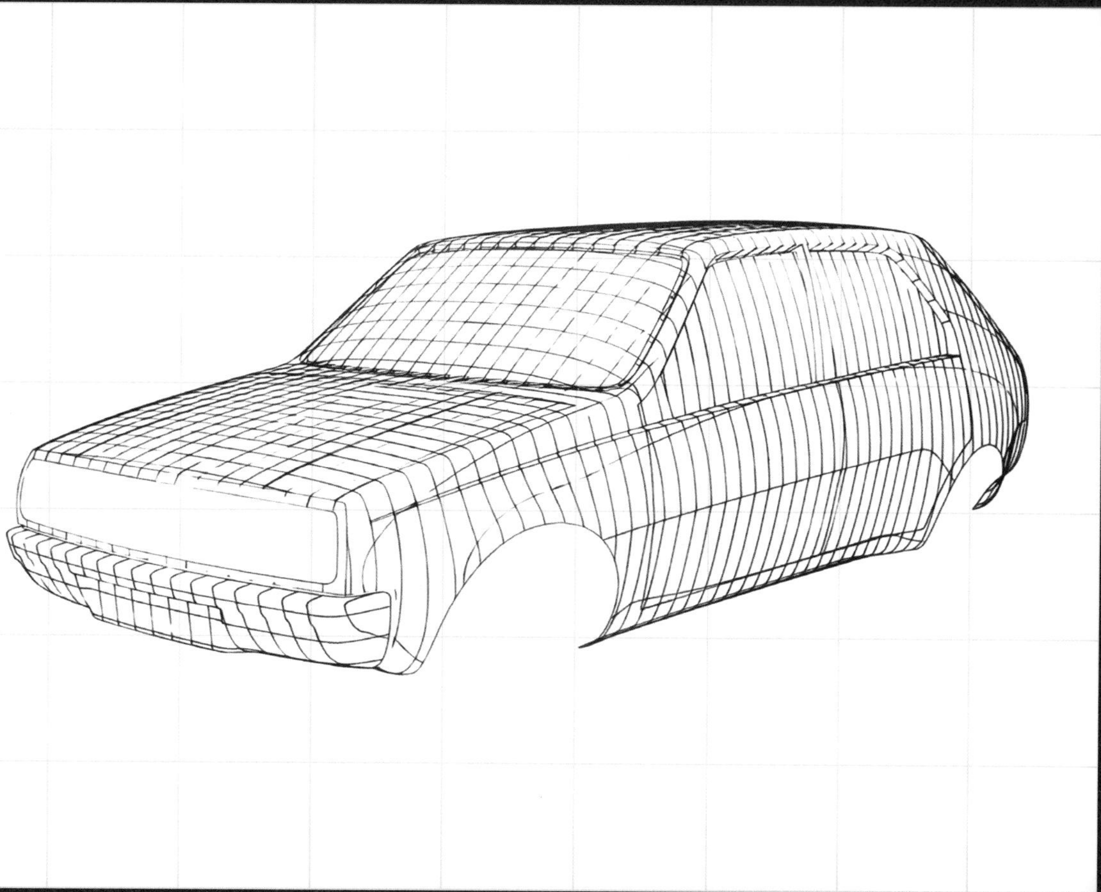

The Walt Disney Concert Hall, Frank Gehry, 2003.

the geometric constraints of conventional design, Gehry collaborated with architect Jim Glymph in 1989 to introduce Dassault Systèmes' CAD/CAM software, CATIA, into architectural practice. Originally developed for aerospace engineering, CATIA enabled Gehry to navigate the extreme geometric complexity of his designs, as exemplified by the **Walt Disney Concert Hall in Los Angeles** (Fig. 10). This project demonstrated **the capacity of 3D CAD to facilitate the realization of highly intricate architectural forms**, solidifying its value as an indispensable tool for contemporary designers. 12

12 Haymaker and Fischer, "Challenges and Benefits of 4D Modeling on the Walt Disney Concert Hall Project," 2001.

Between the 1980s and the early 21st century, continuous advancements in data storage, computational power, and cost efficiency further accelerated the proliferation of CAD technology. The introduction of industry-defining software such as CATIA (1982), AutoCAD (Fig. 11, 1982), and Vectorworks (1985) revolutionized architectural workflows, providing architects with greater levels of control over complex geometries. In addition to enabling more precision, CAD facilitated collaborative design processes, allowing multiple stakeholders to engage in iterative revisions with increased efficiency. The ability to experiment with digital models before committing to physical construction further contributed to cost reduction and resource optimization, cementing CAD's status as an industry standard. 13

13 Narayanan, "Gehry Technologies, a Case Study," 2006.

However, despite its transformative impact, CAD was not without its limitations. As architects became increasingly reliant on digital drafting, certain challenges emerged. The repetitiveness of manual CAD operations, the constraints imposed by rigid parametric definitions, and the difficulty of encoding complex design rules within conventional CAD frameworks highlighted the need for complementary technologies. These shortcomings prompted architects and researchers to seek new computational approaches that could extend beyond CAD's deterministic logic, ultimately laying the groundwork for the emergence of algorithmic and generative design methodologies in the decades to follow.

REFERENCES

SOFTWARE Show Catalog
[Book]
The Jewish Museum, New York, 1970

The Unisurf System
[Article]
Pierre Bézier, 1971

Ivan Sutherland & Sketchpad
[Video]
MIT Science Report, 1963

Sketchpad, a Thesis at MIT Lincoln Lab
[Video]
Ivan Sutherland, 1963

CAD Systems
[Video]
Architecture Machine Group, 1976

CAD Lab at MIT
[Video]
MIT Dept. of Mechanical Engineering, 1982

Frank Gehry Uses CATIA
[Video]
2011

The Case for Process Change by Digital Means
[Article]
D. R. Shelden, AD, 2006

Parametricism

Parametric modeling refers to a design methodology that has gradually become an integral part of mainstream architecture software such as Rhino and Revit. Beyond the direct manipulation of sketches through standard geometric editing tools, this methodology allows designers to specify explicit rules as an alternative approach to shaping buildings. The use of such rules, however, significantly predates the advent of parametric tools in architecture, tracing back to early explorations by architects and pioneering software experiments conducted during the latter half of the 20th century.

As early as the 1960s, **parametric architecture was introduced through the work of Italian architect Luigi Moretti**. His project Stadium N served as an early demonstration of parametric modeling's potential (Fig. 12). By defining 19 parameters, Moretti formulated a precise mathematical procedure that directly influenced the final form of the structure. Each variation in the parameter set could generate a distinct iteration of the stadium, illustrating the capacity of parametric design to produce diverse outcomes within a structured system. Moretti's approach not only provided a compelling proof of concept for his time but also foreshadowed the distinct aesthetic language that parametric modeling would later embody. 14

14 Moretti, "Parametrica Architettura," 1968.

Concurrently, experimental design software developments enabled further explorations of parametric principles. In addition to its CAD interface, **Ivan Sutherland's Sketchpad** (1963), previously mentioned, incorporated fundamental parametric features. At the core of this tool was the concept of "atomic constraint," which functioned as a computational translation of Moretti's idea of parameterization. In Sketchpad, every sketch was interpreted by the computer as a collection of atomic constraints — variables that designers could adjust to modify the geometry. Beyond merely altering values, users could redefine the relationships among parameters, granting them the ability to establish and manipulate both the rules and the inputs governing their designs. 15

15 Sutherland, "Sketchpad: A Man-Machine Graphical Communication System," 1964.

In retrospect, Sketchpad stands as a precursor to most contemporary parametric design tools, as it introduced a level of computational control that architects would later refine and expand.

16 Teresko, "Industry Week," 1993.

Nearly 25 years after Sutherland's thesis, Samuel Geisberg, the founder of Parametric Technology Corporation (PTC), introduced Pro/ENGINEER (1988), the first software program that provided users with full access to geometric parameters. Upon its release, Geisberg summarized the parametric vision succinctly: **"The goal is to create a system flexible enough to encourage designers to explore a variety of options, while ensuring that the cost of design changes remains as close to zero as possible."** His statement captured a fundamental aspiration of parametric modeling: to codify design logic into a structured system of rules, enabling rapid and reliable design exploration. This characteristic, which allowed for iterative experimentation and design optimization, largely explains the widespread adoption of parametric modeling in subsequent decades.

17 Schumacher, "Parametricism: A New Global Style for Architecture and Urban Design," 2009.

As these early innovations demonstrated the viability of parametric modeling in architecture, they also laid the foundation for a new generation of parametric architects. Among the many efforts to theorize the impact of parametric modeling, Patrik Schumacher, a German architect and collaborator at Zaha Hadid Architects (ZHA), sought to provide a comprehensive theoretical framework. In his manifesto, **"Parametricism: A New Global Style for Architecture and Urban Design"** (2009), Schumacher argued that the discipline was gradually "converging" toward parametricism, a term he used to define both a design technique and a distinct architectural style. Beyond the theoretical discourse, parametric modeling found concrete expression through the work of key architecture firms, notably ZHA. Zaha Hadid, an Iraqi-British architect trained in mathematics, positioned her practice at the intersection of mathematical principles and architectural form. Her work, including the Kartal Pendik masterplan in Istanbul (Fig. 13), frequently relied on parametric processes. In her projects, architectural decisions were often encoded into parametric procedures, where key variables dictated the resulting forms. This approach contributed to the distinctive fluidity of Hadid's work, which became a defining characteristic of her practice and, more broadly, of parametricism as an architectural movement. In Hadid's footsteps, many other practices embraced this aesthetic, with notable examples including Coop Himmelb(l)au (Fig. 14), Foster + Partners, and BIG.

18 Rutten, "Computing Architectural Concepts: Grasshopper Stories," 2010.

The adoption of parametric modeling accelerated with the advent of visual programming interfaces. **Grasshopper (Fig. 15), developed by computer scientist David Rutten** in the 2000s, was a pivotal tool behind many of ZHA's projects. By introducing a simple, graph-based interface, Grasshopper significantly lowered the barrier to programming-driven design allowing designers to easily define rules and relationships between geometries. In Grasshopper, objects, mathematical functions, and parameters are interconnected in a procedural workflow, enabling architects to

14

3D optimization process of the facade for PANEUM (House of Bread project), using parametric scripting, Coop Himmelb(l)au.

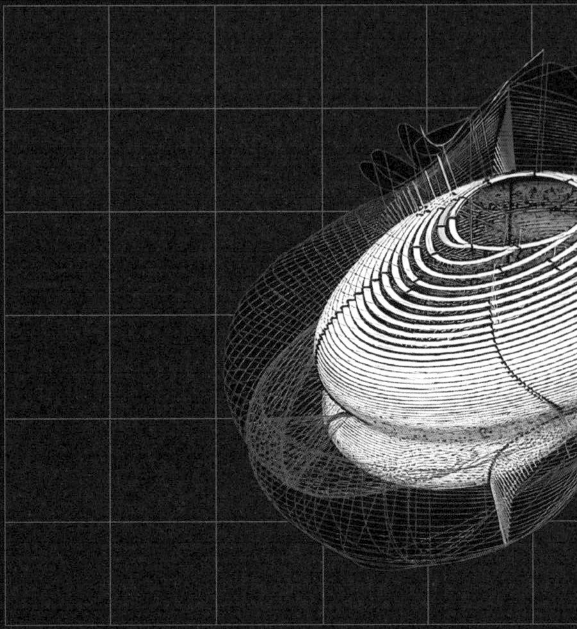

12

Luigi Moretti, models of football stadiums M and N, a swimming stadium and tennis stadium, and a cinema.

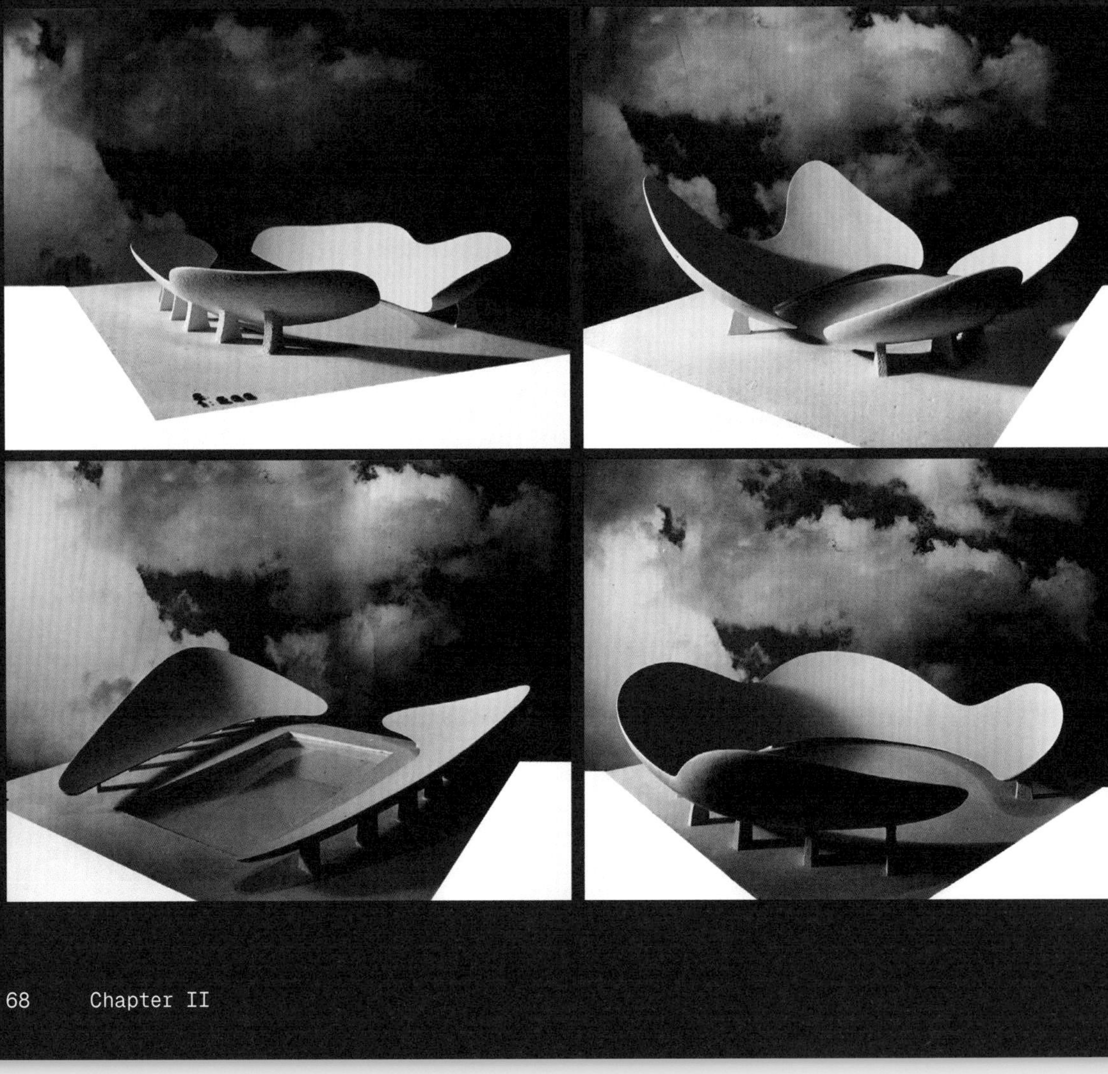

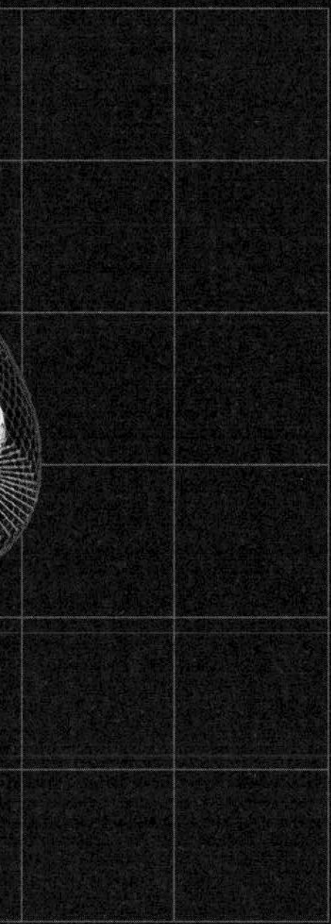

15

Grasshopper, visual programming software, 2018.

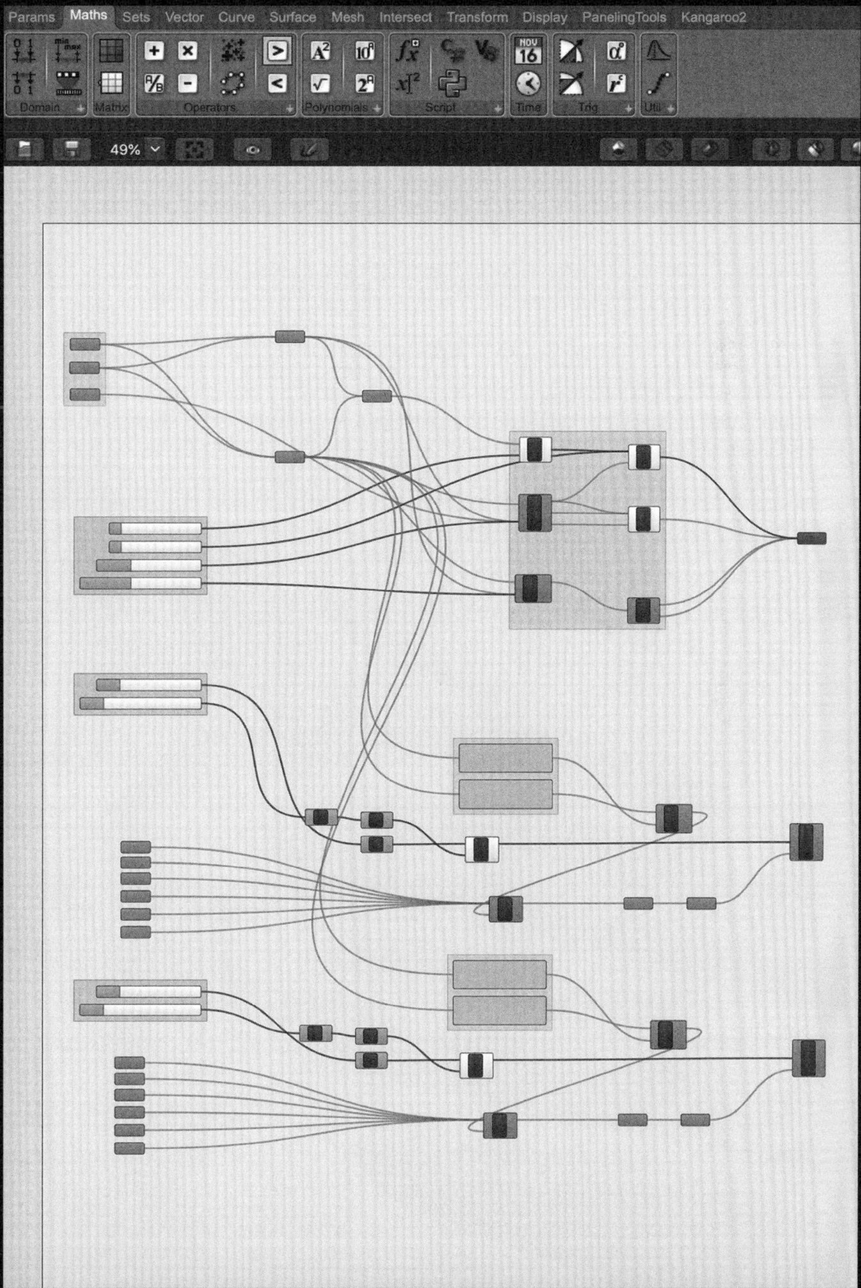

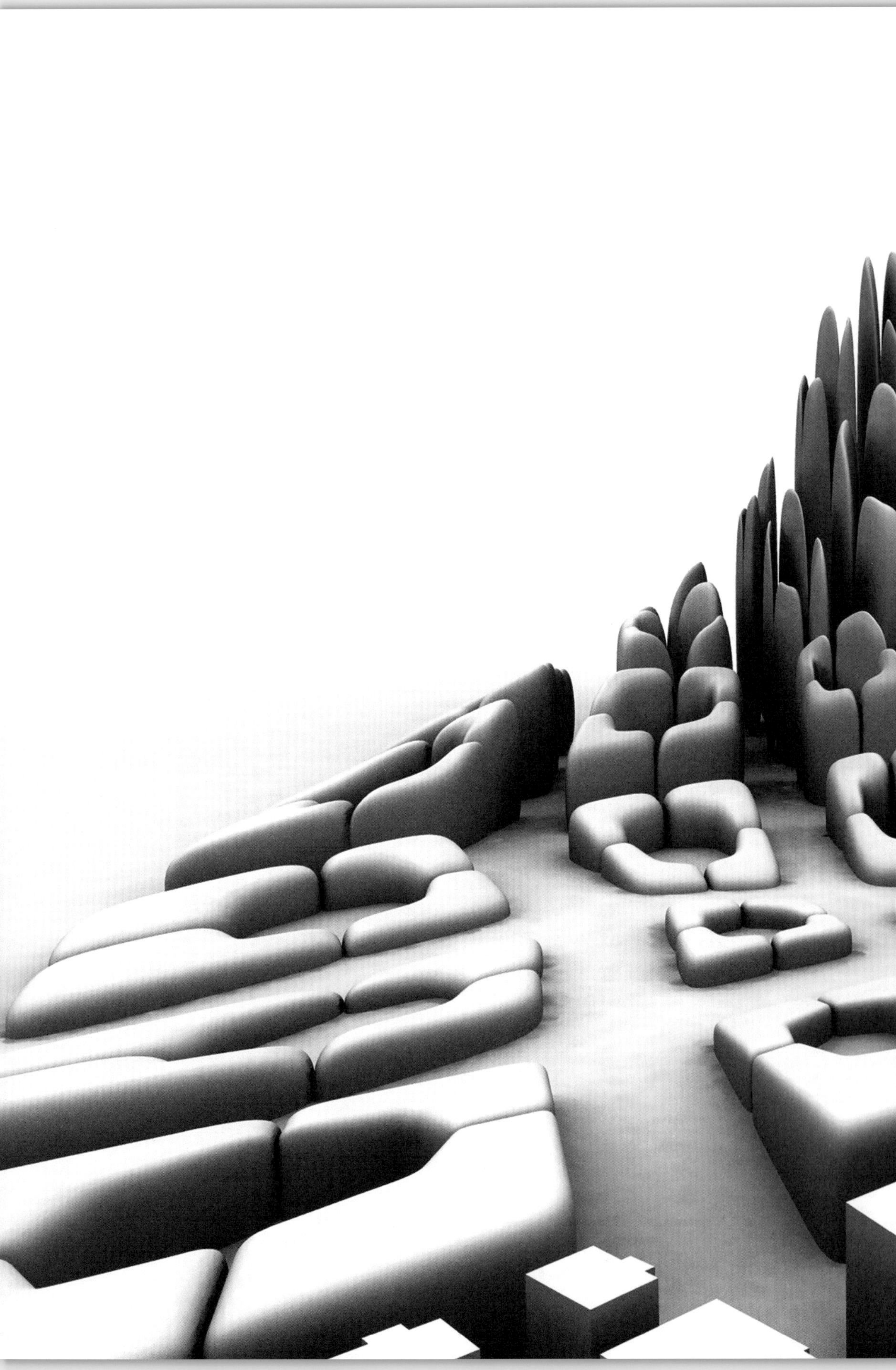

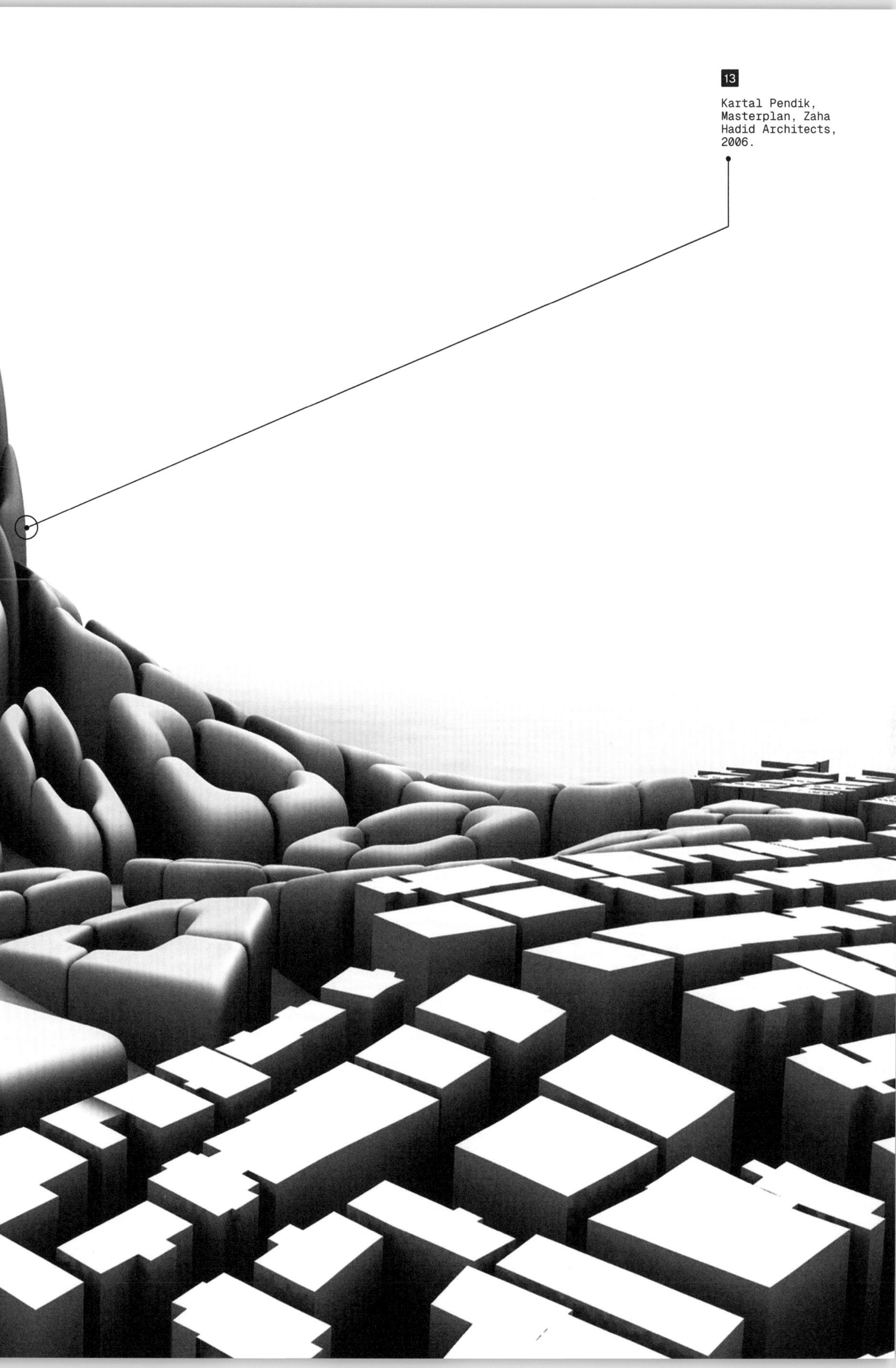

13

Kartal Pendik, Masterplan, Zaha Hadid Architects, 2006.

access computational design methods without requiring extensive coding expertise. The combination of an intuitive interface and a comprehensive suite of features quickly positioned Grasshopper as an indispensable tool for a new generation of designers. By leveraging this new type of software, architects could build their design process upon rules and relationships that allowed for adaptability and scalability. This shift in methodology fundamentally altered how some architectural projects were conceived, encouraging an increasingly systematic approach to form generation. Beyond Grasshopper, another major evolution in the architectural profession emerged in the early 2000s: the development and widespread adoption of **Building Information Modeling (BIM).** BIM sought to integrate and manage extensive metadata associated with building components, encompassing quantities, materials, specifications, and interdependencies. Unlike CAD, which primarily represented buildings through static 2D drawings, **BIM introduced an object-based approach**, where elements not only carried geometric properties but also functional behaviors and relational attributes. This transition marked a fundamental shift toward a more information-rich and structured design methodology, reliant on explicit parameters and predefined rules. In this way, BIM tools such as Revit, ArchiCAD, and others reinforced the parametric logic already established by earlier computational design tools, offering the parametric "tradition" a new form of relevance decades after Sutherland's Sketchpad.

19 Autodesk, "Building Information Modeling, White Paper," 2002.

20 Eastman et al., BIM Handbook: A Guide to Building Information Modeling, 2011.

Despite its transformative impact, parametric modeling has faced challenges and limitations, particularly since the 2010s. While its efficiency-driven logic has facilitated many aspects of design, concerns have arisen regarding its ability to address broader architectural concerns. The prioritization of strict computational processes often risks overshadowing essential spatial, stylistic, and cultural considerations intrinsic to architecture. Furthermore, architecture necessitates the exploration of broad and complex design spaces. Parametric modeling, despite its advancements, frequently falls short of capturing this reality, as the variety of generated design options remains constrained by the rigidity of predefined parameters. Additionally, balancing multiple interdependent parameters can be computationally intensive and challenging, sometimes contradicting the initial goal of streamlining the design process. Beyond technical constraints, some critics argue that parametric modeling rests on a flawed theoretical premise: the assumption that a building's key attributes can be entirely encoded through explicit parameters and rigid rules. In practice, numerous architectural concerns — ranging from sociocultural influences to aesthetic and contextual factors — resist strict computational formulation, posing fundamental challenges to parametric modeling's applicability in architecture.

As computational design continues to evolve, artificial intelligence (AI) has emerged as a potential successor capable of addressing some of these limitations. The integration of AI with architectural practice marks a critical juncture, one that builds upon the computational foundations laid over the past six decades while opening new possibilities for adaptive and intelligent design processes.

REFERENCES

An "Other" Aesthetic: Moretti's Parametric Architecture
[Article]
Alicia Imperiale, 2018

Parametricism as Style
[Article]
Patrik Schumacher, 2008

A History of Parametric
[Article]
Daniel Davis, 2013

The Future of Making Buildings
[Video]
Phil Bernstein, TEDxYale, 2015

Parametricism – A New Global Style for Architecture and Urban Design
[Article]
Patrik Schumacher, 2008

The Kartal Pendik Masterplan
[Video]
Zaha Hadid Architects, 2015

The Challenges of Parametric Modelling
[Article]
Daniel Davis, 2013

Digital Culture in Architecture
[Video]
Lecture, Antoine Picon, 2013

Artificial Intelligence

AI's relevance to architecture was first anticipated by a few theorists who foresaw its potential. These early voices initiated a discussion within the discipline on the possible contributions of AI to architectural practice. A brief look at key milestones can help contextualize current developments.

Nicholas Negroponte was among the first to reflect on the topic. **His work in the 1970s focused specifically on interaction with "intelligent" machines.** He first introduced the concept of a "machine assistant" through his work at the MIT Media Lab's Architecture Machine Group (AMG), particularly in the aforementioned Urban 2 and Urban 5 programs. These early tools were designed to help architects in drawing floor plans by adapting room layouts to optimize adjacencies and lighting conditions, while maintaining alignment with a modular grid. In addition to functioning as an early form of CAD, Urban 5 (Fig. 16, 17) investigated the idea of complementarity between the designer and an "intelligent" agent. The software divided tasks between two distinct layers of information: the machine managed an array of implicit rules, while the user specified explicit parameters. The task distribution of Urban 5 exemplified Negroponte's vision of machine-human complementarity. With this project, Negroponte proposed a new distribution of labor between computers and architects. For instance, when users placed elements on the canvas, Urban 5 would issue warnings if conflicts were detected, such as "TED, TOO MANY CONFLICTS ARE HAPPENING" when blocks overlapped. The machine could also suggest rough layout options for the user to refine. Negroponte's work thus envisioned a more active role for computers in the design process, extending beyond the functionality offered by other CAD research of the time. His work demonstrated the kind of interaction architects might expect from intelligent design software in the future. Around the same time, British architect Cedric Price explored another facet of AI: autonomy. In 1976,

21 Negroponte, The Architecture Machine, 1970.

while serving as a professor of architecture at the University of Cambridge, Price developed the Generator (Fig. 18, 19). Conceived for the Gillman Corporation, the **Generator** envisioned a self-adapting building in which a floor plan organized on an orthogonal grid allowed partitions to be continually rearranged. **A computer was responsible for proposing new layouts**, either in response to user behavior or spontaneously to generate new spatial conditions. At its core, the Generator addressed the potential of machines as autonomous design agents. Price's project offered an early forecast of how AI could be integrated into architectural software, assigning machines a specific, active role in the design process.

22 Hardingham, Cedric Price Works 1952-2003: A Forward-Minded Retrospective, 2016.

23 Furtado et al., "Cedric Price's Generator and the Frazers' Systems Research," 2008.

Since the work of Price and Negroponte, several decades have passed. During that time, early experiments with AI were gradually overtaken by more immediately operational technologies such as CAD, BIM, and parametric modeling. For much of this period, AI remained largely confined to academic research, exerting little influence on mainstream architectural practice. It was not until the second half of the 2010s that AI began to reemerge in architecture, bolstered by the increasing affordability, accessibility, and performance of generative AI technologies. What had once been a subdued presence at the time of this book's first edition has since become a prominent and nearly omnipresent feature of architectural discourse. Still, the current AI landscape in architecture remains fragmented, making it difficult to assess the full extent of its actual footprint. Nonetheless, several clearly observable trends suggest the beginning of a new technological turn for the discipline.

In architecture, exhibitions have long provided a convenient vantage point on the discipline's zeitgeist. By pulling on that same thread today, one can easily trace the increasing presence of AI across exhibitions of the past decade. From the 2019 **"AI and Architecture" show at the Arsenal Pavilion** in Paris to this year's full-scale Biennale **"Intelligens. Natural. Artificial. Collective"** in Venice, the discipline's shifting attention has become clearly noticeable. AI seems to have moved gradually from the periphery of architectural discourse to its very center, as evidenced by the growing number of exhibitions around the world in recent years. To name just a few: "AAA Experiments in AI, Art and Architecture" at Kunsthalle Zurich; "Imagine — A Journey into The New Virtual" at the MAK in Vienna; "Artificial Architecture" at the EPFL Pavillion (École Polytechnique Fédérale de Lausanne); and "Neurons, Simulated intelligence" at the Centre Pompidou in Paris. This institutional enthusiasm is echoed in the academic world. Across major conferences, publications are witnessing a sharp uptick in focus on AI. This trend began around the turn of the 2020s and has continued to grow steadily. Proceedings from conferences such as ACADIA, CAADRIA, eCAADe, ASCAAD, and CAAD Futures are now filled with contributions on this very topic. In parallel, the number of specialized master's programs, open PhD positions, and

24 Pavillon de l'Arsenal, Artificial Intelligence and Architecture, 2019.

25 Venice Biennale, 2025 Venice Biennale: Architecture, 2025.

16

Snapshot of a
3D walkthrough
environment generated
in Urban 5.

17

Interface of Urban 5,
Nicholas Negroponte.

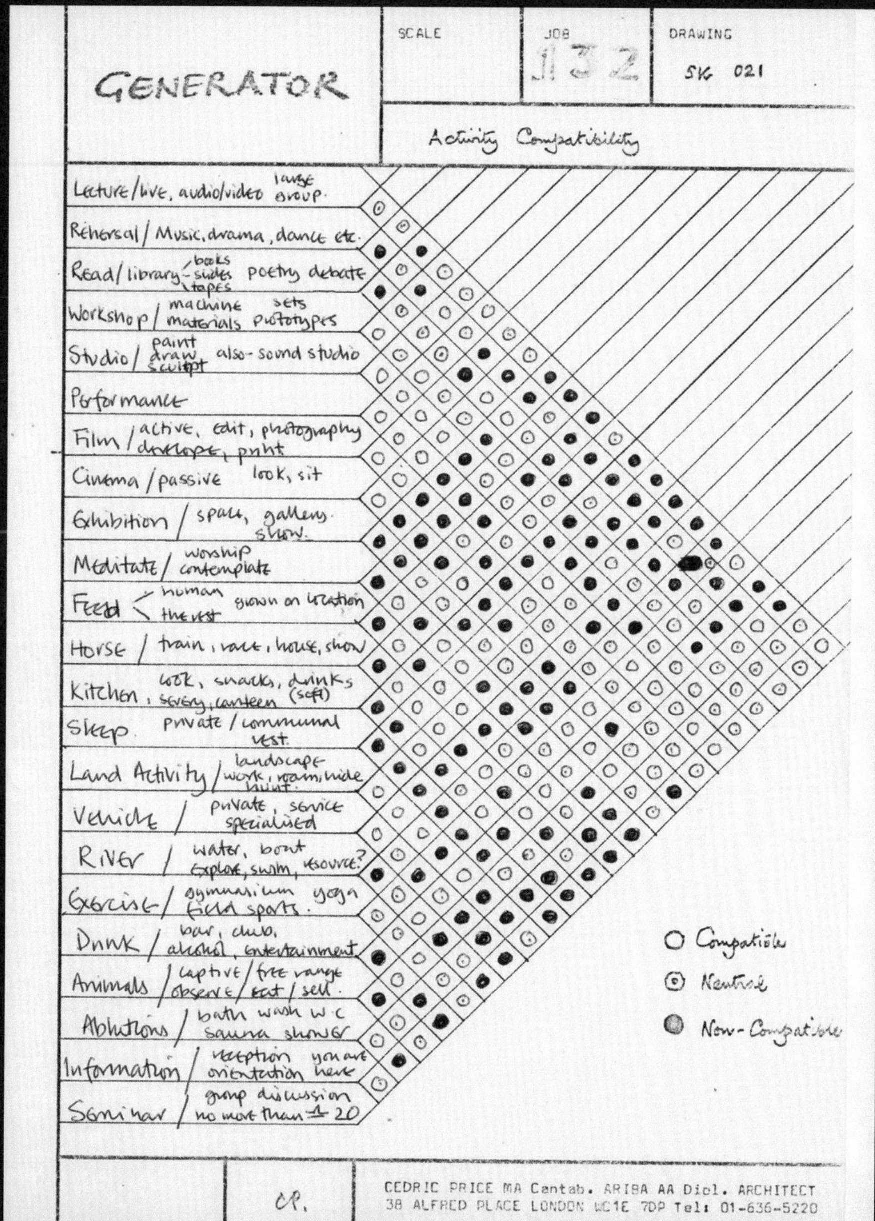

18

Diagram from Cedric Price's Generator project, used to dynamically define compatibility between elements of the building program.

19

View of the working electronic model for the Generator project, 1976-1979.

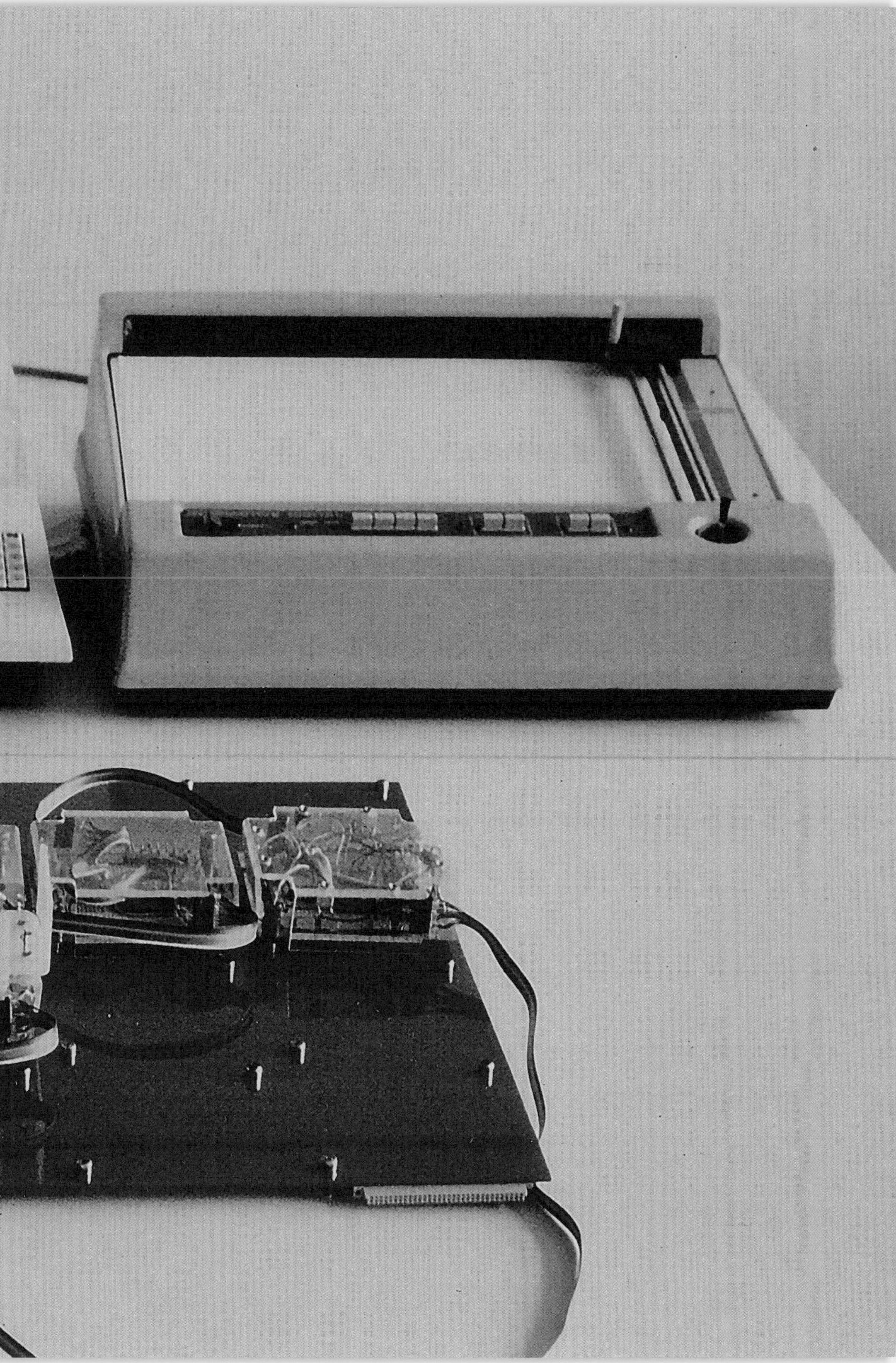

dedicated research groups focused on AI in architecture has increased significantly over the past five years, broadening AI's footprint in academia to a degree that would have been difficult to imagine just a few years ago.

Within architectural practice, there are clear signs that AI has become a tangible presence. **A 2024 report by the Royal Institute of British Architects (RIBA)** found that 41% of architects now use AI at some point in their projects. This figure alone has been enough to spark debate among practitioners, who increasingly seek AI features in their software stack. The current state of mainstream software reveals how much the gradual introduction of AI capabilities has brought this technology closer to architects. From the integration of generative design features in Revit to the growing ecosystem of machine learning libraries for Grasshopper, AI is beginning to permeate the traditional toolkit of the discipline. At the same time, a new generation of lightweight browser-based design software has emerged. Offering affordable and accessible AI-powered design tools, platforms such as Forma (former Spacemaker), Archistar, Hektar, Finch, and Maket represent a rapidly growing web-based ecosystem. Beyond this, the open-source community, rooted in architecture's culture of experimentation, has flourished in recent years. The presence of computational design in the field has been bolstered by these developments, as a growing number of architects contribute to the online community of creative programmers working on open-source AI projects. This movement reflects a larger dynamic: the momentum of AI in other fields, such as engineering and computer science. As these disciplines yield promising results, specific AI applications are being transposed and repurposed to align with architectural agendas. Many of these bridges are built online, through the collaborative sharing of code repositories and open-source AI models. This cross-pollination draws from fields as diverse as self-driving cars and image recognition, where state-of-the-art AI research is being conducted and frequently released as open sourced. In this sense, architecture today benefits from a broader cross-disciplinary research effort — one that provides the field with a growing number of off-the-shelf technological solutions.

26

RIBA, "No Turning Back: 41% of Architects Now Using AI," 2024.

In short, AI has permeated the discourse, research, and practice of architecture. Over the past decade — and particularly in the last five years — a once niche topic has grown into a defining force. From small circles of academics and tech-savvy practitioners, an expansive community has emerged. Not only has the past decade produced a new, fragmented landscape of applications, theories, and actors, but this ecosystem has grown in scale and volume — culminating in AI's central presence at the 2025 Venice Biennale. This ascent from the fringes to the very core of the discipline is what makes a publication like this both timely and necessary. The chapters that follow aim to examine how this rise has taken shape and to explore the foundations upon which architecture's evolving relationship with artificial intelligence is now being built.

REFERENCES

The Architecture Machine
[Book]
Nicholas Negroponte, MIT Press, 1970

Houses That Know the People Who Live in Them
[Article]
Nicholas Negroponte, 1975

Cedric Price's Generator from When Is the Digital in Architecture?
[Article]
Molly Wright Steenson, Sternberg Press, 2017

Architectural Intelligence
[Video]
Molly Wright Steenson, Talks at Google, 2018

Being Digital
[Book]
Nicholas Negroponte, Knopf, 1995

Cedric Price Archive
[Website]
Canadian Centre for Architecture, 1959–1995

Soft Architecture Machines
[Book]
Nicholas Negroponte, MIT Press, 1975

The Creativity Code
[Video]
Lecture, Marcus du Sautoy, 2020

CHAPTER III

AI's Deployment in Architecture

AN EXPERIMENTAL PERSPECTIVE

Leaving history behind us, we now turn to the current state of AI in our industry. The past five years have deeply transformed AI itself. Models, hardware, cost of compute — a complete overhaul of the technology's capabilities has taken shape within the tech world.

New model architectures have superseded those of the early 2020s – namely, diffusion models and transformers have replaced VAEs and GANs. Foundation models have moved to the center of discussion as a new technological paradigm, while large, heavily funded tech companies like OpenAI, Anthropic, and others have begun to industrialize AI at scale, significantly lowering the threshold of access for the general public.

As a side effect, architecture has been inheriting new generations of models and more powerful frameworks to use in research and design. The landscape of investigation – within academia but also across the R&D practices of architecture firms – has been reshaped to align with AI's latest developments. And from the world of research to that of commercial application, more solutions have reached maturity and are being adopted across architecture's tool set. Whether through the back door of traditional software or as standalone web apps, AI has reached large-scale use in a limited set of scenarios, while other use cases are still waiting for this technology to improve.

That is why, as the terrain has shifted dramatically since the first edition of this book, we hope this chapter will offer a timely and useful snapshot of this phenomenon's full magnitude.

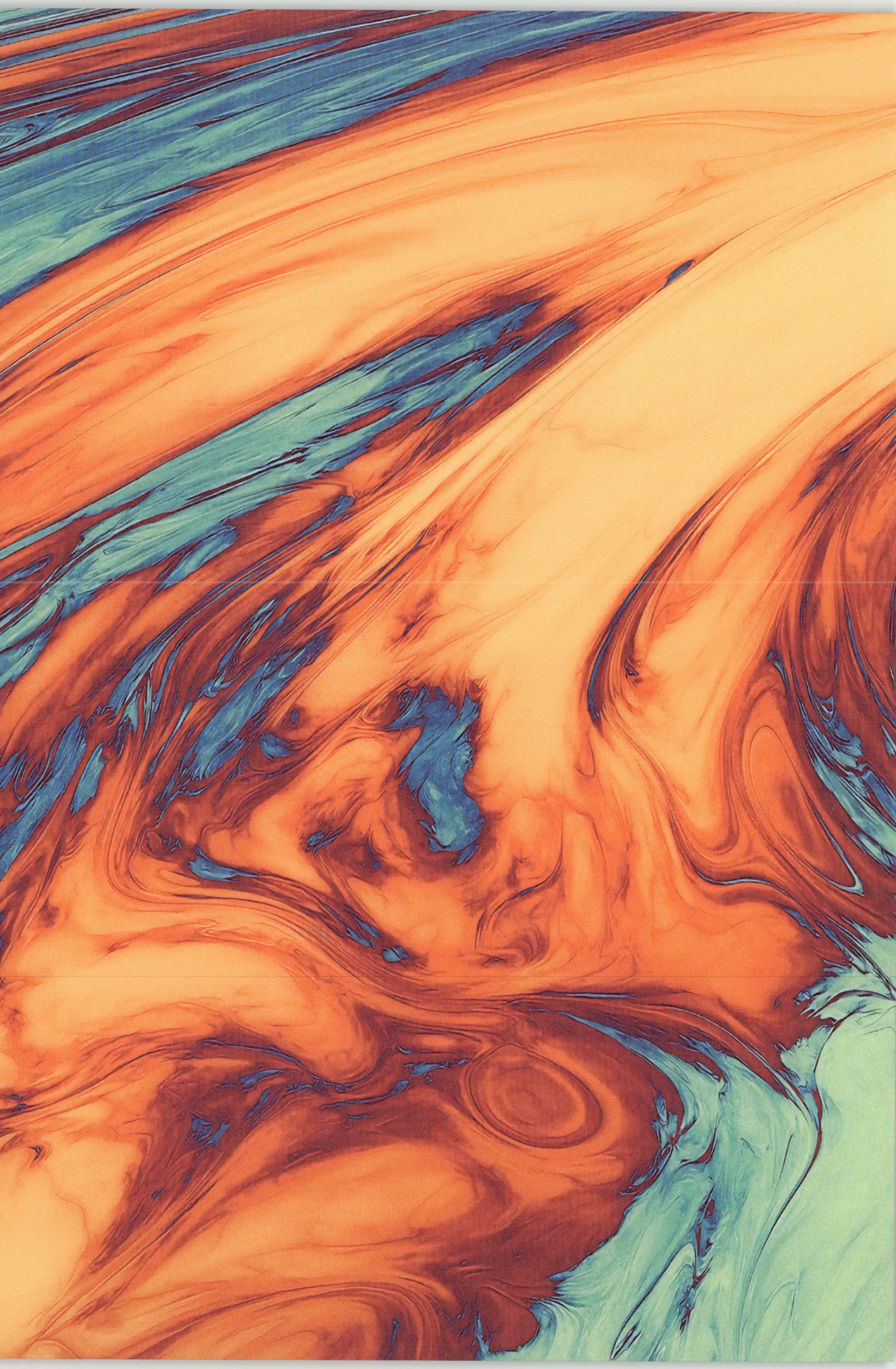

Artificial Intelligence 101

Since its inception at the Dartmouth workshop in 1956, artificial intelligence (AI) has evolved significantly, taking on many forms. Over the past 60 years, each successive iteration has strived to transform the original vision into practical technologies, leaving us today with a somewhat fragmented landscape. That is also why, if this chapter hopes to clarify AI's core concepts in practical terms, it must attempt to lay out useful categories, frameworks, and definitions essential to its understanding. Figure 1 sets the stage: six decades of research have shaped domains and subdomains across the discipline. This classification will help position AI's latest developments within this technology's broader ecosystem.

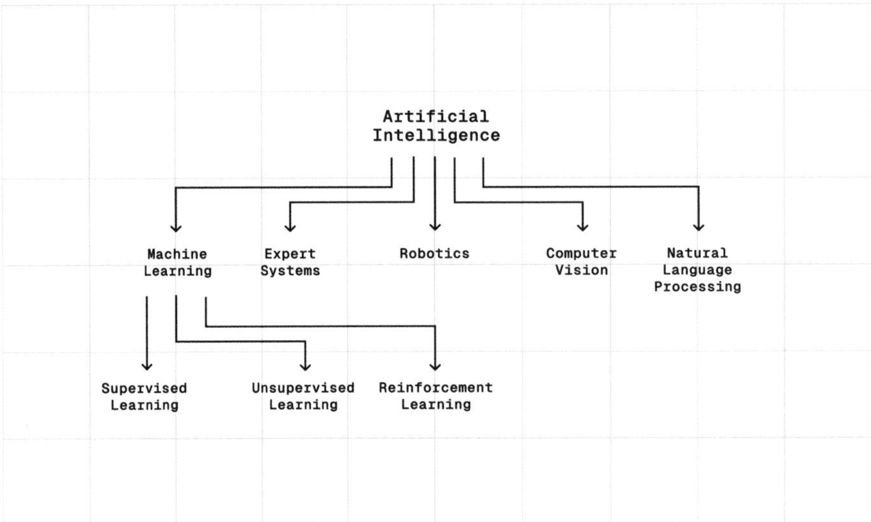

1

Mapping AI categories.

Learning = Training

Starting our journey must begin with the explanation of a notion that is integral to the very existence of AI: learning. That is, the bottom-up acquisition of features through repeated observations. In simpler terms, machine learning models can approximate a phenomenon through an iterative exposure to vast quantities of data. This process, called "learning" — or "training" — corresponds to a tuning phase during which the model will either succeed or fail at capturing some of the observed phenomenon's complexity. Once trained, the model can be used to predict or mimic the same phenomenon under new settings or different parameters.

In this way, machine learning operates a pivot: by embracing an observational approach, it distances itself from descriptive techniques. A canonical example helps clarify this approach: modeling the boiling point of water. It is common knowledge that the physical state of water depends on its temperature and ambient pressure. Rather than taking a descriptive approach by formulating the equation that ties temperature and pressure together, AI would instead browse through collections of data points — also called "observations" — to approximate the same phenomenon.

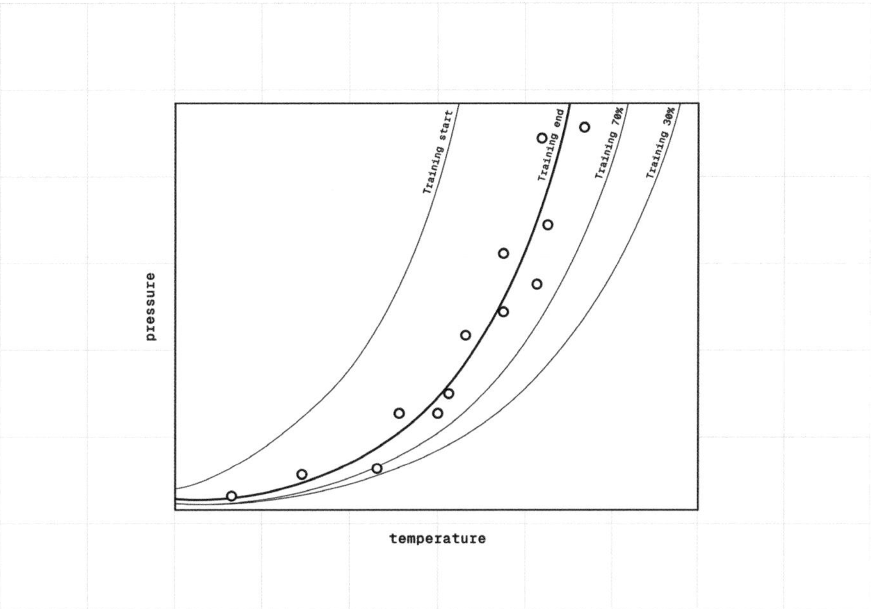

2 Example of a machine learning model gradually learning the distribution of water temperature and pressure data points.

Such observations can be obtained by repeatedly recording pairs of temperature and associated pressure values at different moments during water's heating process. During the learning phase, an AI model tries to improve its ability to predict the temperature at which boiling occurs, given the ambient pressure, using a feedback loop mechanism. Throughout training, the model compares its estimates to the actual values in the dataset. Faced with a residual difference between the two, the model recalibrates itself until it reduces this gap as much as possible. Training concludes when the user deems that the machine has adequately acquired the "mapping" between a variable and an "objective value." In other words, this learned mapping can be conceived and visualized as the model's gradual attempt to fit a curve that best describes the distribution of observations (curves in Fig. 2). Though the above example is fairly simple, it illustrates the broader idea behind machine learning-based techniques: iteratively inducing certain characteristics found in the observed data and encapsulating these approximations in a trained and sufficiently accurate model.

Finally, it is worth noting another distinctive aspect of machine learning: the user's degree of control over computation. With descriptive technics, like those used in architecture for parametric modeling, the user is entirely responsible for formulating each step of the computation and its associated parameters. In machine learning, however, while the model's architecture is designed by the user, the tuning of the parameters — and even, in some models, the definition of these parameters — occurs within the model itself. Users retain control through a handful of high-level settings, known as "hyperparameters," which allow them to guide the general direction of the learning process.

Neither a "white box" (a fully controllable algorithm) nor a "black box" (a sealed system offering no user control), machine learning occupies the **"gray box"** middle ground in the computation landscape. This term, as introduced in our discipline by Andrew Witt, aptly describes the balance that machine learning strikes between user control and computational complexity. As models grow in intricacy and gain the capacity to approximate increasingly challenging problems, the legibility and interpretability of their inner workings may fade. In machine learning, therefore, users constantly work along a threshold between interpretability and complexity, striving to maintain adequate model transparency while leveraging the power of their complex architectures.

[1] Witt, "Grayboxing," 2018.

From ML to Architecture

In recent years, the architectural discipline has had the opportunity to benefit from the accelerated development of AI. Models conceived in other fields, for entirely different applications, have been used and repurposed by architects and researchers across a range of use cases. The complexity of certain concepts and tasks in architecture offers multiple avenues for exploration using the diverse AI models available today. To illustrate this point — and to bridge the gap between a high-level understanding of AI and the tangible realities of architecture — the following example offers a didactic demonstration. In this experiment, an AI model is taught to arrange rooms within a predefined apartment footprint, while respecting the positions of the entrance door and the facade windows. Using a database of image pairs (Fig. 3), the model gradually learns the mapping from one condition to the other: from an empty footprint to a roughly programmed apartment layout.

To document the model's progressive acquisition of this task, Figure 4 shows results produced throughout the training process. Each image corresponds to an attempt by the model to organize the space based on a given input footprint and its current training stage. From the early steps of the process (top left) to the final hours of training (bottom right), the synthesized image quality steadily improves.

Figure 5 provides four snapshots taken at distinct moments during training, offering a clearer overview of the model's incremental progress. From Image [A] to Image [D], the spatial layout becomes progressively more coherent.

3

Typical pair of input-output images from a training set.

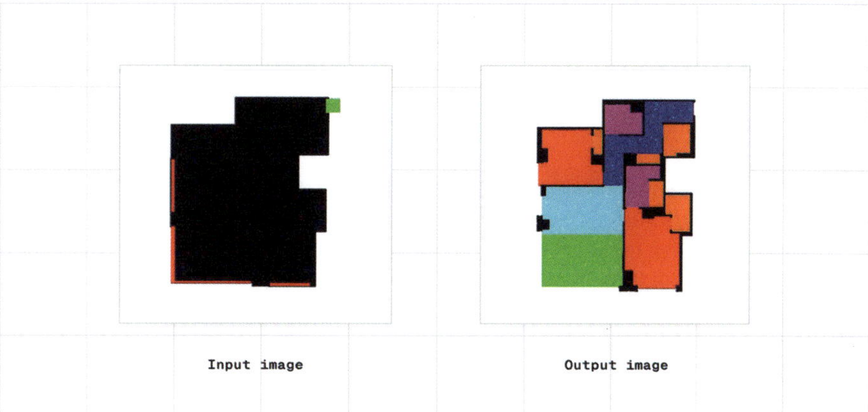

The first attempt ([A]) merely mimics the apartment's footprint. Then the notions of facade and program begin to emerge ([B]), though without spatial coherence. In the next stage ([C]), the model starts to emulate spatial enclosure, as partitions between rooms are added more systematically and adjacencies between spaces become increasingly plausible.

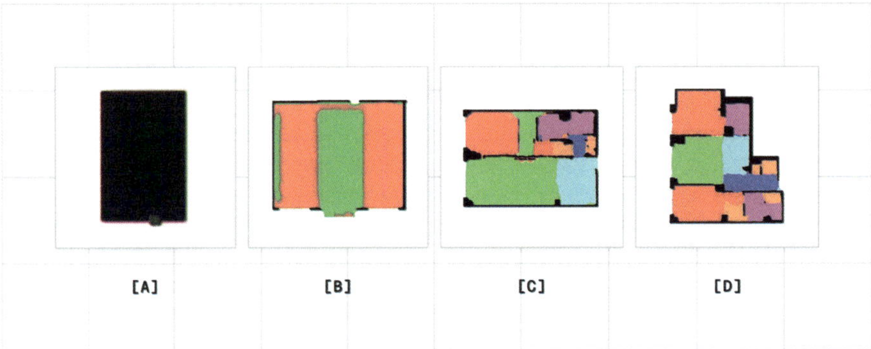

5

Four stages in the training sequence.

Finally, once training is completed ([D]), the model produces a floor plan that appears to reflect basic layout principles: facade openings, somewhat valid room adjacencies, initial partitioning of space, etc. While this marks a major improvement over earlier generative methods, the process still has clear limitations. The generated plans do not yet qualify as valid architectural floor plans: flaws such as room proportions and questionable adjacencies remain. Moreover, these solutions address only formal criteria, leaving issues of contextual relevance unaddressed in this example. Still, the generated floor plans can serve as early drafts — initial proposals to be refined and augmented by the architect. These images can act as early-stage options, helping to stimulate the design process. The relevance of the generated layouts also depends greatly on the quality of the training data — a reminder of the importance of architectural expertise in both curating and training such models.

Finally, AI is not free of bias — biases that are intrinsic to its learning strategy. A trained model may internalize assumptions embedded in its training data. Because the learning process is not entirely transparent to the end user, such biases can go unnoticed. Part of the challenge of training AI models lies in our ability to detect these biases and correct the training accordingly.

4

Typical training sequence.

The Latent Space

The notion of latent space, though seemingly abstract at first, helps us understand the stakes of machine learning training. From the standpoint of a model's internal mechanics, training an AI model means building a coherent internal representation. The analogy of "mental model" points to this reality: latent space corresponds to a continuous domain, located at the core of most AI models today, that encapsulates a compressed and simplified representation of the data presented to the model during training.

At this point, it is worth mentioning a few of its most important characteristics. First, if an AI model is properly trained, each dimension of its latent space will correspond to a feature of importance in the observed data. Ideally, these dimensions will also be independent of one another. Second, it is crucial to understand that the feature each dimension encodes is not directly defined by the user, but rather is gradually learned by the model over the course of training. Finally, in latent space, similarity is translated into proximity; in other words, things that look the same are close to one another in this n-dimensional domain. Looking at an example helps clarify how latent space functions and why it matters. If a model were trained to generate images of characters from various fonts, its latent space would capture the different features involved in font design. Among these, the model might detect characteristics such as italicization, size, and stroke thickness, and assign them to specific dimensions (Fig. 6). Fonts would be placed in latent space relative to these dimensions. A "walk" in latent space — meaning the act of selecting points along a path in this space — would generate different font outputs (here [1], [2], and [3] in Fig. 6). More interestingly, the balance of features in the generated fonts would be consistent: [2], selected between [1] and [3], would yield a font that blends features from [1] and [3]. The richness of features captured in latent space can capture — and the legibility of its structure,

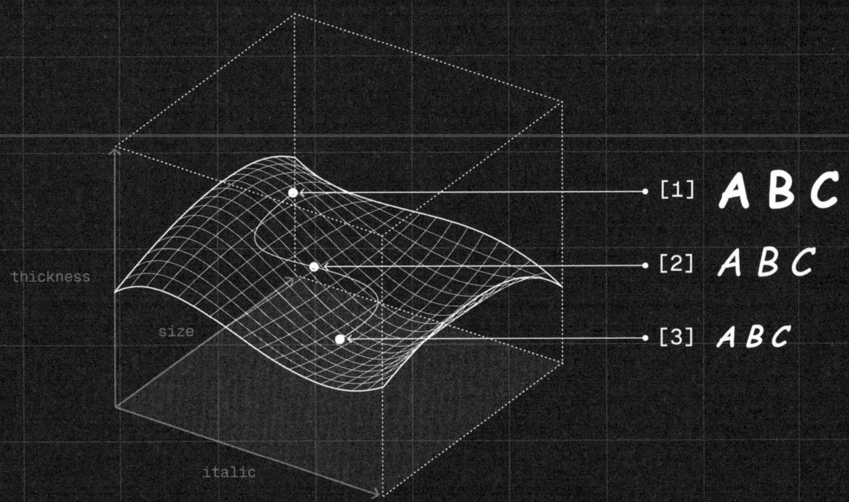

6

Diagram of a “walk” in latent space, and the sampling of three distinct font styles.

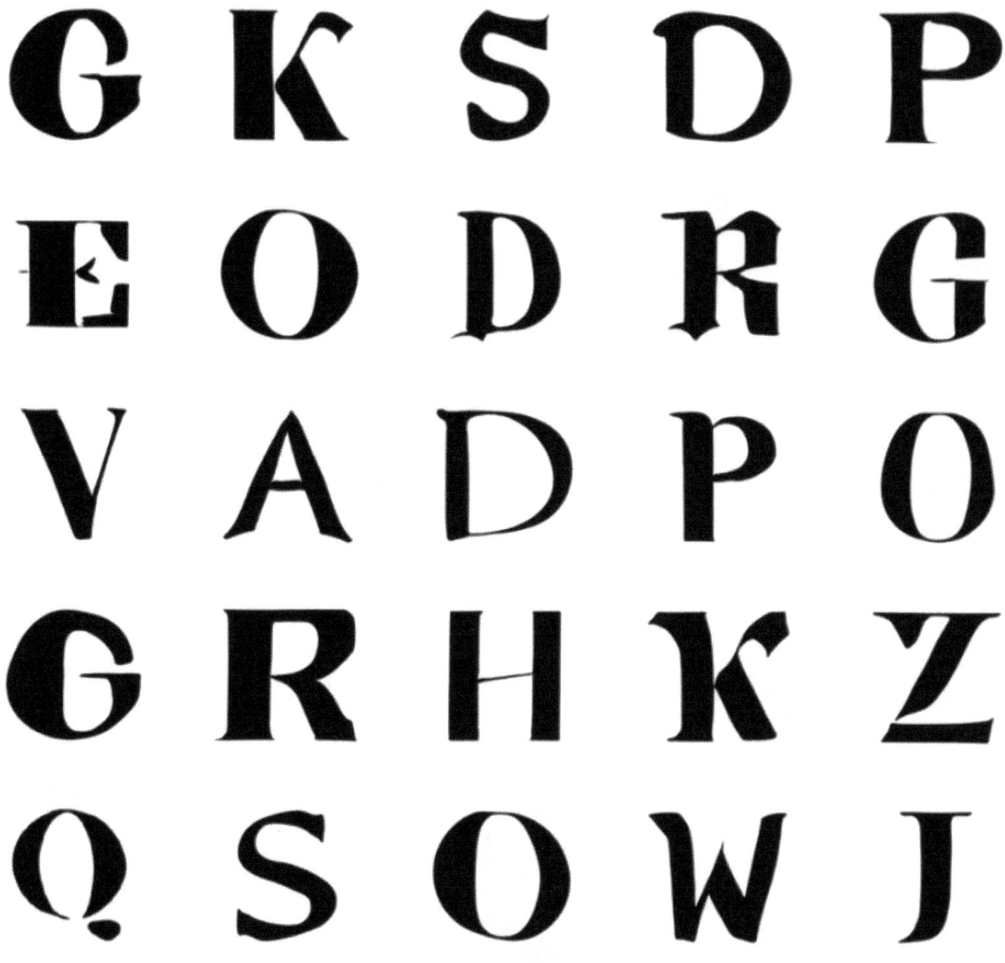

which offers an easy-to-navigate n-dimensional map — makes it both a powerful tool for controlling the generation of complex designs and a domain of investigation in itself. The following chapters and articles will illustrate and explore these characteristics in more depth.

For designers, latent space can serve two complementary but distinct purposes: imitation and exploration. Expanding on the above font example, Figure 7 and 8 show results of letters generated using the latent space of a model trained for that purpose. The precision of the images in Figure 7 demonstrates how realistic this "imitation game" can be. Rather than generating unique designs, this replication can serve designers in specific situations, by providing adequate proposals across various

7

Imitation: letters with somewhat regular font styles, generated by sampling the latent space of a trained model.

8

Exploration: letters with hybrid font styles, generated by sampling the latent space of the same model.

contexts. However, another use case — possibly more immediately relevant to designers — is the possibility of exploring the formal richness found in the "margins." Between the rigid classifications of conventional fonts, for instance, lies a wealth of hybrid styles waiting to be discovered. Figure 8 presents results sampled from across the same latent space and yields a very different impression. By sampling specific moments of the latent space, the collection of generated fonts challenges conventional font classifications and typologies. The letters obtained blend together features picked up from different fonts while merging them into new designs. Rather than merely replicating, this exploration unlocks alternative styles and forms, derived from the initial training set. In this way, AI becomes not only a tangible tool but also a source of inspiration, assisting practitioners in their search for new designs.

The Mosaic of Machine Learning

Machine learning is a field rich in recent breakthroughs and initiatives. These applications span across industries — from speech recognition to image synthesis, all the way to robotics. Consequently, the variety of existing approaches that populate this domain can come across as fairly confusing to the general public. While a comprehensive categorization remains a complex task, a few concepts can help map out the current landscape of investigations. Three lenses in particular can help structure a simplified yet useful classification: learning strategy, building blocks, and model architecture.

Learning Strategy

Machine learning is commonly divided into three subcategories, depending on the training strategy used: supervised, unsupervised, and reinforced. Supervised learning investigates the application of machine learning to the mapping of known input-output data pairs. The boiling water example explained earlier typically illustrates this approach: the model emulates a mapping using labeled data. Unsupervised learning, on the other hand, attempts to model patterns found within the data without specified output values. In other words, the data presented to the algorithm is unlabeled; it is then up to the model to identify trends that emerge from this raw stream of information. Reinforcement learning refers to a third way of conceiving the training process: rather than consuming preexisting data pairs, the model simulates a sequence of steps, receives rewards for certain outcomes, and recalibrates its behavior to improve its score. Over time, the model "reinforces" its ability to perform, as a reaction to its quantified accuracy throughout a broad sequence of steps. These three types of learning strategies help structure a first, rough categorization of the machine learning landscape.

Building Blocks

"Tell me the data you have, I'll tell you the building blocks you need." The ability of a machine learning model to process information and generate accurate predictions depends on the architecture of the neural network it uses, and on how well that architecture can process the input data. Text, images, sequences of numbers, sounds — different data formats call for different types of network building blocks. The advent of the deep learning era has seen the invention of a wide variety of new building blocks, each increasingly tailored to a specific kind of data.

Artificial neuron — The artificial neuron can be considered the mother of all network architectures. As the first formal definition of a computational neuron, it is the least specialized building block. Within its architecture, information flows from a set of inputs, which are weighted, summed, passed through an activation function, and finally output as a single value (Fig. 9). This principle derives directly from early work by McCulloch and Pitts, Rosenblatt, and others who, in the 1940s and '50s, laid the foundations of modern machine learning. Most networks used today across countless commercial applications are built using this basic component or variations of it.

9

Artificial neuron architecture.

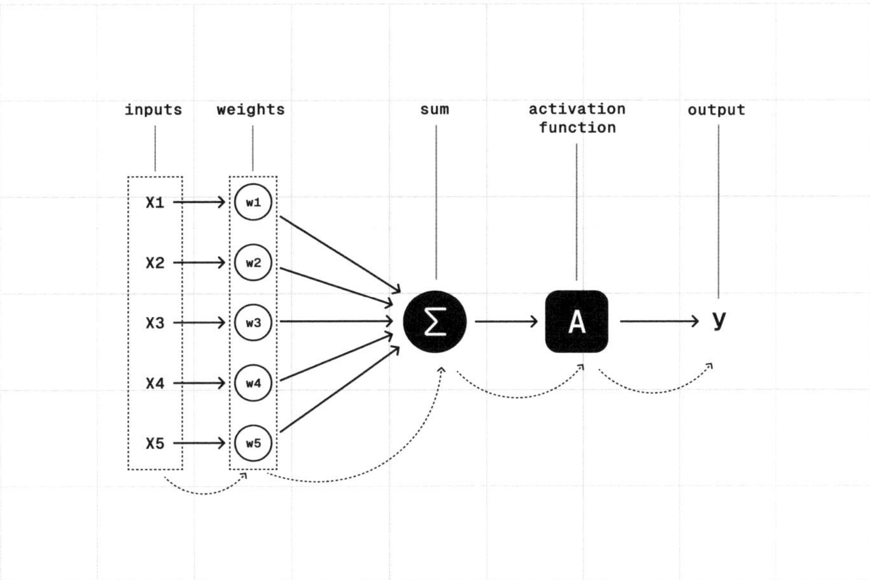

This category of neurons, when assembled into artificial neural networks (ANNs) (Fig. 10), facilitates the modeling of computation as an emergent property of a distributed and diffuse process, loosely inspired by the intricate mechanisms of information processing in the human brain. Within these networks, artificial neurons operate as fundamental computational units, each possessing a set of parameters — commonly referred to as weights — that govern their function and adaptability. These neurons are systematically organized into layered architectures, forming complex network structures capable of learning and generalizing from data inputs.

The internal configuration of ANNs is highly flexible, allowing for significant variation in structure and functionality. Users can adjust numerous parameters — including the number of neurons per layer, the depth of the network, and specific training parameters — to tailor the architecture to the requirements of distinct computational tasks. Moreover, individual layers within a network can be specialized to execute distinct functions, such as filtering relevant features, activating specific patterns, normalizing input distributions, or pooling spatial information to enhance efficiency. These specialized operations contribute to the overall adaptability and efficacy of ANNs, making them applicable across a wide spectrum of computational challenges.

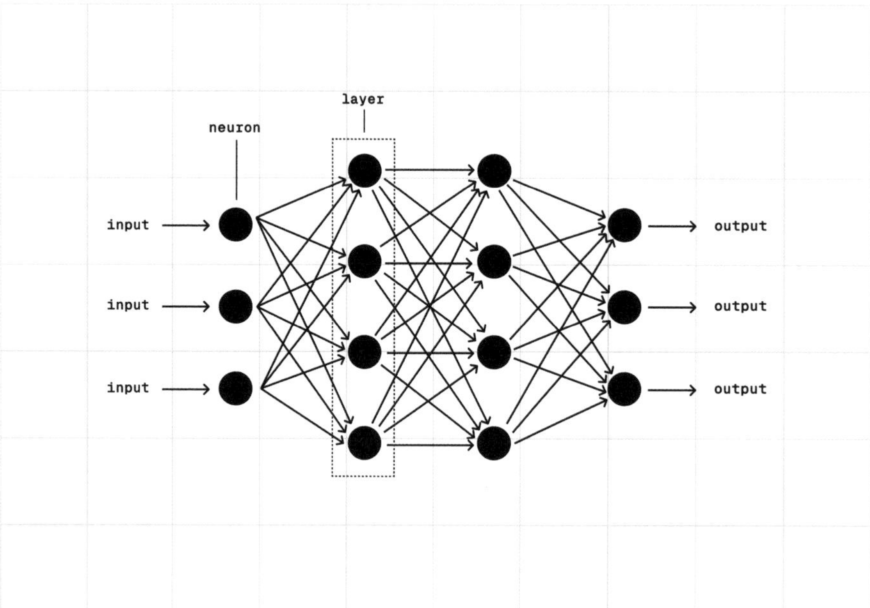

10

Simplified diagram of an ANN architecture.

A closer examination of ANN architecture provides deeper insight into the internal mechanisms that govern the training process. Fundamentally, learning within an ANN occurs through the dynamic flow of data across its structure, during which the network's neurons iteratively adjust their respective weights through a feedback-driven optimization process. This mechanism enables the network to refine its ability to recognize patterns, make predictions, and generalize from input data. Initially, input data propagates through the network in a unidirectional manner — a process referred to as "feedforward" computation. During this phase, neurons apply their weights to incoming signals, transforming raw inputs into increasingly abstract representations as they traverse the network. Once the feedforward computation reaches the final layer, the network produces an output, which is then evaluated against an expected result. This comparison triggers the second key phase of the learning cycle: "backpropagation." (Fig. 11) At this stage, the network calculates the degree of error in its prediction and propagates this information backward, adjusting the weights of specific neurons. In this way, the ANN gradually improves its predictive accuracy over successive training cycles. Through numerous repetitions of feedforward propagation followed by backpropagation-based correction, the network undergoes progressive optimization, ultimately enhancing its capacity to perform complex tasks with increased precision.

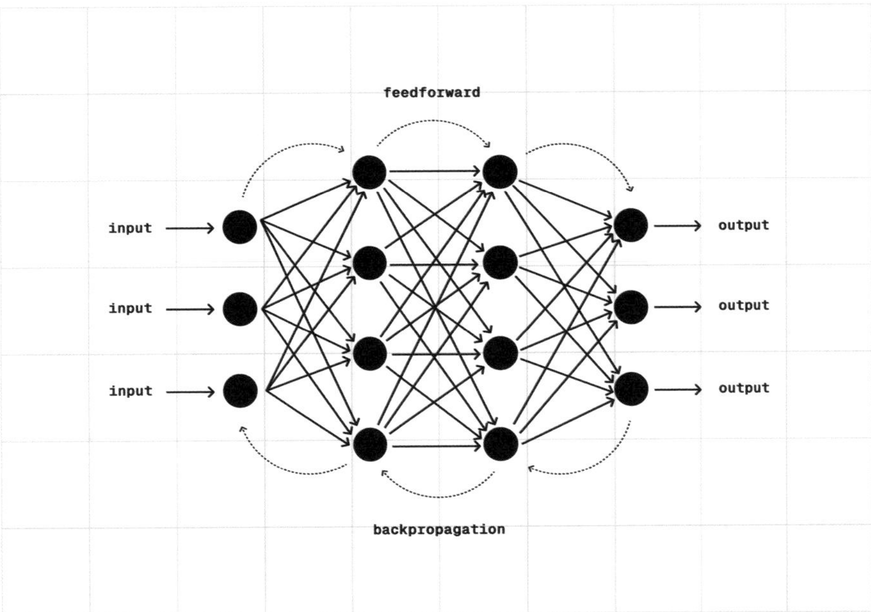

11

Training an ANN: feedforward and backpropagation.

Convolution — Convolutional neural networks (CNNs) are another essential category, whose development has profoundly shaped the course of machine learning. In essence, CNNs are a type of artificial neural network that enables ML models to process images and recognize spatial patterns, in a way that mimics how the human brain interprets visual information. At their core, CNNs consist of layers of artificial neurons equipped with filters (also called kernels) that slide over images to detect features like edges, shapes, textures, etc.; as images pass through these layers, CNNs learn to recognize increasingly complex patterns (Fig. 12). The flexibility of CNNs allows researchers to customize various aspects — such as the number of layers and the size of the filters — enabling them to tailor such building blocks to ever more specific tasks, such as object recognition or medical image analysis.

Like ANNs, training a CNN involves a two-step process: first, the image is processed through the network in a "forward pass" to generate a prediction; then, in a "backward pass," the CNN evaluates its accuracy and adjusts the filters to improve future predictions. This iterative learning process allows CNNs to gradually refine their accuracy. In hindsight, CNNs represent a key breakthrough in machine learning research, as they enabled neural networks to learn from large volumes of visual data with much greater accuracy than earlier architectures. Thanks to this advancement, neural networks became much more relevant for a wide range of applications, from image classification to advanced medical diagnostics.

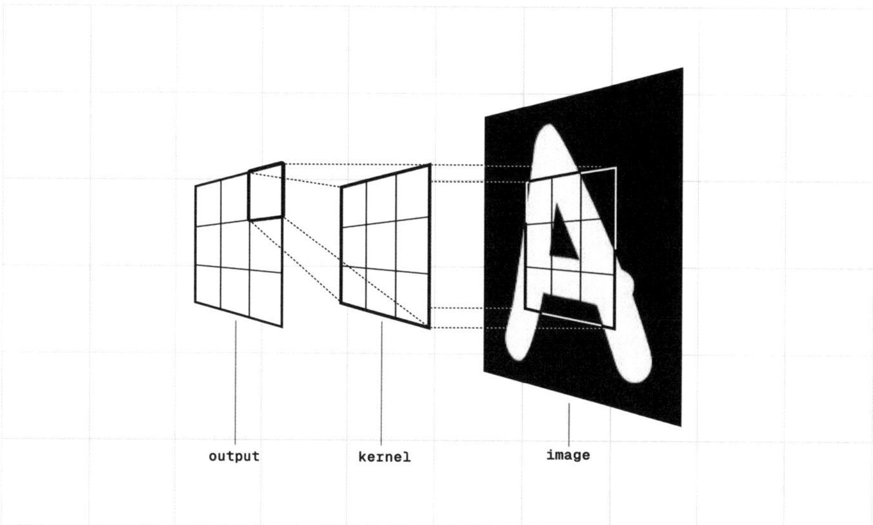

12

Simplified diagram of a convolution operation.

Recurrent neuron — Recurrent Neural Networks (RNNs) are a class of artificial neural networks designed to process sequential data, making them well suited for tasks such as time series analysis and natural language processing. Their key strength lies in their ability to retain information from previous inputs, allowing them to capture contextual dependencies across a sequence.

Unlike feedforward networks described earlier, RNNs handle sequences of varying lengths by maintaining an internal memory that updates with each new input. For example, when processing a sentence, the network refines its predictions by integrating prior context (Fig. 13). This iterative process enables RNNs to adapt dynamically to patterns within the data. As with the other architecture discussed, learning involves two key steps: first, the network processes the input while updating its internal state; second, it evaluates prediction accuracy and adjusts its parameters through backpropagation. As for other architectures, repeating this cycle over time improves the network's performance.

RNNs are widely used in applications such as speech recognition, text generation, and financial forecasting, and many other use cases requiring the prediction of sequential information. As a building block, RNNs also form the foundation for more advanced architectures, such as Long Short-Term Memory (LSTM) networks and Gated Recurrent Units (GRUs), etc.

13

Simplified diagram of a RNN architecture.

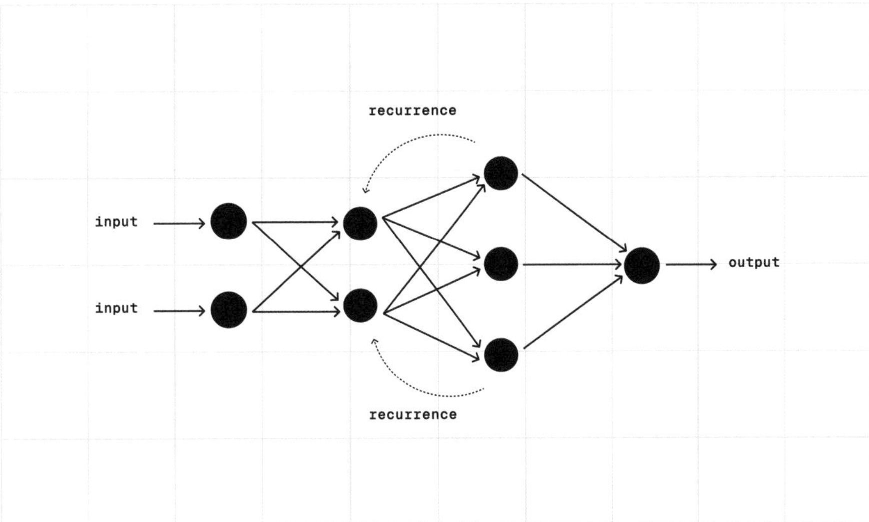

Model Architectures

By leveraging these basic building blocks, recent decades have seen a simultaneous rise in both the performance and complexity of machine learning models. At the core of this fast-paced succession of micro-revolutions lies the evolution of model architectures. In what follows, we unpack this genealogy of architectures, with a particular focus on those models that have led to the current momentum in generative AI.

VAEs — Since their introduction in 2013, Variational Autoencoders (VAEs) have been recognized as a major milestone in AI research. This model architecture helped AI reach a new threshold in its ability to generate compelling content across a range of formats. VAEs approach learning as a process of synthesizing information: learning is understood as the task of compressing data to extract its essential features, and then decompressing it back into its initial form. To achieve this, VAEs combine two distinct components: an "encoder" and a "decoder" (Fig. 14). The encoder abstracts the input data by compressing it while retaining key dimensions. The decoder then unpacks the information by bringing it back to its initial format. As it performs this

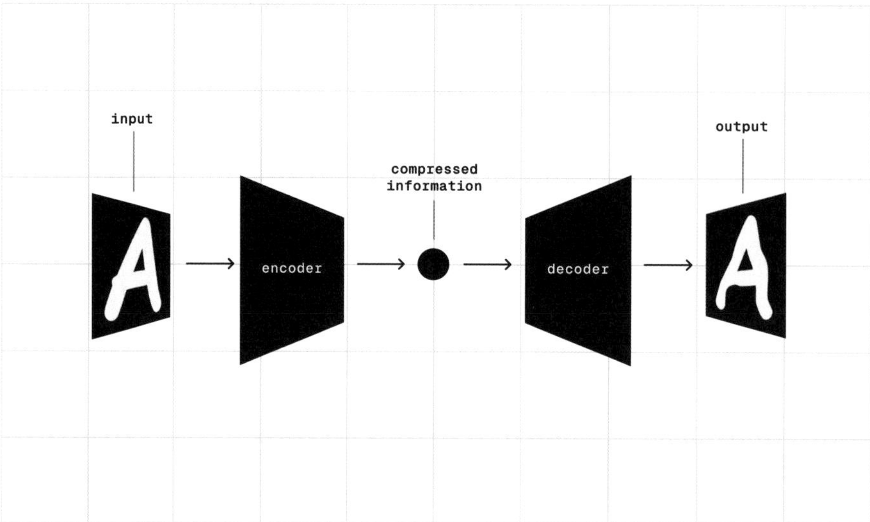

14

Simplified diagram of a VAE architecture.

decompression, the decoder can generate variations of the modeled phenomenon. In other words, VAEs can emulate a given phenomenon by generating multiple, distinct versions of it. This ability to model and reproduce the diversity found within the data constitutes their "generative" power. In recent years, VAEs have been applied in a range of creative fields — including furniture design, fashion, photography, and architecture — offering large numbers of design options suited to each domain.

GANs — Generative adversarial networks (GANs) are a more recent innovation that continues to produce meaningful results. First introduced by Ian Goodfellow et al. in 2014, GANs focus on the generation of data across multiple formats, such as images, graphs, and more. Their architecture relies on the interaction of two competing models — a "generator" and a "discriminator" — to steer the learning process (Fig. 15). Given a dataset, for instance, a collection of images, the discriminator works to improve its ability to recognize real data, while the generator tries to create synthetic images that can pass as real. The discriminator, in turn, provides feedback to the generator about the quality of its outputs. This back-and-forth between generator and discriminator allows for the progressive improvement of image generation throughout the training phase of a GAN model. GANs represent one of this decade's most significant breakthroughs, offering a radically different approach to learning: based on feedback between two agents, rather than the self-correcting loop of a single model. It is also a leap forward in terms of the quality of the results.

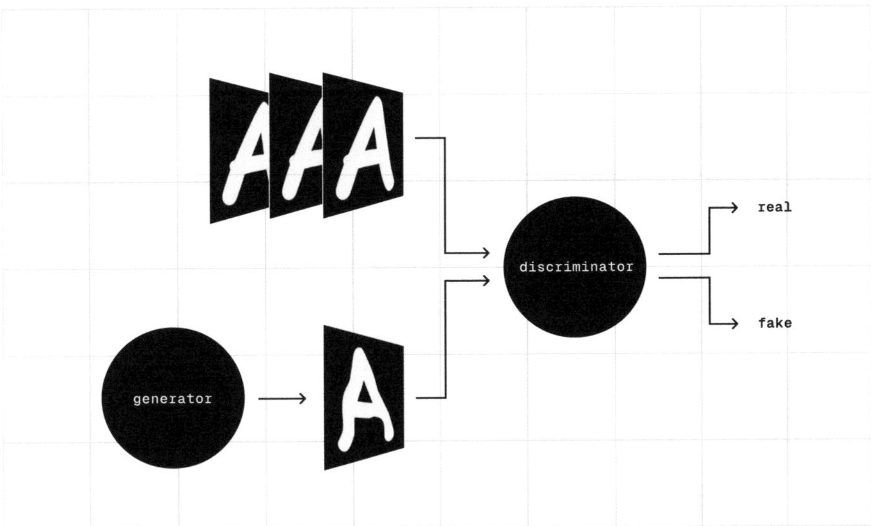

15

Simplified diagram of a GAN architecture.

Diffusion models — Diffusion models are another approach to generative AI that has gained significant traction in recent years. These models focus on the gradual transformation of noise into coherent data, such as images or text. Their architecture, **first proposed by Sohl-Dickstein et al.** in 2015 and **later refined by Ho et al.** in 2020, is based on the principle of reversing a diffusion process (Fig. 16). Given a dataset, a diffusion model first learns to add noise to the data in a step-by-step manner, gradually transforming it into pure noise. Then, it learns to reverse this process, starting from random noise and progressively denoising it to generate new, high-quality samples. As with other architectures, this forward-and-reverse mechanism allows for the creation of increasingly complex and realistic outputs over the course of training.

2 Sohl-Dickstein et al., "Deep Unsupervised Learning Using Nonequilibrium Thermodynamics," 2015.

3 Ho et al., "Denoising Diffusion Probabilistic Models," 2020.

Diffusion models have received significant attention because they offer a more stable and controllable generation process than earlier methods. Technically, their success stems from a distinctive learning strategy that breaks down the generative task into many small, manageable steps, allowing for fine-grained control and incremental correction throughout the generation process.

Commercially, this technology has seen widespread adoption through its large-scale deployment by companies such as OpenAI (DALL·E 2, DALL·E 3), Stablity AI (Stable Diffusion), Midjourney, and others.

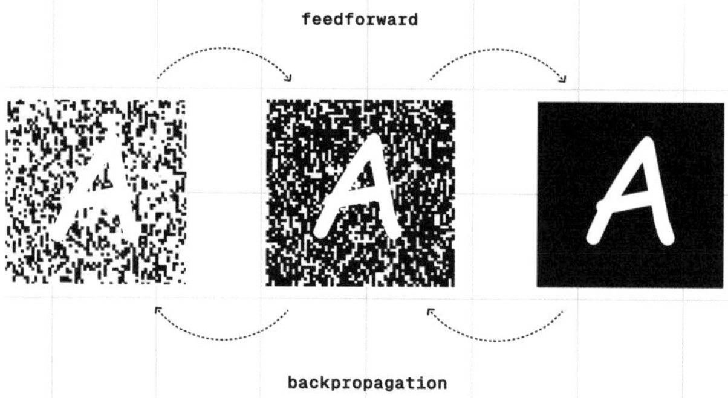

16 Steps of a diffusion process.

Transformers — Transformer models represent a fundamentally different class of AI architectures. This family of neural networks has significantly advanced fields such as natural language processing **since its introduction in a 2017 paper by researchers at Google**. Unlike earlier models that process data sequentially, transformers use a mechanism called "attention" to analyze entire sequences at once, making them highly efficient. At their core, transformers learn relationships between elements in a sequence — such as words in a sentence — through a process called "self-attention," which compares each element to every other element to determine relevance and importance. Their architecture consists of an encoder and a decoder, each composed of multiple layers (Fig. 17).

4 Vaswani et al., "Attention Is All You Need," 2017.

Additional components, including an embedding layer, positional encodings, and multi-head attention mechanisms, contribute to the model's ability to capture the nuances of the input data. During training, transformers optimize these components to perform a range of tasks, including translation, summarization, and text generation. Transformers have become the foundation for many state-of-the-art language models, also known as large language models (LLMs), including GPT (generative pre-trained transformer) and BERT (bidirectional encoder representations from transformers). Their flexibility and power have also led to adoption in various fields beyond natural language processing, such as computer vision and bioinformatics — making transformers a cornerstone of modern AI research and deployment.

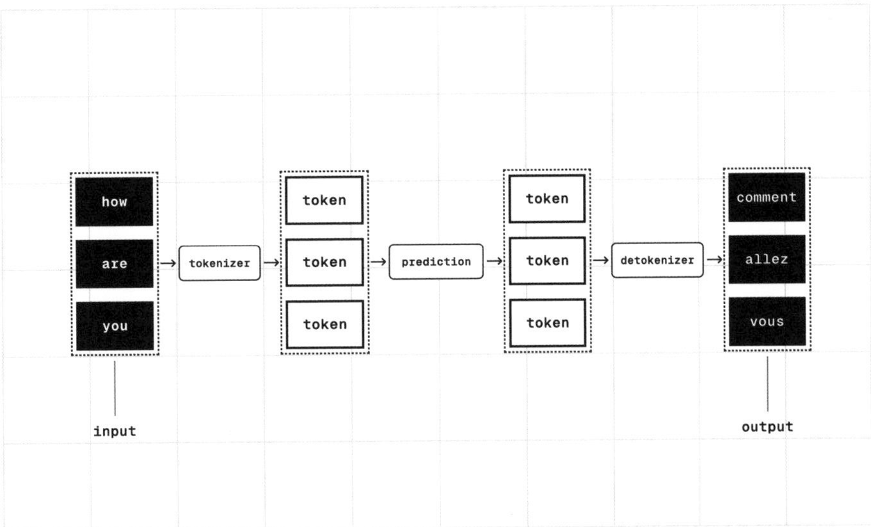

17 Simplified diagram of a transformer architecture.

Multimodal models — Multimodal models have gained increasing importance in recent years due to their ability to leverage artificial intelligence across multiple types of input data and achieve a more comprehensive and nuanced understanding of complex tasks. These models focus on integrating diverse forms of information — such as text, images, audio, and video — processing and analyzing them simultaneously, in a way that mirrors how humans perceive and interpret the world. Given a dataset with various input types, a multimodal model learns to correlate information across different modalities. For instance, it might analyze both the text of a social media post and its accompanying image to better understand its context and sentiment. Typically, a multimodal model consists of separate encoders for each input type, a fusion mechanism to combine the encoded representations, and a decoder to generate the final output (Fig. 18). During training, the model optimizes these components to perform tasks that require cross-modal reasoning, such as visual question answering or multimodal sentiment analysis. This approach represents a significant leap forward in AI capabilities, offering a more holistic method for data analysis and generation, often resulting in more accurate and contextually rich outputs. The technology has enabled remarkable advancements across a range of fields, making possible more robust and versatile AI systems capable of tackling complex, real-world tasks that involve multiple sensory inputs. Models like Mistral's Pixtral model and OpenAI's GPT-4o best exemplify how multimodality has gained momentum — not only in scientific research but also in commercial deployment.

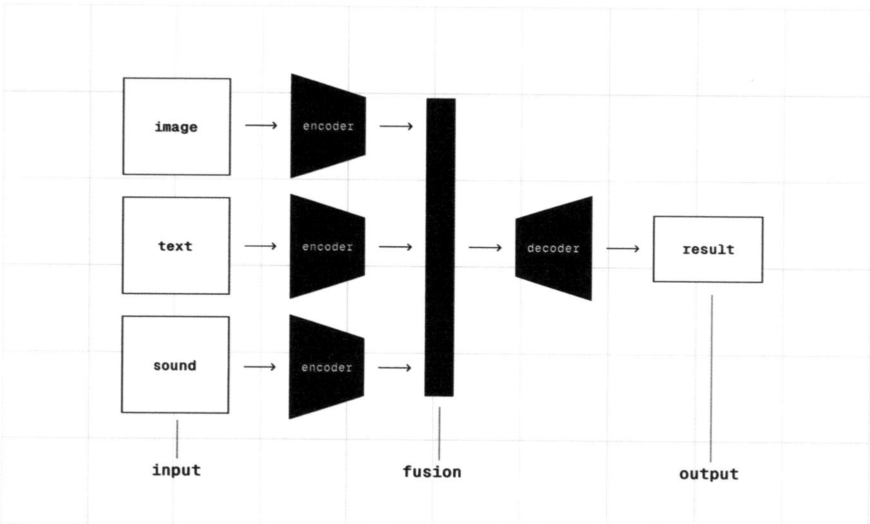

18

Simplified diagram of a multimodal model architecture.

REFERENCES

But What Is a Neural Network? (Part 1)
[Video]
Tutorial, 3Blue1Brown

But What Is a Neural Network? (Part 2)
[Video]
Tutorial, 3Blue1Brown

Backpropagation, Intuitively
[Video]
Tutorial, 3Blue1Brown

LLMs Explained Briefly
[Video]
Tutorial, 3Blue1Brown

Transformers (How LLMs Work) Explained Visually
[Video]
Tutorial, 3Blue1Brown

But What Is a Convolution?
[Video]
Tutorial, 3Blue1Brown

Why Computer Vision Is a Hard Problem for AI
[Video]
Documentary, Quanta Magazine, 2023

Can Large Language Models Understand Meaning?
[Video]
Documentary, Quanta Magazine, 2024

The Zoo

With the foundational concepts now established, and before turning to the current state of AI applications within the architectural domain, a brief interlude of experimentation seems a necessary step. In recent years, not only has the diversity and sophistication of available AI models expanded dramatically, but so too has access to these tools. This democratization has ushered in a period of unprecedented exploration, allowing a broad spectrum of users to engage directly with the technology.

In this context, this chapter introduces what might be considered a digital "zoo" — a curated selection of AI models that have significantly shaped the contemporary AI landscape. Our aim is to offer readers the opportunity to interact directly with these models. Rather than merely discussing their capabilities in abstract terms, we provide a means to explore their behaviors, limitations, and potential firsthand. In doing so, we underscore the importance of familiarity not only with the conceptual implications of AI, but also with its tangible functionality.

To support this exploration, each model is accompanied by a QR code that links to a streamlined digital interface. These interfaces are intentionally designed to be intuitive and accessible, requiring no prior technical expertise. In a matter of moments, readers will be able to experiment with each model and develop a rough understanding of how AI operates across different domains and modalities.

Trellis
[Image to 3D]
Open

Stable Fast 3D
[Image to 3D]
Open

DimensionX
[Image to 3D]
Open

InstantMesh
[Image to 3D]
Open

Hunyuan 3D
[Image to 3D]
Open

Whisper
[Audio to Text]
Open

Text-to-Audio
[Text to Audio]
Open

XTTS
[Audio to Audio]
Open

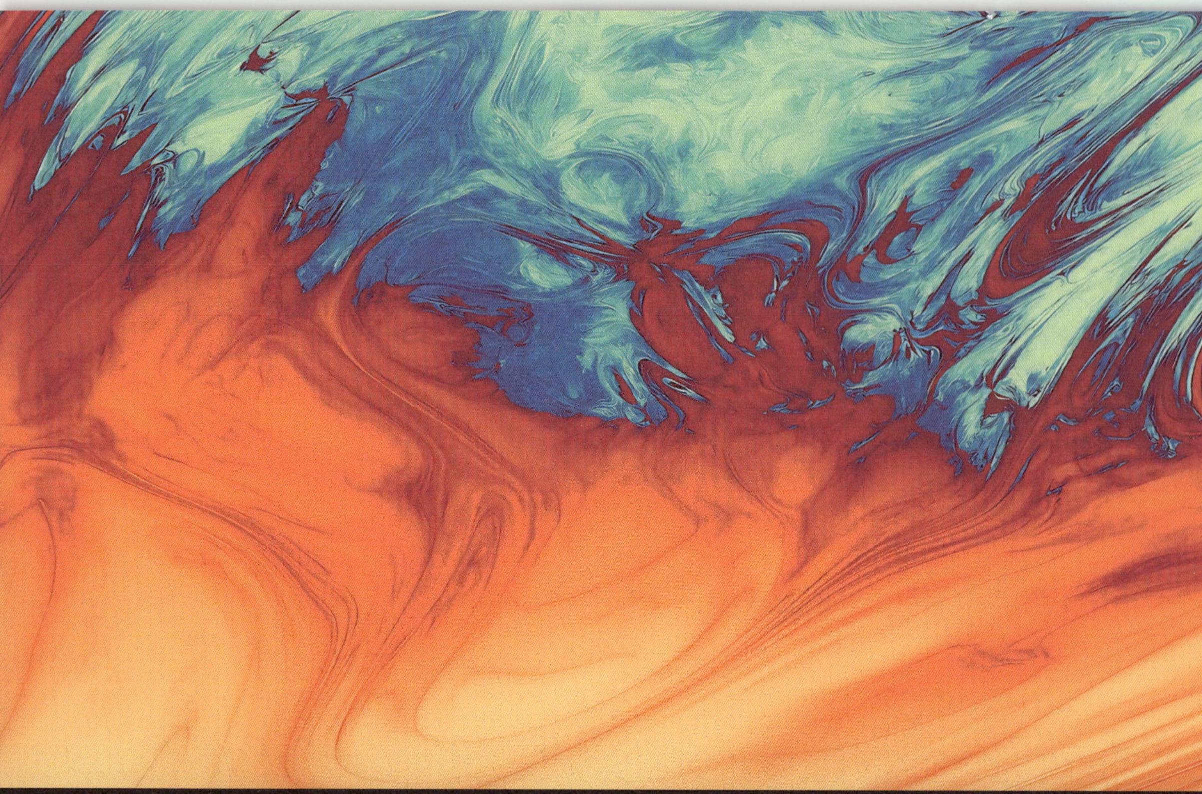

GPT-4o
[Multimodal Model]
Open

Pixtral
[Multimodal Model]
Open

Stable Diffusion 2.1
[Text to Image]
With signup

Flux 1
[Text to Image]
With signup

Imagen 3
[Text to Image]
Open

Flux Schnell
[Text to Image]
Open

Midjourney
[Text to Image]
With signup

DALL·E Mini
[Text to Image]
With signup

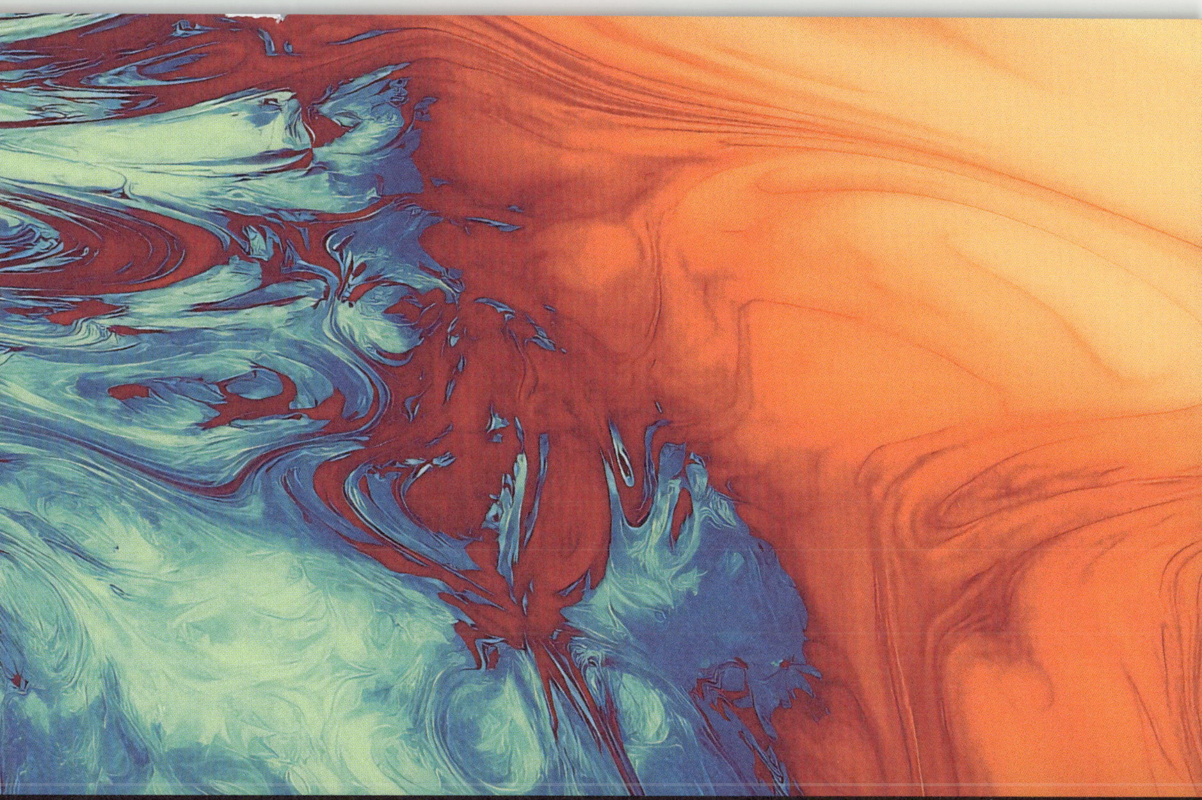

Recraft v3
[Text to Vector]
Open

Background remover
[Image to Image]
With signup

Image outpainting
[Image to Image]
With signup

Image upscaler
[Image to Image]
With signup

Neural style transfer
[Image to Image]
With signup

MusicGen
[Text to Audio]
With signup

Music 01
[Text to Audio]
Open

Bark
[Text to Audio]
With signup

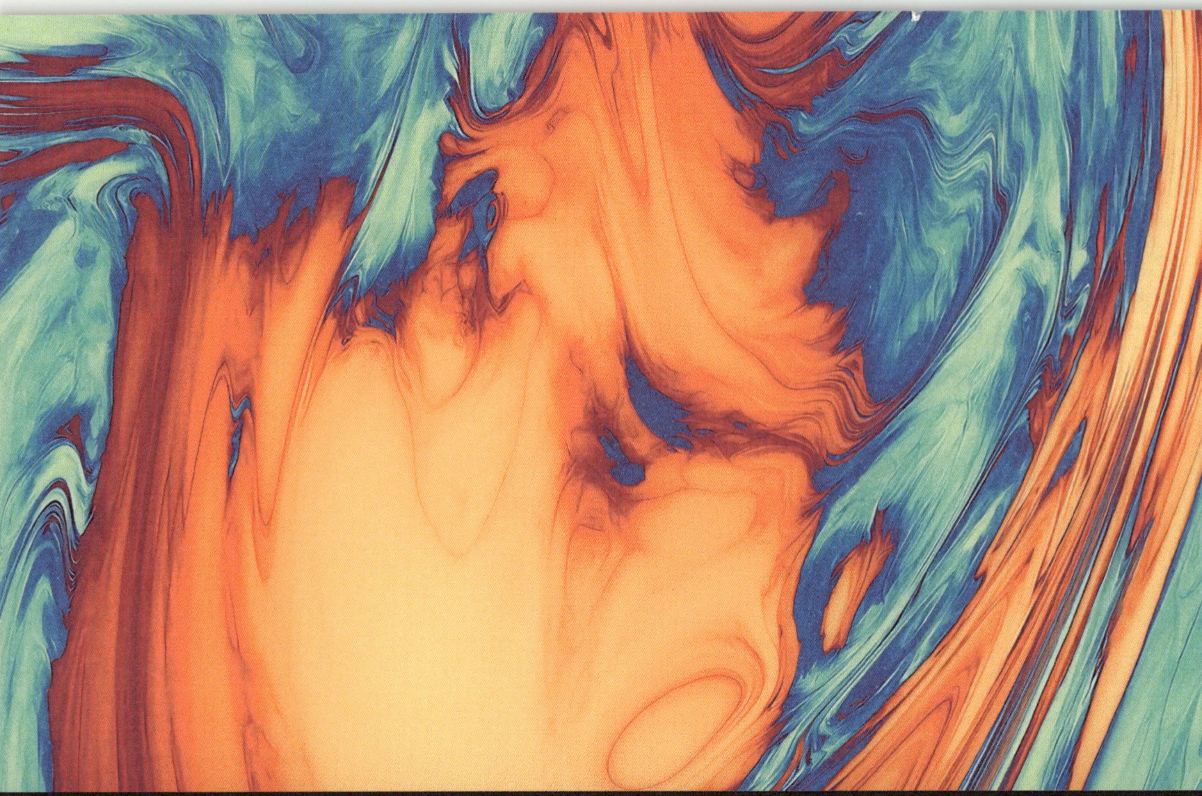

Stable Video Diffusion
[Image to Video]
With signup

Kling 1.6
[Image+Text to Video]
Open

Sora
[Text to Video]
Open

Gen-3-Alpha
[Text to Video]
Open

Wan 2.1
[Text to Video]
Open

Kokoro Text to Speech
[Text to Audio]
With signup

Yolo-World
[Object Detection]
With signup

Detic
[Object Detection]
With signup

ControlNet
[Image to Image]
With signup

LoRA
[Style+Text to Image]
With signup

LGT Net
[Others]
With signup

InstructPix2Pix
[Image+Text to Image]
With signup

Veo 2
[Text to Video]
Open

Claude 3.5
[Text to Text]
Open

DeepSeek R1
[Text to Text]
Open

DeepSeek V3
[Text to Text]
Open

On Pace

We emerge from this gallery of models with a somewhat flat hierarchy. It is, however, crucial to understand the timeframe and velocity of these models' development — while keeping an eye on the deeper, structural changes in the ecosystem that have powered this evolution. If recent years have shown anything, it is that AI is a technology in rapid motion. Grasping the pace of technological substitution that underpins the development of successive generations of AI models is essential. Within just a decade, the evolution of machine learning architectures has advanced at remarkable speed. The chronology presented here (Fig. 19) serves one purpose: to outline the tempo of these changes and the staggered succession of model innovations.

VAEs, introduced in **2013 by Diederik P. Kingma and Max Welling**, remained a thriving area of research until around 2020. 5

5 Kingma and Welling, "Auto-Encoding Variational Bayes," 2013.

GANs, introduced by Ian Goodfellow and his colleagues in 2014, were a major focus until approximately 2022.

Transformer architecture, introduced by Vaswani et al. in the seminal 2017 paper "Attention Is All You Need," has matured and remains a core component of AI research.

Diffusion architecture, as exemplified by DALL·E and Stable Diffusion, emerged in 2020 and remains in active development today.

Multimodal models, the most recent addition to this timeline, can be traced back to 2022. They are now central to both academic discourse and commercial deployment, and have already yielded production-ready systems.

Taken together, this timeline reveals a clear trend: AI models are becoming increasingly sophisticated and versatile, evolving from specialized architectures toward more general-purpose systems capable of handling diverse types of data and tasks. This rapid progress is enabled by three underlying trends that have driven AI innovation over the past decade: a steady rise in model complexity, improvements in computational efficiency, and the exponential growth of commercially available processing power. The following sections briefly address each of these forces to help situate the current moment at the intersection of these broader developments.

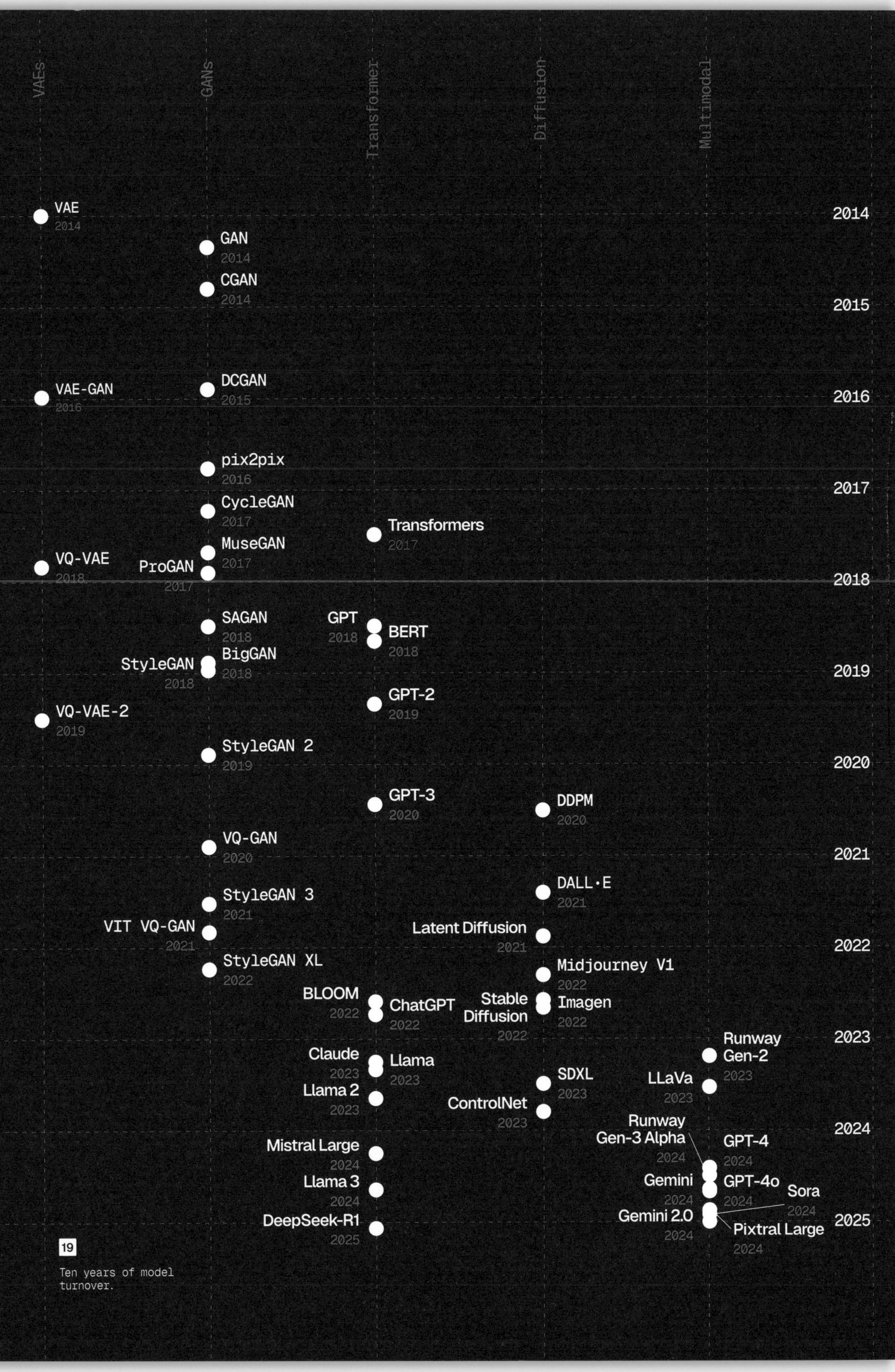

19

Ten years of model turnover.

Models Have Grown in Complexity

AI model complexity can be measured by the number of parameters a model contains. Since the onset of the deep learning era, the number of parameters in leading models **has doubled approximately every five to six months**. This pace distinguishes the current period from earlier phases of AI development. A look at milestone models (Fig. 20) provides a clear picture of this sharp increase in scale:

AlexNet (2012) — ~60 million parameters
VGGNet (2014) — ~138 million parameters
BERT-Large (2018) — 340 million parameters
GPT-2 (2019) — 1.5 billion parameters
GPT-3 (2020) — 175 billion parameters
PaLM (2022) — 540 billion parameters
GPT-4 (2023) — Estimated to be over 1 trillion parameters

This rise in model size is tied to the emergence of what the field now calls **"foundation model."** In essence, the research community has come to recognize the importance of decoupling two stages: on the one hand, the development and training of very large, general-purpose models; on the other, the adaptation of these models for specific, downstream applications. This division of labor has underpinned research efforts over the past five years and has propelled companies like OpenAI, Mistral, and Anthropic to the forefront of foundation model development.

6 Epoch AI, "Compute Trends Across Three Eras of Machine Learning," 2022.

7 Bommasani et al., "On the Opportunities and Risks of Foundation Models," 2021.

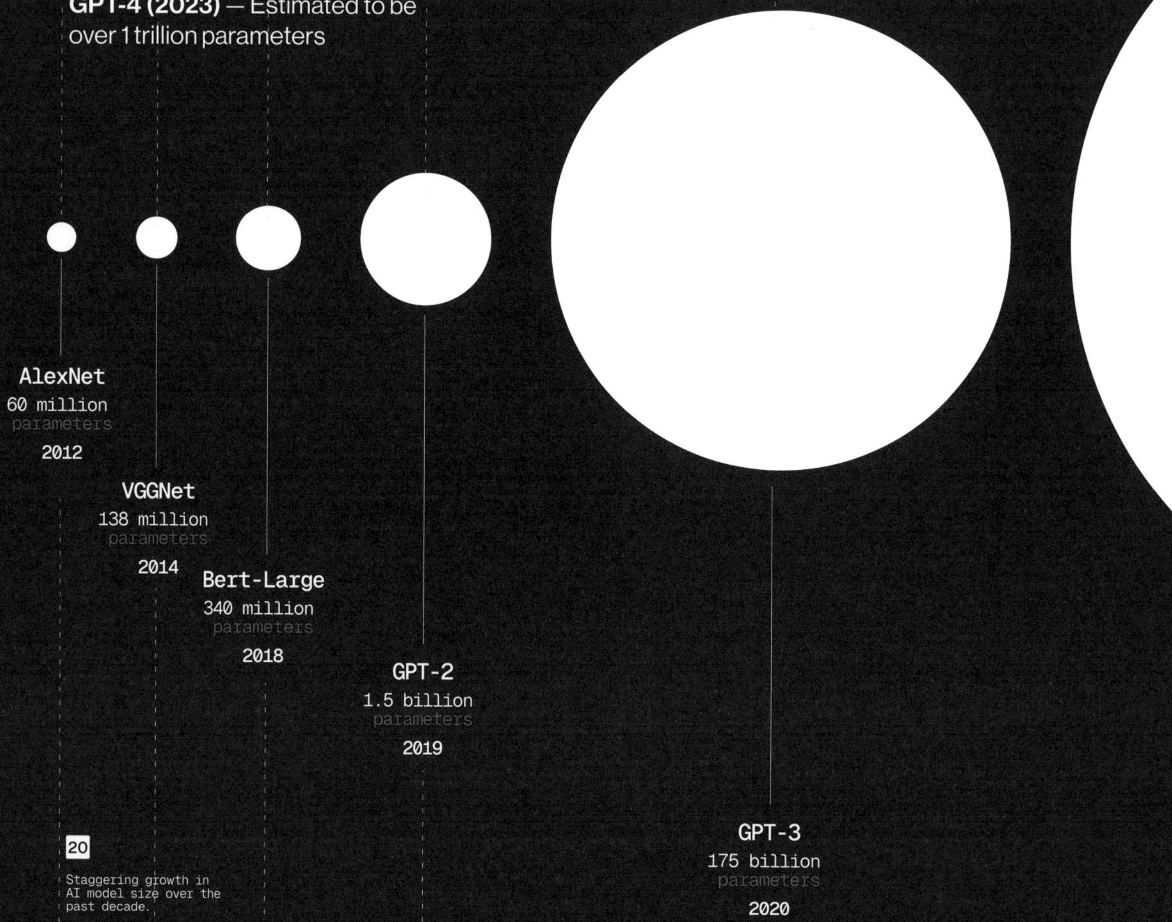

20 Staggering growth in AI model size over the past decade.

PaLM
540 billion
parameters
2022
GPT-4
> 1 trillion
parameters
2023

Models Have Become More Efficient

Not only have models increased in size — their underlying algorithms have also improved, allowing them to perform the same tasks with significantly less compute over time. To quantify this trend: the amount of compute required to achieve a given level of performance in language models **has been declining at a rate of roughly threefold per year** (Fig. 21). This rise in computational efficiency has been driven by advances in model architecture, improved optimizers, and other algorithmic innovations. These developments show that algorithmic progress also has a critical role in advancing AI.

8 Epoch AI, "Algorithmic Progress in Language Models," 2024.

21

Graph of improvement in computational efficiency across AI model generations.

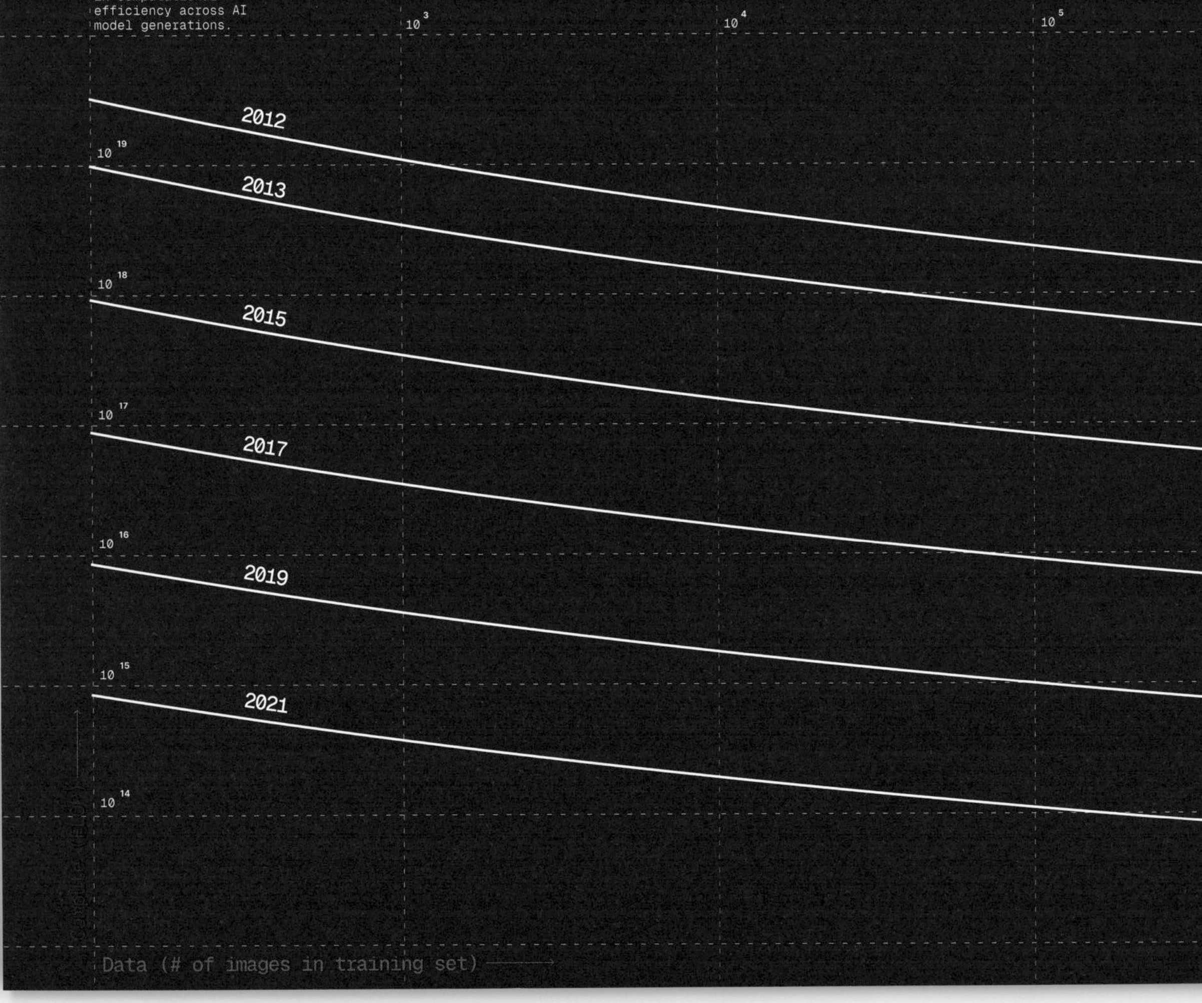

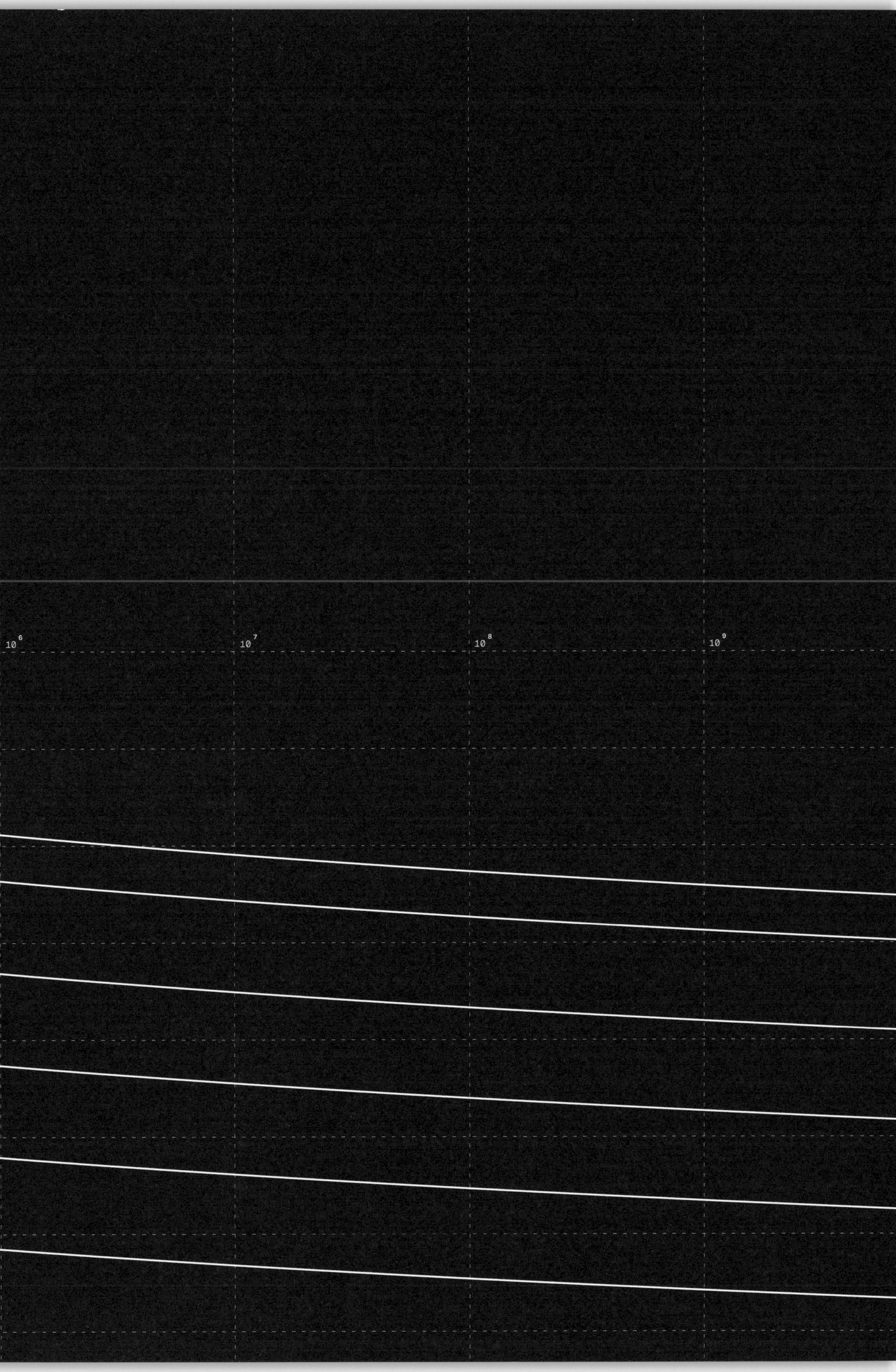
10^6
10^7
10^8
10^9

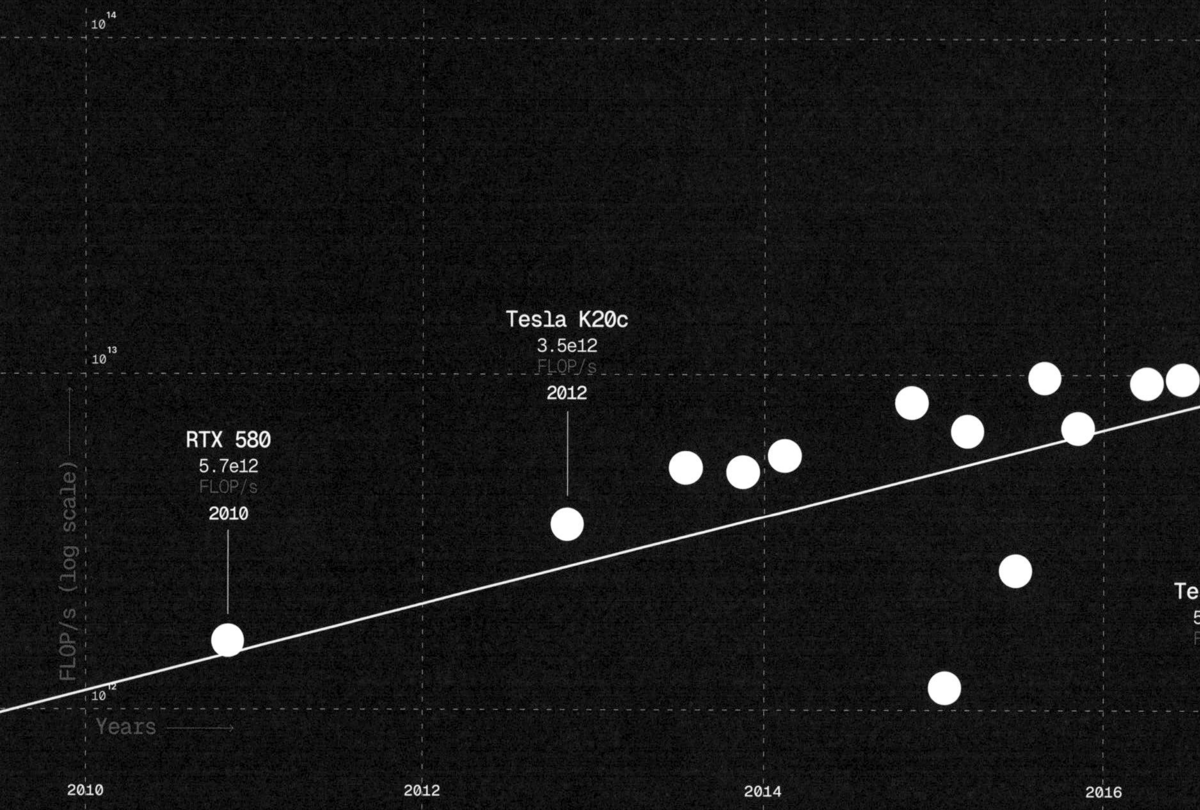

22

Rapid increase in GPU hardware power over the past ten years.

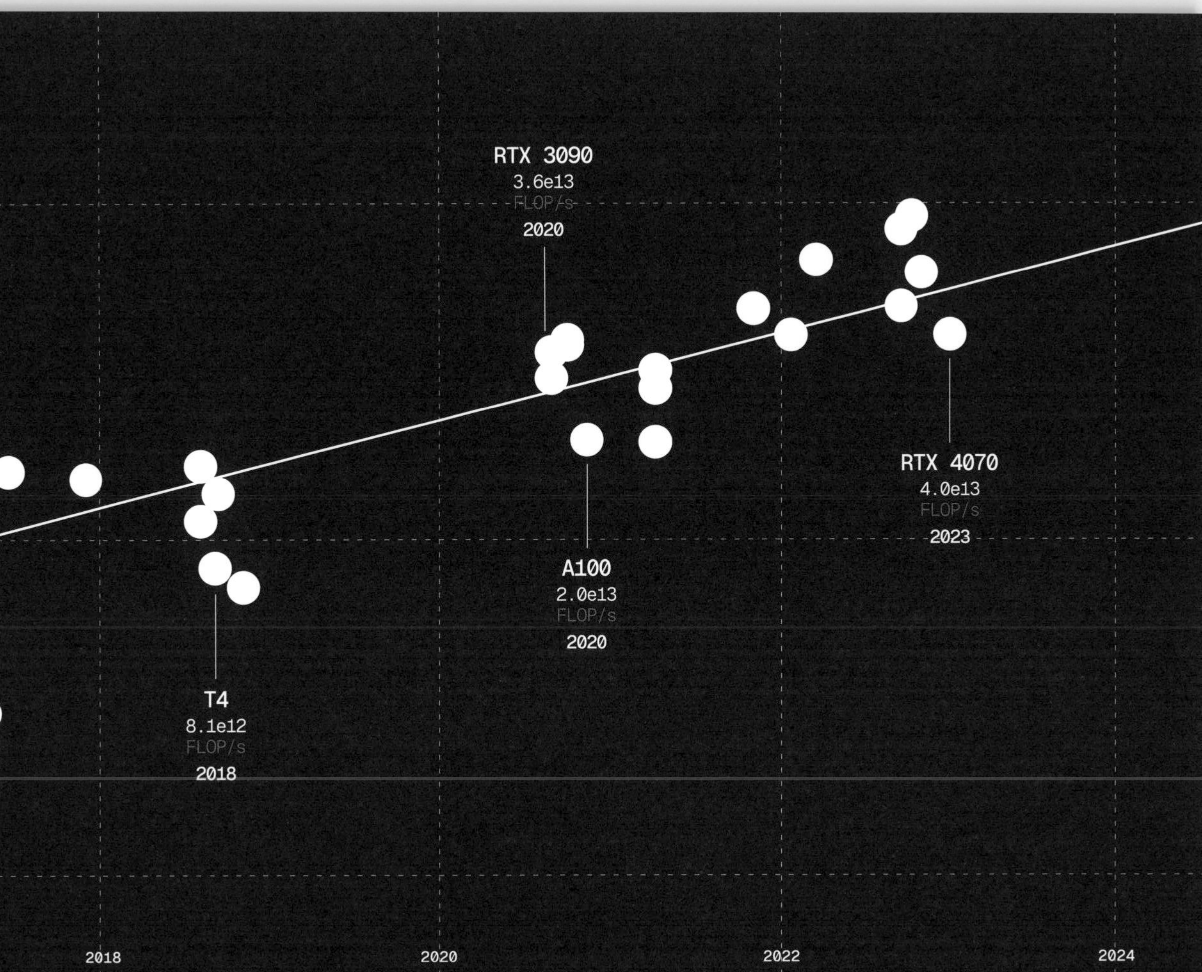

Hardware Has Become More Powerful

AI models rely heavily on the hardware used for both their training and large-scale deployment. This is why increasingly powerful chips, manufactured by providers such as Nvidia, Arm, and others, have formed the backbone of the deep learning revolution. More specifically, as AI shifted toward parallel computing — particularly through the use of graphical processing units (GPUs) — the power of commercially available GPUs has become a key factor in the competitive landscape among AI developers. To illustrate the trend we have been witnessing over the past 15 years with a single metric: FLOP/s performance — the amount of data (counted as floating point operations) a piece of hardware can process per second, **has doubled approximately every 2.3 years across the 47 machine learning hardware accelerators commonly available on the market** (Fig. 22). This steep increase in computational power has been one of the primary engines driving companies' ability to train foundation models, which in turn has enabled the current boom in generative AI.

9 Epoch AI, "Trends in Machine Learning Hardware," 2023.

On Depth & Value Chain

Today, the development and training of large generative AI models takes place at only a handful of highly technical companies worldwide, including OpenAI, Google, Anthropic, and Mistral. However, downstream from these few players, an entire ecosystem has emerged. This broader landscape includes actors who either adapt these models or simply use them as-is for their own specific use cases. Architecture, among many other fields, now contributes to and benefits from this growing value chain. Understanding this ecosystem is essential for positioning the discipline of architecture within the broader evolution of the current moment. To unpack the dynamics at play, we can start by considering what this technology implies for different stakeholders. The complexity and cost of working with AI models varies dramatically, from highly technical processes requiring deep expertise to more accessible workflows available to general users. This already suggests the presence of different types of stakeholders across the value chain. Today, this landscape can be roughly divided into four tiers, ordered by increasing cost and complexity (Fig. 23), which we briefly outline here before turning to other aspects.

Modelers represent the first category of this spectrum. At this stage of the value chain, we find stakeholders tasked with producing and training new, state-of-the-art neural network architectures. The extreme technical complexity of this work requires world-class engineering talent, while the ever-increasing size of models — and therefore the cost of training them — means expenditures are extremely high. To illustrate: the full training OpenAI's GPT-4 model is reported to have cost around $100 million. This single figure reflects the steep barrier to entry at this stage, where competing requires a level of technical expertise and funding that only a few can match. Moreover, breakthroughs in model architecture depend heavily on the ability to assemble top research teams capable of pushing the limits of existing scientific knowledge. Conversely, the production of foundation models today is largely the domain of a small number of tech companies (such as Mistral, RunwayML, OpenAI, Alphabet, and others), and a few top-tier academic institutions. Through open-source releases or commercial offerings, these players provide the basis for downstream innovation.

Retrainers represent the immediate next step in the value chain. This category refers to those who partially retrain existing foundation models or rewire shallower machine learning architectures to tackle complex use cases. These types of deep adaptations are pursued by countless industrial players with internal R&D teams, tech ventures, or academic institutions — often working at the intersection of computer science and other disciplines. This trend may best express the profound impact AI has had over the past decade. Scientific departments — increasingly even the humanities, including fields like social sciences, law, and architecture — have begun to collaborate closely with computer science researchers. These efforts can be seen across university campuses and are reflected in the growing academic literature, where generic machine learning frameworks are applied to an ever-broader range of topics. In architecture, for instance, a quick glance at recent proceedings from conferences like CAADRIA or ACADIA shows how deeply this technology has permeated the work of researchers in the field. Still, this stage of the value chain requires some level of engineering expertise to retrain models effectively, along with sufficient funding to support that work. As a result, retrainers today are mostly found in institutional settings, whether in industry, academia, or tech startups. It is a stage that remains largely out of reach for companies without a structured engineering culture, or at the very least, tech enthusiasts.

Enter the next category: **fine-tuners**. This group represents the direct result of a technological shift that has taken shape over the past decade. Fine-tuning refers to the shallow repurposing of existing AI models. In terms of neural network architecture, it typically involves the quick retraining of only the final layers of a model, adapting it to a new use case. With recent breakthroughs like LoRA, DoRA, and others, fine-tuning has become a low-cost process that requires little to no engineering expertise. As a result, the adaptation of models has become dramatically more accessible in recent years, particularly among tech enthusiasts. A thriving DIY culture has emerged online, giving rise to communities of fine-tuners who gather around platforms such as AUTOMATIC111 (an open-source, Grasshopper-like visual programming tool that allows users to run, fine-tune, and chain open-source models) and collaborative platforms like HuggingFace and CivitAI. This democratization has spread widely across the creative industries, where countless tech-savvy designers have begun repurposing models to support their production workflows. While institutional actors, including companies and universities, also benefit from this ecosystem, what distinguishes this stage of the value chain is the vibrant online creative communities it has helped foster.

At the very end of the spectrum, we find **users**. This final stage of the value chain is perhaps the most obvious: consumers today widely recognize AI as a tool that can support their everyday productivity. Without any fine-tuning or deep repurposing, hundreds of millions of users now access AI-powered services online to accomplish daily tasks. To give a striking example: in January 2025, ChatGPT alone had over 100 million active users. The scale of this phenomenon is directly tied to its ease of access. While no technical expertise is required to use AI models, a set of informal know-hows has emerged around the art of working with models like Midjourney, ChatGPT, Le Chat, and others. Users are encouraged to provide context — information surrounding their request, such as personal data, relevant background knowledge, or task-specific input — and to develop proficiency in what is now loosely called "prompting": the ability to formulate clear, targeted requests in order to obtain valid and useful responses from an AI model. In this world, architecture is no exception. Like many other professions, it stands to benefit from the support these tools can provide.

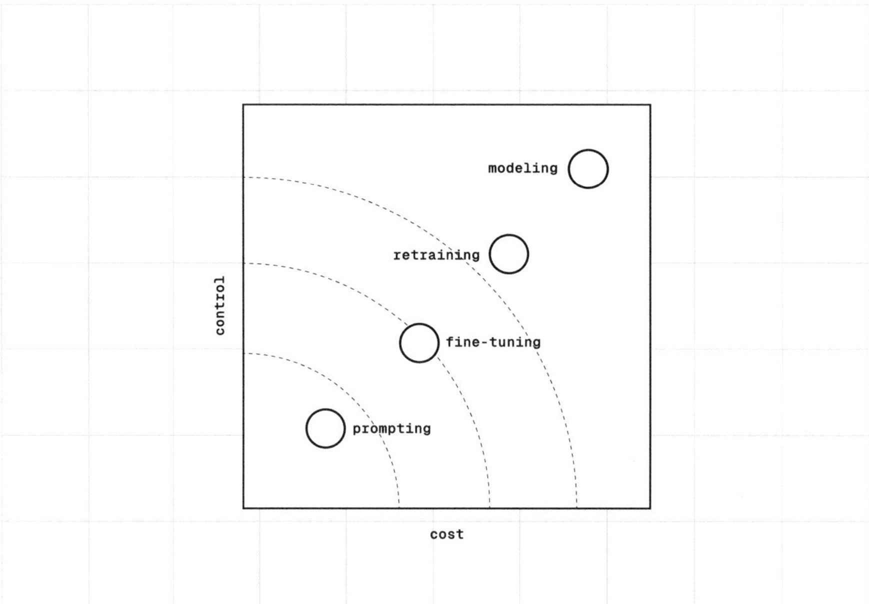

23

Diagram of AI's value chain, Cost vs. control.

One might ask: How does our discipline position itself, and where can it realistically find a place? Where will architecture stand in the future within AI's value chain (Fig. 24)? This section aims to clarify where architects and architectural practices might locate themselves within this fast-moving ecosystem. A look at the current state of the field already provides some answers. Architects today stand between two thresholds — a floor and ceiling: between the role of user and that of light retrainer. The user status is now self-evident. It is a trivial fact that architects can draw on tools like ChatGPT to help draft a client brief, or use Midjourney to generate polished, speculative renderings. The use of Midjourney by MVRDV in internal workshops, for instance, reflects this widespread reality. More intriguing, though perhaps less immediately obvious, is the growing presence of architects as fine-tuners and retrainers, a development that merits closer attention. A spirit of experimentation among younger practitioners has, in recent years, produced a new crop of designers using fine-tuning techniques to adapt models to specific aesthetics. The work of Hassan Ragab and Ismael Seleit from Foster + Partners exemplifies this trend. Through fine-tuning frameworks such as Automatic1111, ControlNet, and LoRA, as well as commercial tools like Runway, some architects are expanding their toolkit to include model adaptation, shaping outputs like drawings, perspectives, and other representation forms to align with their particular stylistic goals.

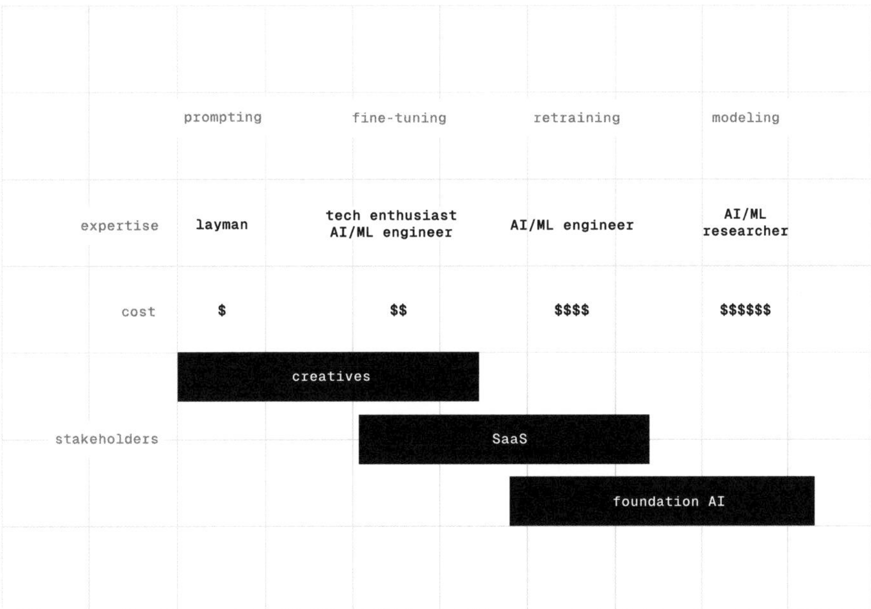

24 Understanding AI's value chain and the position of creatives within it.

One step further upstream, some architects have taken on the role of retrainers, though in more specific contexts. In academic settings or within certain technology-driven companies, more intensive forms of engagement are emerging: projects that reconfigure existing models or undertake deeper training runs. These architects often depart from traditional practice paths to pursue more research-oriented careers. Examples include work at institutions such as MIT, Simon Fraser University, Autodesk Research, and Forma (formerly Spacemaker), where architects contribute to top-tier research that goes beyond the fine-tuning stage. These efforts benefit from a "trickle-down" dynamic, in which breakthroughs developed in the broader tech sector are subsequently tailored to meet the needs and specificities of the AEC (architecture, engineering, and construction) industry.

Finally, as we move along this spectrum — from users, to fine-tuners, to retrainers — it is important to note the steep drop-off in numbers. While many architects now use AI tools for basic tasks, far fewer operate at the level of retraining. This disparity reflects several structural factors, including the limited capacity of the AEC sector to fund R&D, uneven levels of tech literacy among practitioners, and architecture's broader difficulty in integrating into interdisciplinary or venture-driven innovation ecosystems. Taken together, these conditions help explain the discipline's current distribution within the AI value chain.

REFERENCES

Can AI Scaling Continue Through 2030?
[Article]
Report, Epoch AI, 2024

Training Compute of Frontier AI Models Grows by 4–5x per Year
[Article]
Report, Epoch AI, 2024

Tracking Large-Scale AI Models
[Article]
Report, Epoch AI, 2024

Algorithmic Progress in Language Models
[Article]
Report, Epoch AI, 2024

AI Across Scales

Having laid out the core concepts and terminology necessary to understanding AI, we now turn toward the practical reality of this technology in architecture. The following pages attempt to map existing, tangible models, software, and research papers to provide an accessible overview of what is either already available or currently in development. At a glance, the discipline seems to have crossed the threshold from experimentation to adoption over the past five years. Yet the actual presence of AI in architecture is not a uniform or singular phenomenon. Rather, it constitutes a far more uneven and heterogeneous landscape that this chapter attempts to capture. From a distance, at least three clear tendencies emerge.

Uneven maturity — The varying levels of maturity among generative AI models across different modalities result in widely differing contributions to architecture today. The stark contrast, from the current ubiquity of image generation to the early-stage demonstrations of 3D generative models, illustrates how much each medium's level of development conditions the depth and relevance of AI's impact, ranging from the profound to the experimental or superficial.

Ongoing substitution — Models that were mainstream just four years ago, such as GANs and VAEs, have gradually been supplanted by newer architectures, including diffusion models and transformers. This latest generation has propelled both research and applications. In parallel, the distinction between foundational models and their domain-specific adaptations, as discussed earlier, has also reshaped AI's role in architecture, as it has in many other fields.

Widened spectrum — AI's emergence in architecture has brought with it a kind of fragmentation. The spectrum of contributors has broadened dramatically in just five years, from in-field, AEC-centric research projects to out-of-field tools and mainstream platforms industrializing AI features at scale. At the same time, the channels through which AI enters the discipline have also diversified, ranging from integrations in legacy software to the standalone web applications.

To help navigate the growing number of ongoing applications, we have chosen to counter this general fragmentation by applying a rather simple thematic outline to this chapter. Experiments, use cases, channels, and contributors are grouped here according to different architectural scales:

Building scale (p. 128) — Gathers current experiments focused on conventional architectural representations such as sections, floor plans, facades, etc.

Perspectives (p. 134) — Presents recent developments in AI research concerning its use to generate realistic perspective views, as well as the state of commercial tools.

Structures (p. 140) — Covers current research at the intersection of architecture and civil engineering related to the analysis and generation of structural systems.

Performance (p. 146) — Focuses on the use of AI in forecasting of building performance, including CFD analysis, daylight analysis, and related simulations.

Urban scale (p. 152) — Looks at the growing field of research on AI-generated urban masterplans and reviews the current state of commercial applications.

3D (p. 158) — Concludes with an overview of current research into 3D generation and the emerging promise of large world models.

To each scale its experimental landscape — to each facet, its particular relationship with AI tools and software. Compared to the state of the field when the first version of this book was published three years ago, this panorama reveals a substantial transformation. Through the overview provided in this chapter, we hope to provide, if not an exhaustive account, then at least an up-to-date snapshot of current experiments, along with a clear view of the AI-enabled solutions now shaping architecture.

Building Scale

As discussed earlier, the latest generations of AI models provide architects with increasingly sophisticated tools for controlling, constraining, and guiding the generative process. While AI has been applied to multiple facets of architectural design, its most pronounced impact so far has been in 2D representation — particularly at the building scale. This includes the generation of floor plans, sections, and facades, which has benefited extensively from recent AI-driven advances.

This recent wave of applications builds upon an earlier generation of research initiatives that emerged approximately five years ago. That first phase of AI-driven architectural research was predominantly characterized by the use of variational autoencoders (VAEs) and generative adversarial networks (GANs). These early explorations showcased AI's potential in generating architectural layouts, including the arrangement of rooms, structural elements, and facades. Notable projects such as **House-GAN** (Nauata et al., 2020) and **ArchiGAN** (Chaillou, 2020) provided preliminary demonstrations of how AI could assist the architectural design process, albeit with significant limitations in control and scalability.

1 2

Nauata et al., "House-GAN: Relational Generative Adversarial Networks for Graph-Constrained House Layout Generation," 2020.

Chaillou, "ArchiGAN: Artificial Intelligence x Architecture," 2020.

Subsequent refinements built upon these early contributions, introducing greater levels of constraint and precision. HouseGAN++ (Nauata et al., 2021) improved upon its predecessor by incorporating additional architectural constraints, leading to more practical and structurally coherent layouts. Similarly, **FloorplanGAN** (Luo et al., 2022) focused on the generation of housing unit layouts while achieving vector-based representations, enhancing their adaptability to real-world design workflows. Parallel to these advances in spatial layout generation, researchers also leveraged StyleGAN models to explore architectural stylistic control. Kyle Steinfeld's **GAN Loci** (Steinfeld, 2019) applied StyleGAN to replicate the characteristic aesthetics of suburban neighborhoods, demonstrating the potential of

3 4

Luo et al., "FloorplanGAN: Vector Residential Floorplan Adversarial Generation," 2022.

Steinfeld, "Imaging Place Using Generative Adversarial Networks (GAN Loci)," 2019/2022.

5

Meng, "Exploring in the Latent Space of Design," 2022.

AI in architectural stylistic synthesis. Building on this concept, **Shengyu Meng utilized StyleGAN2** (Meng, 2021) to generate building facade images with controllable stylistic properties, taking an important step toward mapping the latent space of architectural representation. Despite their promise, these GAN- and VAE-based approaches faced significant challenges, particularly concerning scalability, interpretability, and the ability to generalize across diverse architectural typologies.

6 7 8

Shabani et al., "HouseDiffusion: Vector Floorplan Generation via a Diffusion Model," 2022.

Hong et al., "Cons2Plan: Vector Floorplan Generation from Various Conditions," 2024.

Leng et al., "ArchiDiffusion," 2024.

The field has since transitioned into a second phase, marked by the adoption of more advanced generative techniques — specifically, diffusion models. Papers such as **HouseDiffusion** (Shabani et al., 2022, Fig. 25) and **Cons2Plan** (Hong et al., 2024) exemplify this new era of architectural AI research. These projects demonstrate how diffusion models have not only increased the quality of generated outputs but also introduced greater control over the generative process. By leveraging graph-based conditioning, models such as Cons2Plan allow architects to specify programmatic and spatial constraints, ensuring that generated designs adhere to functional and contextual requirements. The flexibility of diffusion models has also allowed for more experimental approaches. A notable example is **ArchiDiffusion** (Leng et al., 2024), which extends AI's capabilities beyond mere layout generation to include structural design specifications, further blurring the boundary between conceptual exploration and engineering feasibility.

9 10 11

Galanos et al., "ArchiText: Language-Driven Generative Architecture Design," 2023.

Luo et al., "DStruct2Design," 2024.

Du et al., "Text2BIM," 2024.

Simultaneously, the emergence of transformer-based architectures has further expanded AI's role in architectural design. One of the earliest applications of large language models (LLMs) for architectural generation was **ArchiText** (Galanos et al., 2023, Fig. 26), which explored the potential of text-based models for generating floor plan configurations. Since then, more advanced projects have continued to push the boundaries of transformer applications. **DStruct2Design** (Luo et al., 2024) leveraged LLMs to generate program-conditioned floor plans, demonstrating how AI can bridge textual architectural specifications with spatial design outcomes. Around the same time, **Text2BIM** (Du et al., 2024, Fig. 27) introduced a novel approach to 3D architectural modeling, utilizing LLMs to generate building information modeling (BIM) structures directly from textual descriptions, showing how AI can interface with the complex abstractions and layered representations familiar to architects.

12 13 14

Wang et al., "SceneFormer," 2021.

Paschalidou et al., "ATISS: Autoregressive Transformers for Indoor Scene Synthesis," 2021.

Wei et al., "Planner3D," 2024.

Beyond spatial planning, transformer architectures have also advanced the subfield of indoor scene generation, which deals with the organization of interior spaces, including furniture placement and spatial programming. Projects such as **SceneFormer** (Wang et al., 2021), **ATISS** (Paschalidou et al., 2021), and **Planner3D** (Wei et al., 2024) have demonstrated substantial improvements in generating coherent and context-aware room layouts. These studies highlight how transformers have significantly enhanced the realism and usability of AI-generated interior layouts.

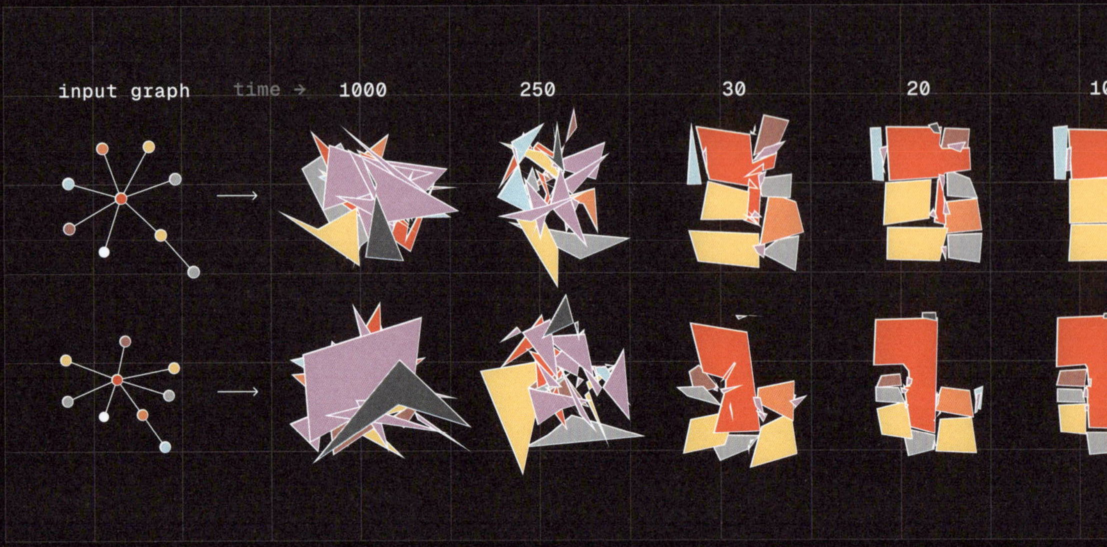

25

Generation steps in HouseDiffusion, from the early stage of the diffusion process to the final output.

26

Interface of ArchiText and a generated floor plan. Galanos et al., 2023.

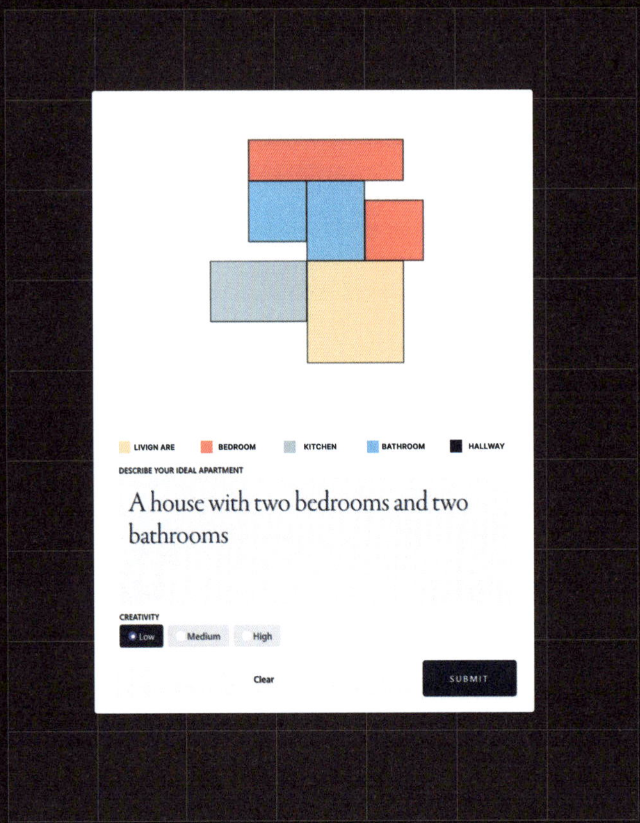

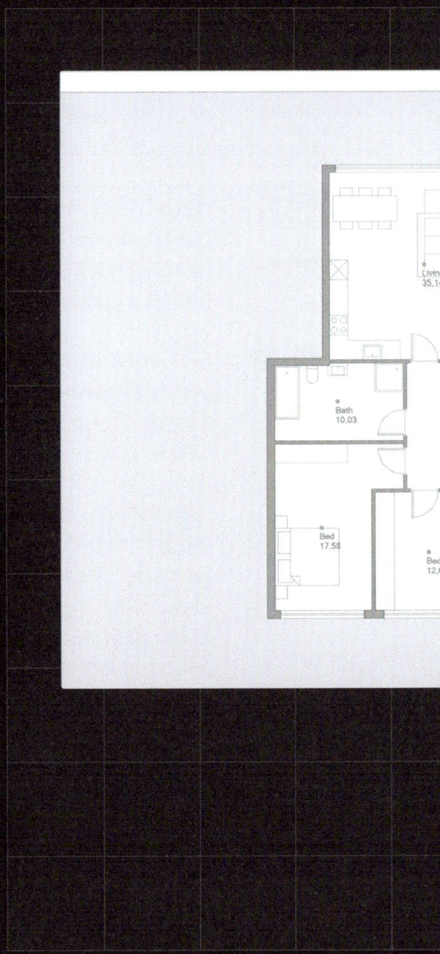

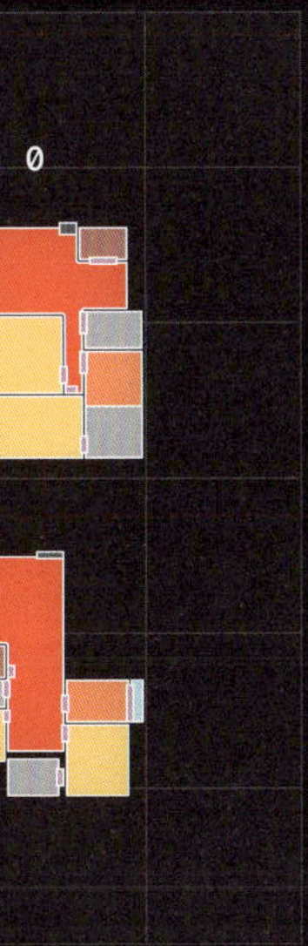

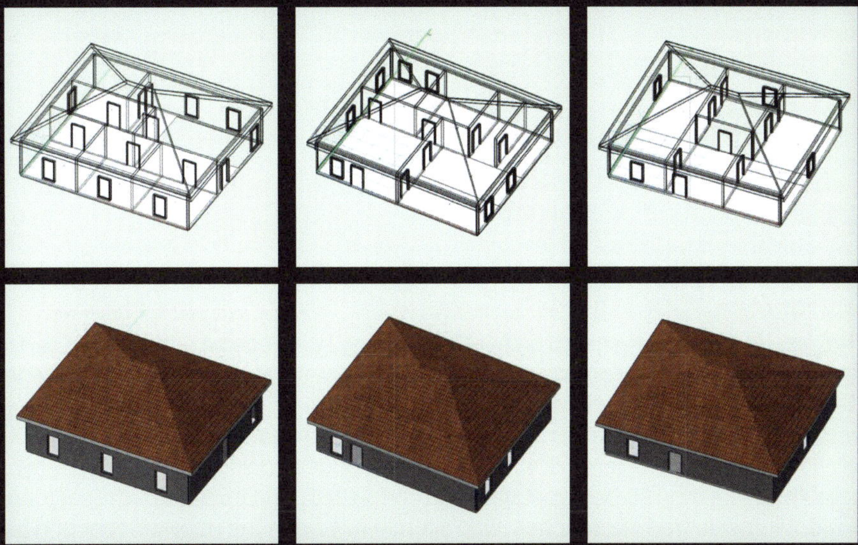

27

Results of Text2BIM model, benchmarking various foundation models. Du et al., 2023.

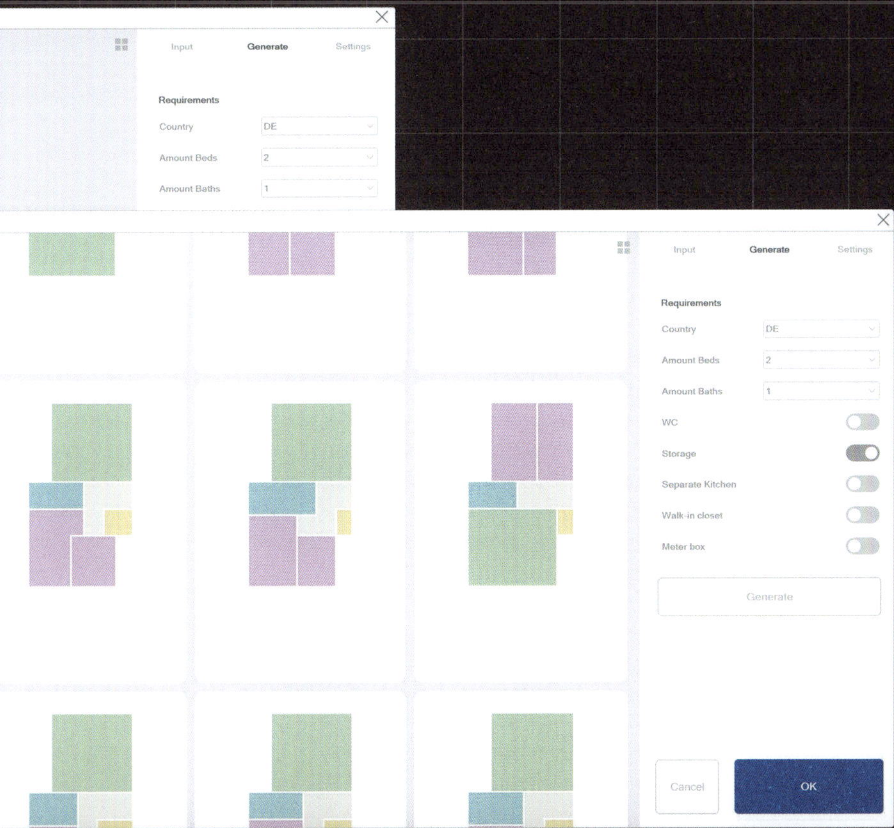

28

The “Generate” feature in PlanFinder, J. van Lith.

The growing body of research on AI at the building scale can be attributed, in part, to the inherent complexity of architectural constraints at this level. Unlike facade generation, which primarily involves stylistic considerations, floor plan and section design require models to balance functional requirements, circulation logic, regulatory compliance, and structural feasibility. The challenge of developing AI models capable of reliably generalizing across typologies and contextual conditions has led researchers to adopt specialized approaches. One avenue has been the development of typology-specific AI models. For example, the **EDU-AI** project (Karadag et al., 2022) introduced a twofold machine-learning model to support classroom layout generation, addressing the unique spatial constraints of educational architecture. Similarly, Liu et al. (2023) explored AI-driven generation of campus layouts, refining models to cater specifically to large-scale institutional design.

15 Karadag et al., "EDU-AI," 2022.

Another approach has been the contextual specialization of AI models, wherein research efforts focus on localized datasets to reduce architectural complexity. A compelling example of this method is Lin et al.'s (2023) work on the generation of historic building facades using conditional GAN (CGAN) models. By restricting the training dataset to a specific neighborhood's architectural style, this study demonstrated how AI-generated designs could align closely with contextual stylistic requirements. This research underscores the broader potential of AI to function as a tool for site-specific architectural adaptation, rather than merely producing generic outputs.

Despite the increasing sophistication of AI research in architectural representation at the building scale, commercial applications remain relatively nascent. While standalone SaaS web applications such as Maket and Finch, as well as integrated plugins like PlanFinder (Fig. 28), have entered the market, their widespread adoption remains uncertain. The primary challenge lies in bridging the gap between research prototypes and real-world architectural workflows. Many of these AI tools excel in early-stage ideation but struggle to integrate smoothly with industry-standard software environments such as Revit, Rhino, Archicad, and others.

Looking ahead, AI's role in architectural generation at the building scale remains an open problem. Future research must address the challenges of integrating multiple representations — floor plans, sections, and facades — into cohesive and context-aware generative models. Additionally, the ability to tackle more complex building typologies and multi-program structures will be crucial for AI's long-term relevance in architectural practice. The emergence of large vision models and large world models holds promise in this regard, potentially enabling AI to process architectural representation in a more holistic manner.

REFERENCES

House-GAN++: Generative Adversarial Layout Refinement Networks
[Article]
Nauata et al., 2021

HouseDiffusion
[Video]
Paper Presentation, CVPR 2023

Architext: Language-Driven Generative Architecture Design
[Website]
Galanos et al., 2023

Practical Machine Learning In Architecture
[Video]
Lecture, Jeroen van Lith, 2023

Perspectives

The generation of perspective views has arguably been the architectural application most profoundly transformed by recent advances in artificial intelligence research. This technological progress has not only streamlined the efficiency of architectural visualization but has also significantly broadened the creative latitude available to designers. The impact of this shift is particularly evident in the current proliferation of stylistically diverse architectural representations, a phenomenon that has flourished across various social media platforms. The rise of diffusion models, coupled with an increasing ability for users to fine-tune and condition the generative process, has led to the development of highly adaptable solutions that are now becoming integral to several aspects of contemporary architectural practice.

The acceleration of AI-driven perspective view generation can be attributed to several key technological breakthroughs. Among them, the refinement of conditioning techniques has played an essential role in improving control over generated outputs. One particularly noteworthy development is **low-rank adaptation (LORA)**, which has emerged as a powerful tool for style conditioning. This technique enables architects to fine-tune pre-trained models, allowing them to generate visualizations that align with specific architectural styles, design philosophies, or personal preferences. Simultaneously, another significant advance, **ControlNet** (Fig. 29), has provided a means for greater topological conditioning. By allowing designers to impose constraints on spatial organization and structural elements of scenes, this framework has facilitated greater precision in the generation of perspective views.

16 Hu et al., "LoRA: Low-Rank Adaptation of Large Language Models," 2021.

17 Zhang et al., "Adding Conditional Control to Text-to-Image Diffusion Models," 2023.

Beyond improvements in control, perhaps the most transformative advancement has been the increase in realism achieved by mainstream diffusion models over the past few years. Models such as Stable Diffusion, Flux, Midjourney, and others have raised the quality of AI-generated architectural renderings to unprecedented levels, reducing the perceptual gap between computer-generated and manually crafted visualizations. This leap in realism, as exemplified in Figure 30, has significantly expanded the potential applications of AI in architectural workflows, making these tools not only viable but increasingly present across architects' toolsets for early-stage design exploration.

The growing sophistication of these AI models has, in turn, catalyzed a proliferation of specialized commercial applications tailored to architectural visualization. Beyond widely known generators like Stable Diffusion and Midjourney, industry-specific solutions such as Interior AI, Visoid, and Palazzo.ai have emerged, offering refined tools explicitly designed for architectural and interior design contexts. Concurrently, major architectural software platforms, including Vectorworks and D5, have integrated AI-powered functionalities, further embedding generative technologies within established professional workflows. This seamless incorporation of AI-generated perspectives into conventional design environments marks a notable shift in architectural practice, where AI is no longer perceived as an experimental tool but rather as an increasingly standard component of visualization processes.

Parallel to this industrialization of AI-driven perspective generation, a wave of experimental initiatives continues to push the boundaries of what these technologies can achieve. Platforms such as Krea.ai (Fig. 30) and Blockade Labs exemplify this frontier of research, where the focus extends beyond static renderings toward more interactive and immersive applications. Blockade Labs, for instance, has pioneered the development of AI-generated 360-degree immersive renderings — commonly referred to as "skyboxes" — which allow users to generate panoramic environments based on textual prompts (Fig. 31). Once synthesized, these environments can be explored dynamically from a single vantage point, with the ability to make real-time, localized modifications. The rapid generation time and immersive nature of these tools signal the potential for AI-driven visualization techniques to evolve beyond conventional static perspectives, reshaping the medium through which architectural design is experienced and communicated.

Despite these recent advancements, several critical limitations remain that currently hinder AI from achieving full applicability in architectural perspective generation. The foremost challenge pertains to control. While AI models have become increasingly sophisticated, they still do not provide architects with the level of precision necessary for later-stage design refinement. This constraint relegates AI-generated perspectives primarily to the conceptual and early ideation phases, where broad explorations of form, style, and composition are more valuable than fine-grained

29

Image generated with ControlNet, with conditioning mask (center). Prompt: "a cheerful modernist bedroom." Input (left), extracted mask (center), result (right).

31

Four 360° skybox views generated using software by Blockade Labs.

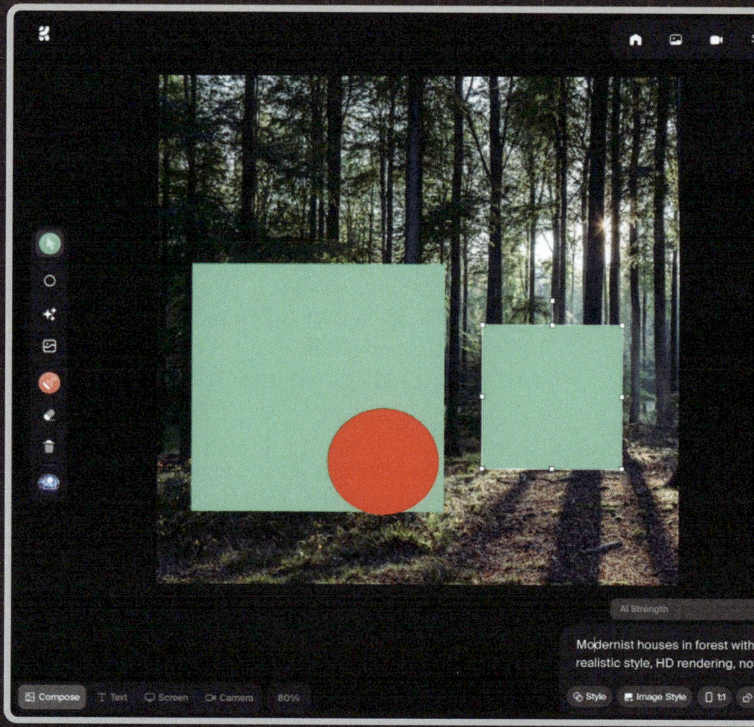

30

Image of the Krea.ai interface, showing a control scene (left), prompt (bottom center), and result (right).

Upgrade Now
21% Daily Credits
Quick Enhance
Fast
Model
Send to Upscale
Save

control over specific design details. Another substantial challenge lies in the issue of scene persistence. Current AI models struggle to generate multiple views of the same architectural space while maintaining consistency across vantage points. This limitation, despite some recent progress in multi-view consistency techniques, poses a significant obstacle for architects who require reliable and coherent visualizations of a single project from different perspectives. Without robust mechanisms for ensuring spatial continuity across generated images, AI remains largely unsuitable for detailed design development and technical visualization.

Overcoming these challenges will be crucial in determining AI's future role within architectural practice. As research continues to refine methods for improving control, consistency, and adaptability, AI has the potential to transition from a tool predominantly used for conceptual exploration to a robust asset capable of supporting architectural visualization across all stages of design. Whether through enhanced conditioning techniques, or new hybrid workflows that combine AI-generated imagery with traditional modeling methods, the coming years will likely see significant strides in the evolution of AI-assisted architectural visualization.

REFERENCES

Architecture and Artificial Intelligence
[Video]
Lecture, Matias del Campo, ICD Stuttgart, 2024

Ripping Up the Gen AI Rulebook
[Video]
BlockadeLab Demo, Adam Levine, 2023

Vectorworks New AI Visualizer
[Website]
Product Release, 2024

How MVRDV Is Using AI to Design Their Buildings
[Video]
Documentary, Steven Rubio, 2024

Structures

In recent years, artificial intelligence has begun to play a significant role in well-defined use cases for structural analysis, operating at the interface between architecture and civil engineering. Whether applied to the optimal placement of structural elements — such as shear wall positioning and structural frame layouts — or used to enhance the topology of structural components by optimizing material distribution and truss configurations, AI has demonstrated its capacity to support various facets of architectural design. Additionally, AI-driven approaches have shown potential in assessing structural compliance with regulations, automating certain aspects of verification that traditionally require intensive computational resources. These successes illustrate the relevance of AI in structural design, yet they must be considered with nuance, as current applications present both advantages and clear limitations. On one hand, AI appears to offer a compelling set of tools that can significantly mitigate the computational costs associated with traditional structural analysis. By streamlining processes that typically require extensive numerical simulations, AI has the potential to democratize structural design methodologies, making advanced computational tools more accessible to architects and designers who may not have direct expertise in structural engineering. On the other hand, structural design remains a domain governed by strict regulatory constraints, engineering imperatives, and safety considerations. Given that AI models are inherently statistical in nature, they often struggle to achieve the high levels of precision and reliability that professionals expect. Unlike purely aesthetic applications of AI in architecture — such as image generation or conceptual design — structural analysis requires absolute accuracy, making AI's current limitations particularly evident in this field.

Regardless of these limitations, the state of the literature has significantly evolved over the past few years. Examining the trajectory of AI applications in structural analysis reveals a pattern similar to that observed in other areas of architectural research.

18 19

Danhaive et al., "Design Subspace Learning," 2021.

Mirra et al., "Comparison Between Human-Defined and AI-Generated Design Spaces," 2021.

Specifically, the field has witnessed a gradual transition from variational autoencoders (VAEs) and generative adversarial networks (GANs) toward diffusion models and transformer architectures, albeit at a somewhat slower pace than in adjacent domains. Since the foundational work of **Danhaive et al.** (Fig. 32), VAE-based approaches have garnered attention for their role in studying and generating structural forms. Several research initiatives have explored the application of VAEs in this context, with notable contributions from ETH Zurich's **Mirra et al.**, who have employed these architectures to design pedestrian bridge structures. This work exemplifies how VAEs can be leveraged for structural synthesis, allowing for the automated exploration of various configurations while maintaining certain engineering constraints.

20 21 22

Liao et al., "Automated Structural Design of Shear Wall Residential Buildings," 2021.

Fu et al., "Dual generative adversarial networks for automated component layout design of steel frame-brace structures," 2023.

Nie et al., "TopologyGAN," 2021.

GANs have also been widely used in structural analysis, yielding numerous downstream applications in recent years. A prime example is **StructGAN** (Liao et al., 2021), a model designed to automate the placement of shear walls within residential floor plans (Fig. 33). More recently, **FrameGAN** (Fu et al., 2023) has extended this approach by focusing on the optimal layout of steel frame-brace structures, while **TypologyGAN** (Nie et al., 2021) has explored the optimization of material distribution based on applied loads and boundary conditions. These projects illustrate the adaptability of GANs for structural design tasks.

23

Zhou et al., "StructDiffusion," 2024.

More recently, however, the pivot away from VAEs and GANs — already evident in other AI-driven architectural applications — has become increasingly pronounced in structural design research. Diffusion models, in particular, have begun to permeate the literature, offering promising alternatives to earlier generative approaches. Using this new breed of models, the study of the placement of shear walls has seen encouraging results. Models like **StructDiffusion** employ diffusion-based techniques to automate both the placement and structural analysis of shear walls, enhancing the efficiency of early-stage design iterations.

24

Mazé et al., "Diffusion Models Beat GANs on Topology Optimization," 2023.

In another subfield of structural engineering — topological optimization, that is, the study of the form and shape of structural components so as to best carry loads — diffusion models have also gained traction. This area had previously been overrepresented by research using VAEs and GANs to predict load paths as image outputs (Fig. 34). More recent projects using diffusion models, such as **TopoDiff** (Mazé et al., 2023), have been exploring new ways in which AI can outperform earlier methods in optimizing the topology of structural elements. Results show that this new generation of models is able to provide more robust predictions.

Simultaneously, transformer-based architectures have started to carve out a niche within structural analysis research. One of the most compelling examples

33

Functional diagram of StructGAN. Lu et al., 2020.

32

VAE-generated efficient roof structures. Danhaive et al.

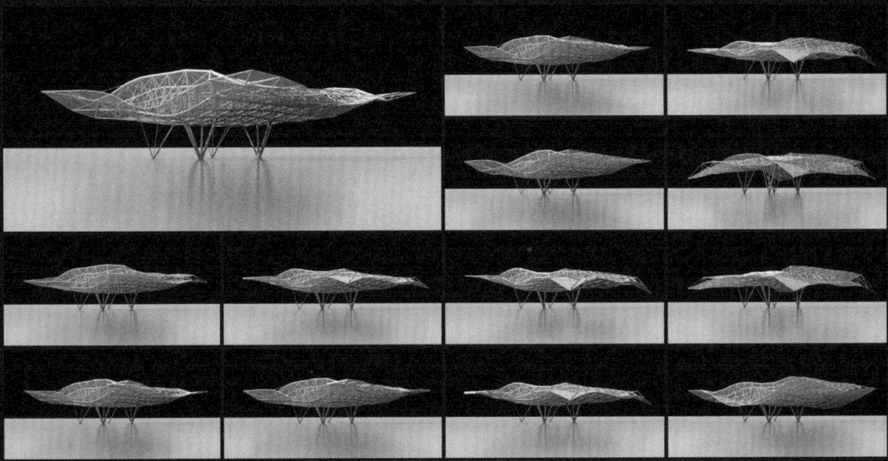

conceptual architectura sketches

34

Sample from the Topy dataset, a well-known benchmark for ML-enabled topology optimization. Black lines show load paths under given input conditions.

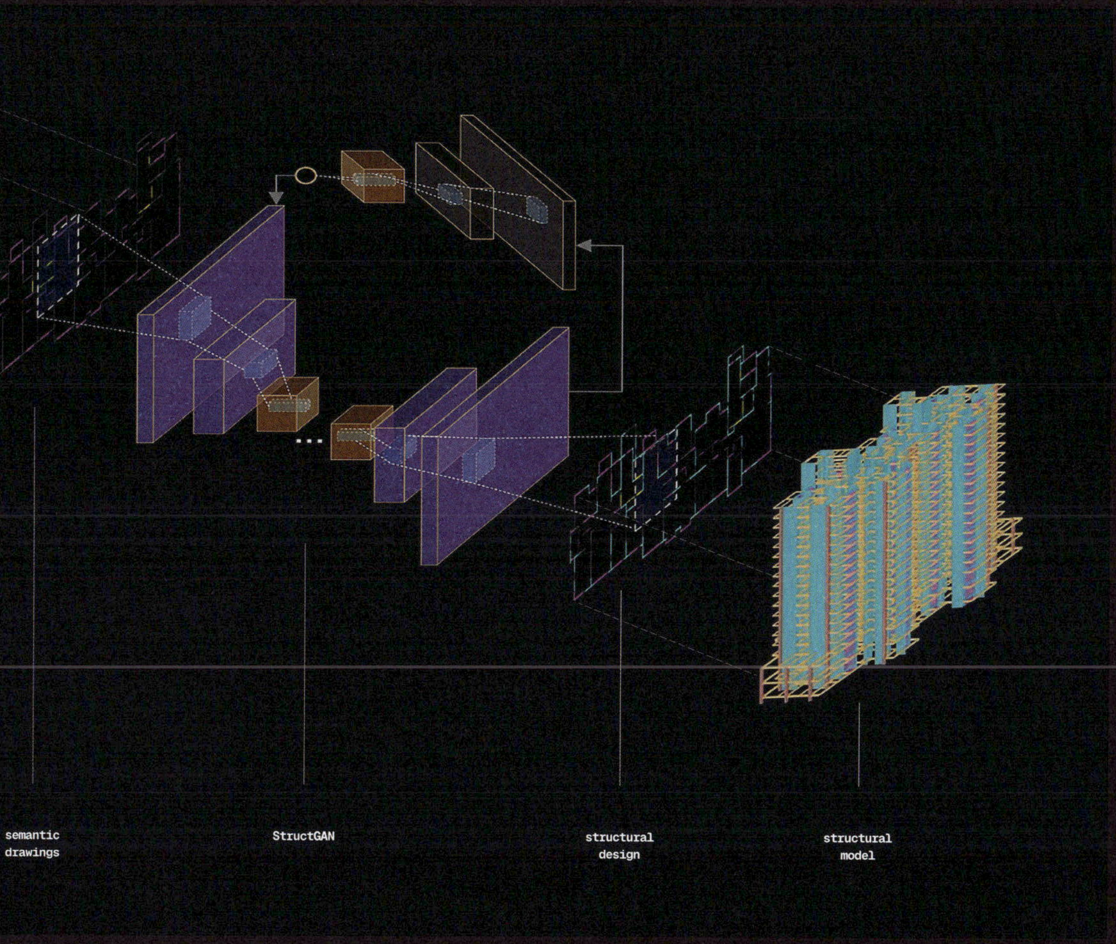

semantic drawings
StructGAN
structural design
structural model

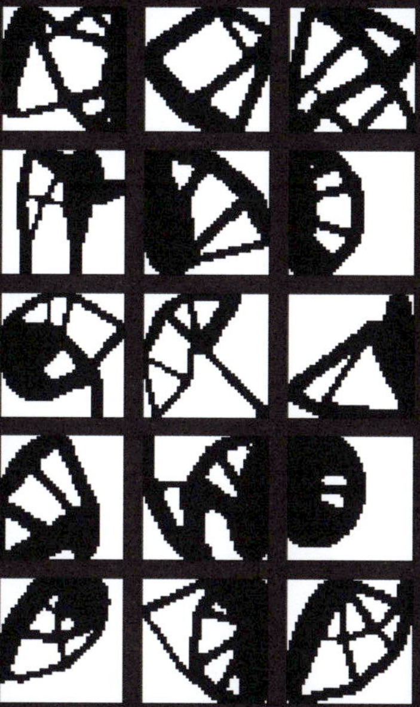

is **TransFrameNet** (Shu et al., 2024), a project that applies transformers to seismic analysis in building structures. This initiative demonstrates the significant potential of transformer models in structural engineering, particularly for tasks that require the processing of complex, interdependent spatial relationships. Given their ability to handle sequential and relational data effectively, transformers may prove especially valuable for dynamic load simulations and real-time structural assessments.

25 Shu et al., "TransFrameNet," 2024.

Despite these advances in the academic and research landscape, the commercial adoption of AI-driven structural analysis tools remains comparatively limited. The architecture, engineering, and construction (AEC) software ecosystem has yet to fully integrate these innovations, leaving a notable gap between scientific research and practical application. Unlike other AI-driven design tools that have rapidly gained traction in architectural practice, structural AI solutions have not yet been widely incorporated into mainstream architectural software platforms. The open-source community has sought to bridge this gap by developing plugins and ad hoc tools, though these remain fragmented and lack the robustness of fully integrated solutions.

It seems clear, for the time being, that while AI's role in structural analysis is expanding, its full potential remains unrealized within architecture due to challenges related to precision, regulatory constraints, and software integration. Moving forward, reconciling research with practice will be essential in determining AI's long-term viability in this domain. As technological advancements continue to refine AI's capacity for control, accuracy, and adaptability, it is likely that these models will gradually become more relevant to architecture's structural analysis workflows.

REFERENCES

Generative AI Design for Building Structures
[Website]
Survey, Liao et al., 2024

Computing for Performance and Delight
[Video]
Lecture, Caitlin Mueller, ACADIA 2021

Artificial Intelligence in Structural Engineering
[Video]
Lecture, Naveed Anwar, 2024

Engineering-Driven Design: A New Foundation
[Website]
Keynote, Bradley Rothenberg, nTop, 2021

Performance

As ecological awareness increasingly influences priorities within the built environment, the demand for rigorous, data-driven tracking of energy performance has become more pressing than ever. Architecture has responded to this challenge by integrating simulation tools early in the design process, enabling the assessment of diverse factors ranging from solar radiation and wind flow to indoor thermal comfort. These evaluations play a critical role in informing design decisions aimed at sustainability and energy efficiency. However, access to such simulation tools has historically been constrained by the expertise, time, and financial resources required for effective deployment — making them largely the domain of experts and out of reach for many architects and designers who could benefit from them.

When the first edition of this book was published three years ago, the influence of artificial intelligence (AI) had already begun to reshape this dynamic. AI was already helping to lower the barriers to predictive modeling, making it more accessible and facilitating its widespread adoption across the AEC industry. By leveraging machine learning techniques, a new generation of surrogate models emerged — offering fast, cost-effective alternatives to conventional simulation engines. These models could generate reliable insights with a fraction of the computational expense, making performance analysis a more feasible and attractive option for a broader range of design teams.

In the years since, AI has continued to permeate the realm of performance forecasting, driven by increasingly sophisticated algorithms such as diffusion models and transformer architectures. These developments are now becoming more prominent in the literature, signaling a shift in how AI is applied within the AEC sector. Research projects based on generative adversarial networks (GANs), such as **DaylightGAN**,

26 Mitev, "DaylightGAN," GitHub, n.d.

focused on predicting natural light distribution within a building, had already set the stage for the current wave of AI-driven experimentation in architectural performance. **ComfortGAN** (Quitana et al., 2020), a model that estimates indoor thermal comfort by considering factors such as spatial configuration and material properties, is another prime example of how AI is transforming performance analysis.

27 Quintana et al., "Balancing Thermal Comfort Datasets: We GAN, but Should We?," 2020.

A particularly illustrative example of these early advancements can be found in the work of Angelos Chronis and his team at the CIL research group at AIT. Their research exemplifies AI's potential to produce highly accurate predictions of solar radiation in and around built forms (Fig. 35). By using surrogate models trained specifically for this purpose, they analyze environmental data to simulate and forecast patterns of solar exposure. Since then, more recent developments have built upon this foundation. The rise of diffusion models has created new opportunities for predicting indoor daylight conditions, with projects such as Li et al. (2024) demonstrating the relevance and effectiveness of diffusion models in generating accurate, real-time simulations of natural lighting inside buildings.

In addition to advances in daylight prediction, AI has shown particular promise in replacing costly computational fluid dynamics (CFD) models, which are traditionally used to simulate wind flow inside and around buildings, as well as indoor thermal comfort. In recent years, researchers have developed AI-driven models capable of generating wind flow maps based on simplified site layouts and building orientations. While these models may not be as precise as traditional CFD simulations, they provide sufficiently accurate insights for early-stage assessments and comparative analysis of multiple design scenarios. A notable example of this trend is the **work by Foster + Partners**, who trained a convolutional neural network (CNN) to predict airflow based on urban massing layouts (Fig. 36). Expanding on this, projects like **Airvox** (Han et al., 2024) have improved the prediction of indoor airflows by scaling these models to the third dimension, using 3D convolutions. Though these are only two examples within a growing body of research, they highlight the transformative potential of AI in CFD analysis. In the coming years, this technology is poised to democratize access to wind flow and thermal comfort analysis across architectural workflows.

28 Musil et al., "Towards Sustainable Architecture," 2019.

29 Han et al., "Airvox," 2024.

The effectiveness of these AI-driven models, however, depends not only on their accuracy but also on their accessibility. In recent years, the emergence of online platforms has played a crucial role in closing the gap between cutting-edge research and practical application. These platforms ensure that predictive modeling tools can be easily accessed by a wider range of practitioners, making advanced performance analysis available to architects without specialized computational expertise. Companies such as Forma (formerly Spacemaker, Fig. 37), Covetool, and InFraReD have

35

Solar radiation predictions around various urban massings, by A. Chronis & team at AIT.

37

Predictive simulations of sunlight (left), daylight (center), and wind flow (right) in Autodesk Forma.

36

Predicted wind flow around tower massings. Foster + Partners.

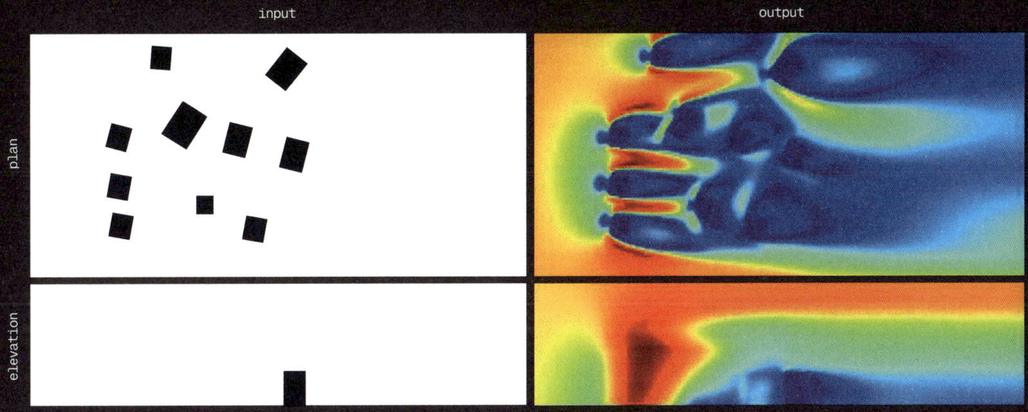

developed user-friendly online platforms that simplify the deployment of AI-based simulations. These tools enable architects to generate predictive insights into building performance without requiring deep technical knowledge, thus democratizing sustainability analysis and embedding high-level performance assessments directly into the design workflow. By lowering the barriers to entry, these platforms not only accelerate the adoption of predictive modeling but also promote a more informed and proactive architectural practice.

Beyond specific applications in performance forecasting, a broader shift is underway within the realm of foundation models, marked by the emergence of models capable of simulating fundamental physical processes across disciplines. Initiatives such as **Archetype AI are pushing the boundaries of AI's capabilities in physics-based modeling**, developing large-scale world models that can generalize across different environments and conditions. These models aim to establish a unified framework for simulating real-world physics, from material behaviors to environmental dynamics. For architecture, this evolution has the potential to raise the level of current AI-driven simulation from isolated performance assessments to holistic, integrated analyses of buildings and urban environments.

30 Archetype AI, "What Is Physical AI?," 2024.

REFERENCES

A Ground-Breaking AI-Driven Climate Simulation Framework
[Website]
Lecture, Angelos Chronis

Re-Inventing Performance Driven Design Through AI
[Website]
Angelos Chronis, MBL Lunch Hours

Analysis in Autodesk Forma
[Website]
Product Demonstration

Early Demonstration of DaylightGAN
[Website]
Petr Mitev & Theodore Galanos

Urban Scale

The urban scale represents yet another critical dimension of the built environment that has experienced a significant and sustained increase in AI-driven generative design research over the past five years. With applications ranging from land use planning and massing studies to road network optimization and urban form classification, AI's role in shaping cityscapes has expanded considerably. As in other domains of architectural design, urban AI research has followed a trajectory of methodological evolution, transitioning from VAEs and GANs to more sophisticated architectures such as diffusion models, transformers, and multimodal learning systems. At the same time, commercial applications of AI in urban planning have become increasingly accessible, offering powerful tools at the intersection of architecture, urban design, and city planning.

Within the research community, early efforts focused on leveraging generative AI to synthesize increasingly realistic urban features while offering users greater control over the design process. Experiments from the early 2020s explored the potential of GANs to generate urban morphologies, demonstrating how AI could synthesize urban block layouts, street networks, and massing configurations. Key projects such as **Urban-GAN** (Quan, 2022), **GANmapper** (Wu et al., 2022), **MasterPlanGAN** (Ye et al., 2022), **InstantCity** (Fig. 38, Wu et al., 2023), **UDGAN** (Gan et al., 2024), and **CAIN-GAN** (Jiang et al., 2024) provided valuable insights into the application of adversarial networks for urban-scale synthesis. These studies showed how GANs could generate urban blocks while incorporating contextual factors such as land use distribution, programmatic zoning, and morphological constraints. Their ability to integrate regulatory constraints, street alignments, and density patterns demonstrated early potential for use as design assistants in planning workflows.

31 32 33

Quan, "Urban-GAN," 2022.

Wu et al., "GANmapper," 2022.

Ye et al., "MasterplanGAN," 2021.

34 35 36

Wu and Biljecki, "InstantCITY," 2023.

Gan et al., "UDGAN," 2024.

Jiang et al., "Automated Site Planning Using CAIN-GAN Model," 2024.

Beyond block-level synthesis, research also explored the generation of complementary urban elements such as road networks. Yang et al. (2023) demonstrated how
37 GANs could be adapted to **generate the inverse of building blocks**: street networks. Their approach enabled the generation of road layouts responsive to a given context. In parallel, VAEs contributed to the development of urban form generation, as seen
38 in projects like **BlockPlanner** (Xu et al., 2021). While this first generation of AI-driven urban planning tools showcased the feasibility of using generative models to shape urban fabrics, they generally lacked mechanisms for precise user control over outputs — a critical limitation for real-world planning applications. Their reliance on implicit learning patterns made it difficult for practitioners to anticipate or adjust specific aspects of the generated urban configurations, limiting their practical utility.

37 Yang et al., "Street Layout Design via Conditional Adversarial Learning," 2023.

38 Xu et al., "BlockPlanner," 2021.

The advent of diffusion models, transformers, and multimodal architectures has marked a turning point in urban AI research. These models have enabled more refined, context-aware urban design proposals by incorporating a broader spectrum of input modalities, including text, images, GIS data, and environmental analytics.
39 The **TEXT-TO-CITY** project (Fig. 39, Zhuang et al., 2024) provided early evidence of this potential by integrating Stable Diffusion to generate urban layouts from textual prompts, allowing planners to steer the generative process using natural language.
40 **ControlCity** (Zhou et al., 2024) advanced this approach by incorporating multimodal inputs — text and imagery — alongside contextual sources such as Wikipedia entries and OpenStreetMap data. By leveraging extensive datasets and conditioning generation on site-specific information, these projects have significantly improved the quality and realism of AI-generated urban masterplans. What makes this new wave of research particularly promising is the increasing ability of models to align with actual planning constraints. Rather than merely generating plausible urban forms, diffusion- and transformer-based models are beginning to incorporate zoning regulations, environmental impact, and infrastructure requirements — raising the relevance of AI for real-world urban design tasks.

39 Zhuang et al., "Text-to-City," 2024.

40 Zhou et al., "ControlCity," 2024.

While research continues to evolve, commercial applications have already gained substantial traction. Over the past five years, a new generation of web-based applications has emerged, catering specifically to urban planners a nd architects. One of the clearest manifestations of this trend has been the rise of AI-enhanced geographic information systems (GIS). **Platforms such as Aino exemplify this new generation**
41 **of online GIS tools**, integrating AI-driven analytics to process and interpret urban data. Aino's recent incorporation of large language models (LLMs) allows users to query spatial datasets in natural language, facilitating richer and more structured urban analysis.

41 Kamenev, "Aino AI v1: First-Generation LLM for Geospatial Analysis," 2025.

38

InstantCity's generation pipeline: from street network tiles to stitched urban map with generated building footprints. Wu et al., 2023.

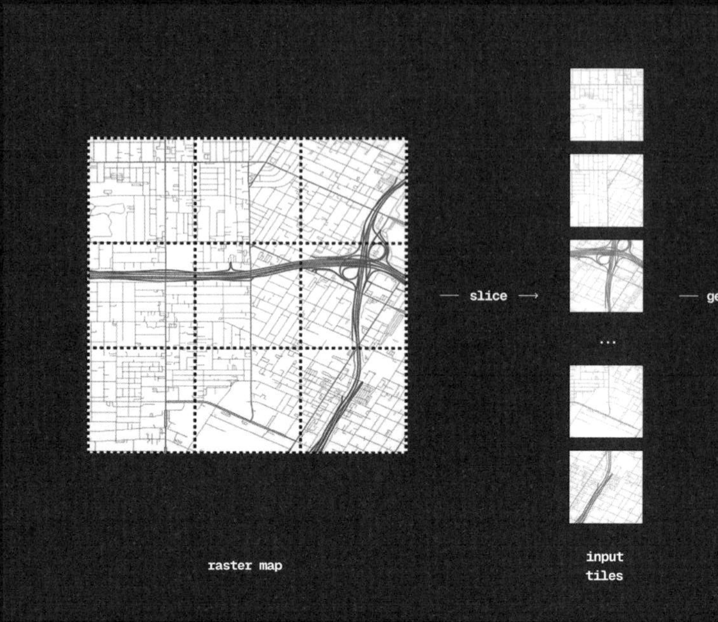

39

Text-to-city generation results for various cities and densities. Zhuang et al., 2024.

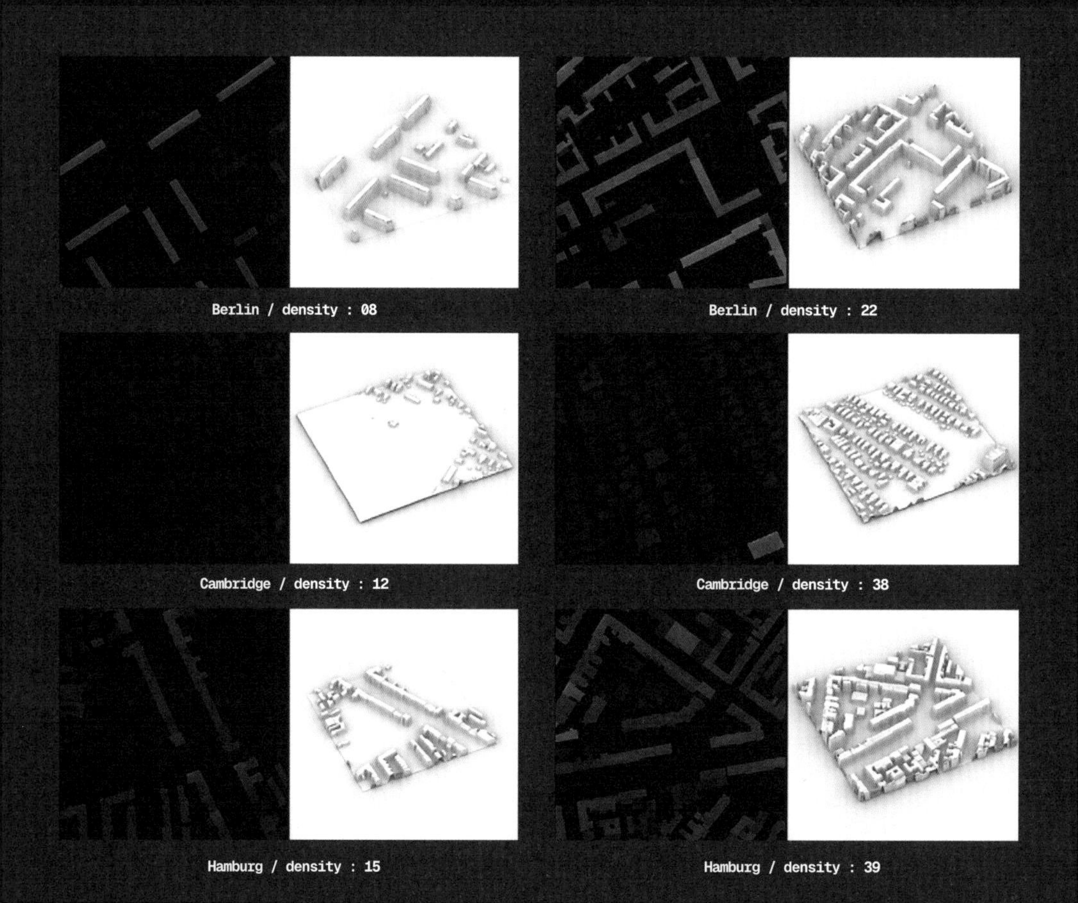

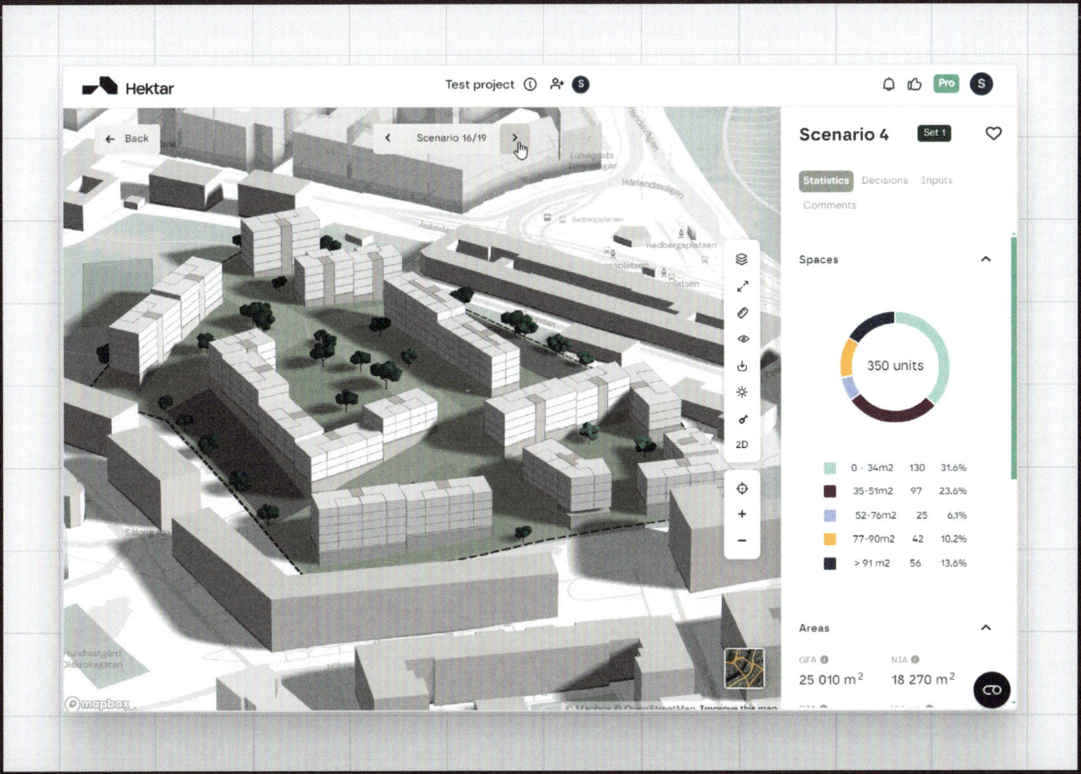

40

Generated urban massings in the Hektar web app, 2024.

In parallel, AI-driven site configurators have become increasingly prevalent in professional workflows. Platforms such as Forma (formerly Spacemaker), Hektar (Fig. 40), Spacio, TestFit, and Finch provide automated massing studies that combine AI with traditional procedural algorithms to generate optimal building layouts based on site constraints. Many of these tools also incorporate AI-based performance assessments, offering predictive insights on wind flow, daylight exposure, and environmental impact. The growing adoption of these tools suggests a shift in how early-stage urban design is approached, with AI now serving as both a generative mechanism and an analytical aid. In practical terms, the integration of such software into everyday design practices has accelerated iterative exploration, allowing practitioners to test more urban configurations in less time.

As research progresses, urban planning remains one of the areas within the built environment most actively supported by AI tools, largely due to the abundance of publicly available urban data. Extensive datasets at the urban scale, such as OpenStreetMap and GIS repositories, have played a crucial role in fueling the development of AI-driven urban planning solutions. Looking ahead, AI's role in urban planning is likely to continue expanding. With the recent introduction of foundation models, a new generation of urban planning projects — trained on vast datasets encompassing diverse cityscapes — could give power AI systems better suited to generate and analyzing urban structures across a wide range of cultural and geographic contexts.

REFERENCES

Generative AI in Urban Planning
[Website]

Prototype Presentation, ArcGIS, ESRI

Aino Demonstration
[Website]

Step-by-Step Guide on Using Aino

Generative AI and Urban Design
[Video]

Discussion, K. S. Ochoa & L. N. Zertuche with T. Sonnenschein

Urban Artificial Intelligence
[Video]

Lecture, Daniel Aliaga, TEDx

The Third Dimension

Research in 3D generation has evolved into a fairly fragmented landscape. The wide array of formats used to model three-dimensional space — voxels, point clouds, meshes, neural fields, B-Reps, etc. — has given rise to distinct subfields, each exploring different applications of generative AI. While recent experiments have produced promising results, key technical limitations continue to hamper full-scale industrialization. As a result, meaningful commercial applications remain in their early stages. In the meantime, the emergence of research into large world models (LWM) seems to provide more robust and generalizable frameworks for addressing the challenges of 3D generation. From the early models of 2010s to the current LWM landscape, this section examines how AI is beginning to resolve key technical limitations in 3D generation.

As a preliminary step in reviewing the current state of experimentation, it is helpful to clarify how 3D is represented by AI models in the literature (Fig. 41). Voxels, a long-standing abstraction, are the three-dimensional equivalent of pixels and model physical shapes as aggregations of discrete spatial units (cubes). Similarly sparse but based on a different primitive, point clouds use vertices (defined by their X, Y, and Z coordinates) to approximate the geometry of physical objects and environments. Closer to the geometric abstractions used in architectural modeling, discrete 3D formats such as B-Rep and meshes represent three-dimensional counterparts to 2D vector graphics, describing shapes through finite geometry composed of edges, control points, and surfaces. More recently, neural fields (NeRFs) have introduced continuous volumetric representations that go beyond discrete formats like point clouds, voxels, and meshes. These 3D representational formats structure the current landscape of generative AI research in 3D. With this taxonomy in mind, we now turn to the literature.

Even more than in other architectural domains, the transition from GANs and VAEs to diffusion models and transformers is particularly visible in "in-field" research, that is, research led by architecture-related labs, academic teams, and scholars focused on applying AI within the AEC sector. Several of these projects illustrate the current trajectory of 3D generation in architecture. Starting with the most sparse formats and moving toward more structured ones, the panorama begins
42 with **BuilDiff** (Wei et al., 23), a project by researchers at the University of Twente. This model combines an encoder-decoder architecture — similar to that of VAEs — with a diffusion model to generate point clouds of generic objects. From points to
43 voxels, **Sketch-a-Shape** (Sanghi et al., 23) by Autodesk Research follows a related approach, using an encoder-decoder in conjunction with a transformer to generate voxel-based representations of generic objects.

Wei et al., "BuilDiff," 2023.

Sanghi et al., "Sketch-A-Shape," 2023.

Many other investigations focus on generating structured outputs more closely aligned with CAD and BIM workflows, bringing results closer to practical use by
44 architects. A strong example is **BrepGen** (Fig. 42, Xu et al., 24), also developed by Autodesk Research. It uses a diffusion-based generative approach to produce 3D CAD objects as boundary representations (B-Reps). The model combines the generative power of diffusion models with an editable output format, making the results more actionable for architectural workflows. On the BIM side, several research projects have adopted BIM-compatible formats. Text2BIM (Du et al., 24), mentioned earlier, and the study by Liang et al. (2024), which uses VAEs to generate BIM models of residential buildings, are notable examples of current efforts to integrate 3D generative models into BIM workflows. Nonetheless, limitations are still hampering wider adoption of current models, as generalizing to more complex and diverse typologies of objects and buildings remains a significant challenge.

Xu et al., "BrepGen," 2024.

That is why it is also essential to scrutinize out-of-field research to understand how 3D generation may evolve. The scale and pace of progress in these projects far outstrip developments in in-field work — a reality now clearly reflected in the literature. Just as foundation models for modalities such as text, image, and sound emerged from research groups at tech companies like OpenAI, Stability AI, and Midjourney, current trends suggest that the same is true for 3D generation. Already, several research projects have surpassed existing benchmarks. DreamFusion, developed by
46 Google Research in 2022, demonstrated how diffusion models could be used to synthesize coherent 3D assets. Just two years later, in 2024, the same team surpassed this early breakthrough with **CAT3D**, using diffusion to render scenes con-
47 sistently across multiple viewpoints. That same year, Meta Research introduced **Meta3DGen**, which further improved output quality and added a texturing stage to the generation pipeline. These models reflect the ongoing race we have witnessed

over the past four years among research groups to produce increasingly performant text-to-3D systems.

This effort, however, has led the scientific community to formulate a broader framework for addressing the generalization of generative AI to the third dimension. This need first arose from the realization that 3D generation presents a far greater challenge than other modalities, due to at least three key factors: scene persistence — the requirement for a model to consistently represent the same spatial environment across multiple vantage points; movement control— the necessity for users to navigate through a 3D representation in order to query and edit the generated scene; and geometrical correctness — the imperative to model the physical and mathematical rules that govern real-world form in order to produce realistic 3D outputs. These challenges have pushed the field toward the foundation model paradigm, prompting researchers to investigate the potential of large world models (LWMs, also referred to as general world models). This emerging terminology reflects a shift in focus: from simply generating 3D scenes to building AI models capable of replicating the underlying laws that govern the physics of our world — an objective that can be approached by leveraging the depth and generalization capacity of foundation models. We are now witnessing the early stages of this new trajectory, as researchers begin investing time and efforts into constructing these LWMs.

Major advances in this area have come from prominent industry players. Notable examples include OpenAI's Sora, **Runway's Gen-3** (Fig. 43), and **WorldDreamer**, a joint research effort by GigaAI and Tsinghua University. By improving consistency in text-to-video generation, these models demonstrate how foundation models can begin to capture physical logic and synthesize realistic, navigable 3D environments. These LWM-based video generators now occupy a central position in the literature, and the research ecosystem is rapidly expanding. While the architecture and methodology that underpin these new models are well understood by researchers, many aspects of their technical success remain under active investigation. In this respect, **"Is Sora a World Simulator?"** (Zhu et al. 2024) offers a detailed study of current developments and critical reflections on the topic.

Along similar lines, but aiming for a different type of output, other players have approached world generation through the lens of navigability or autonomy rather than video generation. The recently founded **World Labs**, led by Fei-Fei Li, has focused on developing models that generate navigable 3D environments (Fig. 44). Early results are already available: World Labs' prototypes successfully synthesize 3D worlds through which users can navigate using keyboard input. These early examples provide a glimpse of the technology's potential for architectural applica-

48 Germanidis, "Introducing General World Models," 2023.

49 Wang et al., "WorldDreamer," 2024.

50 Zhu et al., "Is Sora a World Simulator?," 2024.

51 World Labs, "Generating Worlds," 2024.

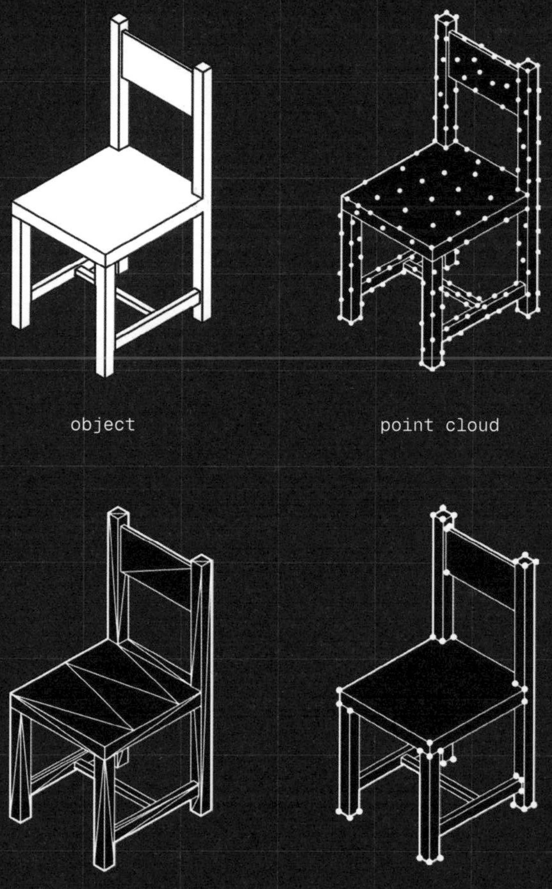

41

Illustration of three types of 3D representation.

42

Stages in the BrepGen generative pipeline. Autodesk Research. Xu et al., 2024.

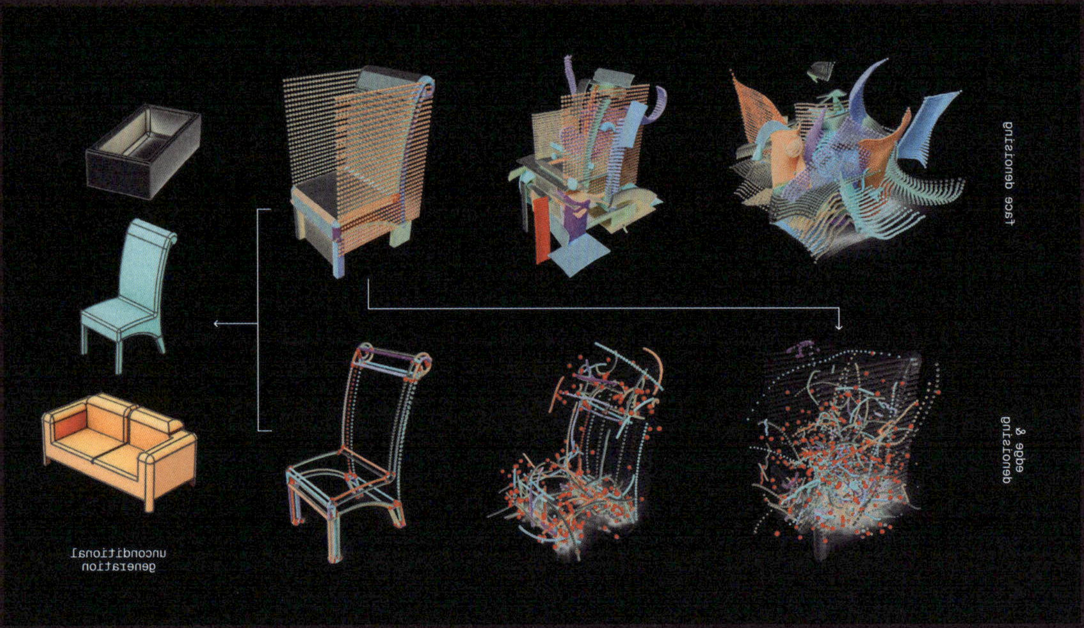

43

Snapshots from videos generated with Gen-3. Runway, 2024.

44

Walkthrough of a 3D-generated environment. World Labs, 2025.

tions. Companies such as Nvidia, with its **Cosmos** project, and Archetype AI have instead directed their research toward accurately simulating real-world physics. While these models are primarily aimed at use cases in robotics and autonomous driving, they may also hold future relevance for architecture.

52 Agarwal et al., "Cosmos World Foundation Model Platform for Physical AI," 2025.

All in all, this review of the various means by which AI currently enables the generation of realistic 3D representations may leave practitioners with mixed feelings. While it is clear that AI is rapidly improving in its capacity to generate 3D content, most results remain too experimental to meaningfully contribute to architecture. The requirements of architectural practice — namely, editability, scene persistence, and geometric precision — still present a threshold that commercially available AI models struggle to meet. Yet the impression conveyed by the examples above is that the pace of development may lift these remaining barriers sooner than we might currently expect.

REFERENCES

Advances in 3D Generation
[Article]
Survey, Li et al., 2024

Introducing General World Models
[Website]
Anastasis Germanidis, Runway, 2023

World Models
[Video]
Presentation, David Ha, 2018

What We See and What We Value: AI With a Human Perspective
[Video]
Lecture, Fei-Fei Li, Allen School Distinguished Lecture Series, 2024

The Missing Pieces

While progress is clearly visible on many fronts — and has prompted the reissue of this very book — it remains essential to identify what is still lacking for AI to fully engage with architecture where it is most needed. Three critical, long-awaited breakthroughs continue to prevent the technology from fully addressing the discipline's core demands.

Vector-based AI generation — The first challenge lies in the development of models capable of discrete generation, particularly the creation of vector-based designs. These contrast with the more prevalent continuous generation methods, such as pixel-based (2D image) and voxel-based (3D) outputs. While progress has been made, current AI models still produce results that are too imprecise to meet the quality standards required for adoption in architectural design workflows.

3D generative AI — The second challenge concerns the ability of cutting-edge models to synthesize realistic and accurate 3D designs. While 2D image generation has reached a degree of maturity and practical utility, high-quality 3D generation remains significantly underdeveloped, trailing in both technical sophistication and commercial readiness. For now, this gap means that architects still contend with models' inability to ensure robust scene persistence.

Large world models — The final and still-developing frontier is the capacity to holistically model synthetic worlds, with all the associated rules, complexities, and dependencies. Current efforts by companies such as World Labs reflect this ambition among researchers and tech developers to build large-scale AI models capable of capturing the underlying logic of world simulation. If successful in the coming years, this line of research could yield immediate benefits for architecture.

Overcoming these current bottlenecks will be essential for any meaningful deployment of AI within our discipline. As the next chapter explores AI's application to architecture's concrete use cases, we will see that early signs of solutions to these challenges are already on the horizon.

REFERENCES

To Make Language Models Work Better, Researchers Sidestep Language
[Article]
Anil Ananthaswamy, Quanta Magazine, 2025

Genie 2: A Large-Scale Foundation World Model
[Article]
Parker-Holder et al., Google DeepMind, 2024

World Model on Million-Length Video and Language With Blockwise RingAttention
[Article]
Liu et al., 2024

The Future of AI Is Here
[Video]
Discussion, Fei-Fei Li with a16z, 2024

CHAPTER IV

Semanticism

ARCHITECTURE'S SEMANTIC TURN IN AI TIMES

As AI continues to permeate architectural practice, many are beginning to question what long-term shifts may emerge in the discipline. Will AI simply serve as a set of auxiliary tools, to improve efficiency within existing workflows, or could it provoke a more fundamental realignment in architectural thinking?

In this context, we believe that AI prompts a renewed focus on semantics as a central framework for describing and generating the built environment. The idea that architecture is fundamentally about meaning rather than merely form or function is not new, yet AI's rise may lend this perspective new relevance. The term "Semanticism" offers a useful lens through which to view this evolution, capturing the idea that AI-supported design operates under a paradigm in which "form follows meanings." Architecture in the age of AI may become increasingly concerned with encoding, analyzing, and synthesizing built forms in relation to their underlying semantics.

Initially introduced in the first edition of this book, Semanticism was proposed as an emerging paradigm in architectural thinking, one that integrates AI's analytical and generative potential with architecture's enduring concern for finding the right abstraction to formulate the very essence of built forms. With the rapid acceleration of generative AI in recent years, this idea has matured. In this chapter, we unpack how Semanticism came to be and sketch out its specific features.

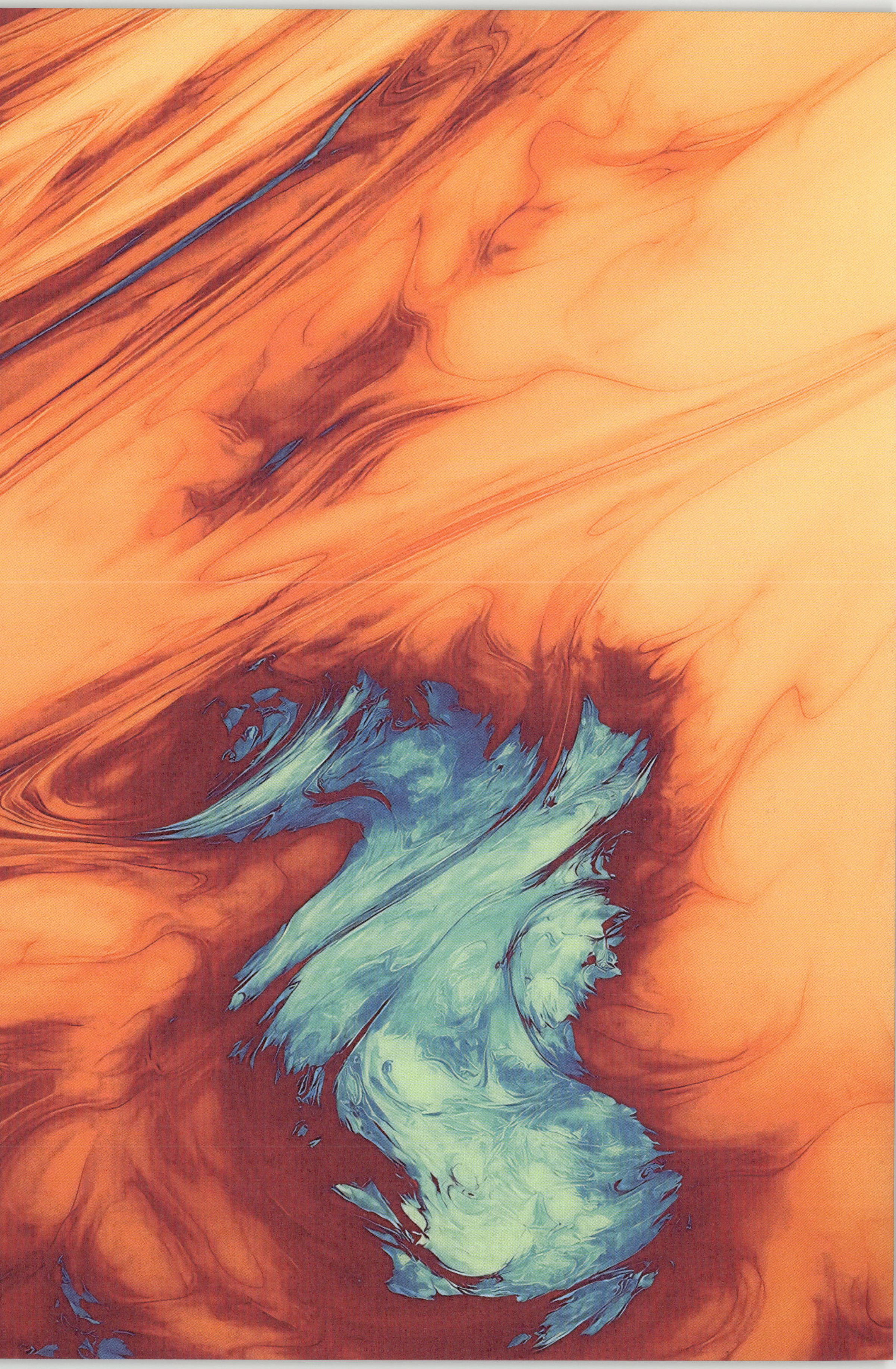

The Revolution That Already Was

The gradual rise of AI as a decade-defining technology is now an established fact. In that sense, some of its major milestones already lie behind us. Looking at its impact on other fields can provide a useful vantage point from which to grasp what may lie ahead for architecture. Most notably, an early and ongoing discussion in the field of linguistics forecasted the evolution now taking place across many creative disciplines. Over the past 70 years, successive traditions have shaped the discourse among linguists by opposing fundamentally different approaches to how meaning in language is formed. This debate, internal to linguistics, is essential for architects to understand — not as a mere analogy, but as a foundational reference for anticipating future shifts in architecture.

The Grammatical Moment

The intellectual history of grammar in linguistics throughout the 20th century can be traced through a complex interplay of philosophical logic, formal language theory, and cognitive science, beginning most pivotally with Gottlob Frege's seminal work, "**Begriffsschrift**" (1879). By the end of the 19th century, language was increasingly examined from an analytical standpoint. Frege sought to create a formal language for pure thought, modeled on the clarity and rigor of mathematics, in which propositions could be logically composed and analyzed through a strict syntactic framework. This notion of language as a structure capable of expressing logical relations became foundational not only to analytic philosophy but also to the subsequent development of formal grammars. Frege's innovations deeply influenced Bertrand Russell, whose explorations of logic and language culminated in works like "**Principia Mathematica**"

1 Frege, Begriffsschrift, 1879.

2 Russell & Whitehead, Principia Mathematica, 1910.

(co-authored with Alfred North Whitehead), which aimed to reduce mathematics to logical foundations. Russell's distinction between the surface structure of ordinary language and the deeper structure of logical form planted the seeds for later linguistic theories that aimed to model language at similar levels of abstraction. These philosophical inquiries laid the groundwork for the formal study of grammar in the 20th century, where linguists began to frame language not merely as a historical or cultural phenomenon but as a systematic, rule-governed system that could be scientifically modeled.

3 Saussure, Cours de linguistique générale, 1916.

This transition accelerated in the early to mid-20th century with the rise of structural linguistics, particularly in Europe with Ferdinand de Saussure, whose posthumous "**Cours de linguistique générale**" (1916) shifted the linguistic focus toward the abstract structures underlying language use. Saussure's distinction between "langue" (the underlying system) and "parole" (instances of speech) resonated with the formalism of Frege and Russell, emphasizing that meaning arises from differential relations within a system, much like logical notation. In the United States, Leonard Bloomfield advanced structuralist rigor through methodologies that emphasized formal description over semantic content. His behaviorist stance prioritized observable data, which, while limiting semantic inquiry, set the stage for the algorithmic approaches to grammar that would follow.

4 Chomsky, Syntactic Structures, 1957.

Yet another revolution in grammatical theory came with Noam Chomsky, whose 1957 book "**Syntactic Structures**" marked a radical departure from previous approaches. Drawing on formal language theory, Chomsky introduced generative grammar, a model of grammar that could produce all the grammatical sentences of a language and none of the ungrammatical ones. His theory posited that language is underpinned by a finite set of rules capable of generating an infinite number of utterances, reflecting the recursive and hierarchical nature of syntax.

From Frege to Chomsky, the 20th century witnessed the evolution of grammar as a distinct, new approach within linguistics. Over time grammatical principles crystallized into several foundational assumptions:

- Language is the product of words assembled through logic-driven, explicit rules;
- Meaning can be studied and generated through this rule-based system;
- Words function as building blocks within larger, hierarchical syntactic structures.

With these few assumptions in mind, we can now turn to other traditions within linguistics and better understand the stark contrast between these various movements.

From Semantics To Computational Semantics

In contrast to grammar, semantics offered an alternate approach to explaining the structure of meaning in language. It arose from the observation that syntactic structures alone cannot fully account for linguistic meaning. For example, the sentence "The whale is parked in the parking lot" is grammatically sound but semantically absurd. Grammar alone cannot capture the illogic of the statement. Semantics emerged to address such discrepancies, where purely syntactic analysis fails to provide an adequate methodology for understanding meaning. The field branched into subdomains such as cognitive semantics, phrasal semantics, and lexical semantics, all rooted in the same insight that the contextual and relational dimensions of language offer a better chance of explaining how meaning works.

With the advent of computerization, semantics began to exert influence far beyond linguistics. Programming languages and, later, the World Wide Web incorporated semantic principles into their underlying structures. **The Semantic Web**, as articulated by Tim Berners-Lee — the so-called father of the Internet — is a perfect example: the modern Web is built on an infrastructure of nodes and links whose naming and organization reflect the content they host. Nodes are tagged with semantic categories; connections are labeled according to the type of relationships they describe. The Web Ontology Language (OWL) formalizes and records this structure. At the same time, computational semantics introduced new methodologies grounded in statistical analysis. To model the kinds of relationships that semantics had long been concerned with, linguists began using statistical analysis to abstract texts and words as statistical distributions. Under this new framework, the study of meaning evolved into the analysis of distributional properties: similarity or dissimilarity in language became measurable as distance between elements in a multidimensional space.

5 Berners-Lee, "The Semantic Web," 2000.

From the early days of semantics to its digital transformation, this subfield of linguistics has maintained a consistent set of convictions that set it apart from earlier, grammar-based approaches:

- The sole syntactic structure of language is not sufficient to exhaust the information that it encodes;
- If different contexts give to the same word widely different significations, then a more robust study of language must embrace the contextual and relational nature of meaning;
- Words make sense only as they relate to the whole (the sentence, the paragraph, the text, the corpus); only their study within this broader scope can clarify their contribution to the meaning of language.

Building on these convictions, machine learning has propelled semantics to a new level, significantly expanding its scope and applications to the present day.

When Semantics Met Machine Learning

In recent decades, the encounter between linguistics and data science — and, subsequently, machine learning (ML) — has significantly advanced the computational turn in semantics that began several decades ago. Rooted in information theory and statistical learning, this shift to computational semantics introduced methodologies that were previously either impossible or prohibitively difficult to implement. Among the many advancements, three stand out as foundational to this transformation.

A first major contribution was the scalability of linguistic analysis. Prior to machine learning, analyzing large corpora (millions or billions of words) required painstaking manual coding or fragile rule-based systems. Machine learning enabled the automatic discovery of patterns across massive datasets. Tasks like part-of-speech tagging, syntactic parsing, and semantic role labeling — once slow and error-prone — became automated with high accuracy. Crucially, ML models could adapt to different languages, genres, and domains without requiring exhaustive manual reprogramming for each case.

Second, machine learning introduced the ability to handle ambiguity and variation in natural language. Human language is rich in polysemy, metaphor, and context dependence — elements that traditional computational systems struggled to accommodate. ML models proved far more capable of capturing probabilistic representations of words, phrases, and meanings. By mapping language in feature space, meaning became measurable as distance between vector-encoded words (Fig. 1), concepts, and contexts. In this way, technologies like word embeddings (e.g., Word2Vec, GloVe) and later contextual embeddings (e.g., BERT) were able to capture nuanced shades of meaning in context — something earlier approaches could not achieve at scale.

Third, the leap in text generation was even more profound. Before ML-based systems, text generation was largely template-based: fixed sentence structures filled with variable slots. This made outputs repetitive and unconvincing. With ML, particularly sequence-to-sequence models and later transformer architectures, it became possible to generate coherent, original, and stylistically appropriate text without handwritten templates. Tasks like automatic summarization, translation, and even open-ended storytelling became achievable with little or no manual intervention in the actual wording.

Above all, these evolutions of semantics, leveraging data science and machine learning, have propelled this subfield of linguistics onto the global stage. No longer confined to academia, computational semantics now powers many of the most recent innovations, from machine translation to web search. Setting aside its internal variations, the most recent evolution of semantics can be distilled into a few core assertions:

Above all, these evolutions of semantics, leveraging data science and machine learning, have propelled this subfield of linguistics onto the global stage. No longer confined to academia, computational semantics now powers many of the most recent innovations, from machine translation to web search. Setting aside its internal variations, the most recent evolution of semantics can be distilled into a few core assertions:

- Semantics established the importance of context; computational semantics introduced quantitative methods; machine learning scaled and reinforced both;
- With machine learning, meaning — understood as information — can be studied using statistical learning at scale; the meaning of a word becomes a product of its position within a distribution;
- Machine learning enables the systematic modeling of language ambiguity and high-level abstraction.

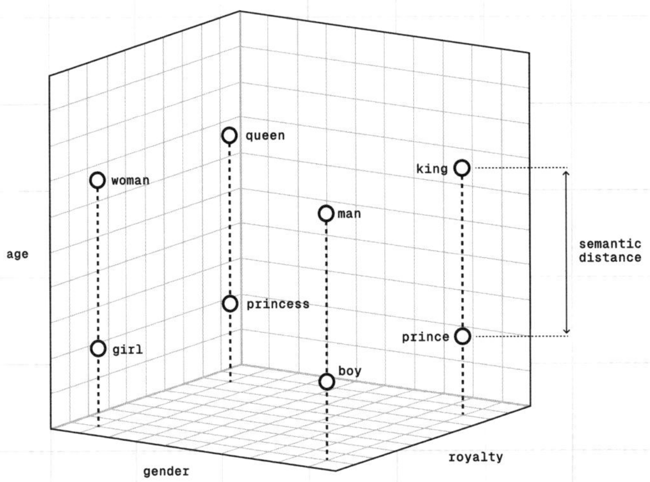

1

A canonical example of a semantic space, where words, mapped along specific features, can then be compared by computing their relative semantic distance.

A Matter of Principles

The evolution of linguistics described above has been, first and foremost, deeply practical: it introduced a powerful new set of tools to support text analysis and generation. Today, AI allows academics, writers, translators, and others to bypass many labor-intensive tasks, prompting a reexamination of long-standing conventions. At a more fundamental level, however, a number of epistemic assumptions have begun to shape the contemporary zeitgeist. When tools are based on statistical learning, the underlying ethos of entire disciplines starts to shift. Three core principles help illuminate the magnitude of this evolving mindset.

The first principle is that no creation exists in isolation — it is always part of a broader distribution of possibilities. A word, a text, a film, a sculpture, a visual composition: none of these are truly singular, isolated events. Each is one possible expression drawn from a wider array of potential outcomes. Borrowing from statistical reasoning, we might say that any creation is a sample from a larger problem space, a selected point within a broader distribution.

Second, every characteristic of a design — its style, tone, language, genre — can be understood as a dimension within that problem space. In AI contexts, these features are mapped onto dimensions of a feature space. For instance, labels such as "baroque," "classical," or "modernist" represent values along a "stylistic" axis. Here, AI contributes to the creative process by reframing qualities not as abstract descriptors but as quantifiable, computable metrics, measurable against any creation.

Third, AI blurs the boundaries between different modes of representation, reinforcing the idea that any format can be translated into any other. Just as AI transformed language translation, enabling the projection of any language into another, other media are now benefitting from similar possibilities. A 2D image of an object can be reconstructed as a 3D volume; a textual description of a space can be rendered as multiple 2D or 3D visualizations; sound can be transposed into texture. As AI enables geometry, sound, video, and text to be translated into one another, a new fluidity emerges in the creative act, permeating practices across disciplines.

Architecture has matured within this shifting epistemic landscape and has absorbed, almost by capillarity, the concepts, frameworks, and tools that now set it on an entirely new trajectory.

Architecture's Abstraction Journey

From the early days of the grammatical theory to its present-day encounter with AI, the history of linguistics has held acute relevance for architecture. If anything, this chronology seems to foreshadow what lies ahead for the discipline, and how it may continue its scholarly tradition of identifying the correct abstractions to describe and act upon built form. This effort, with its longstanding tradition, has shaped architectural discourse for centuries, long before the emergence of generative AI. As architecture has gradually absorbed terminology and concepts from linguistics, the discipline's recent intersection with computation and deep learning is poised to exert a profound influence. In the presence of AI, architecture is once again being called to refocus on semantics — a concern deeply rooted in its own intellectual history.

The Grammatical Tradition

As the conversation surrounding formal languages matured within linguistics, their relevance gradually expanded to architecture. The field began to adopt parallel principles, as theorists and practitioners recognized the potential of rule-based design methodologies. Shape grammars and parametric modeling represented high points in this movement, marking a shift toward the explicit formulation of design rules. **James Gips and George Stiny's pioneering research in the early 1970s** established a framework for describing architectural compositions as structured rule sets (Fig. 2). Their seminal 1971 work provided one of the first comprehensive demonstrations of how formal logic could be applied to spatial design.

6 Stiny & Gips, Shape Grammars and the Generative Specification of Painting and Sculpture, 1972.

With the rise of computational design, these principles evolved into more intricate rule-based systems. Parametric modeling, fueled by advances in visual programming, allowed architects to encode design logic into machine-readable instructions.

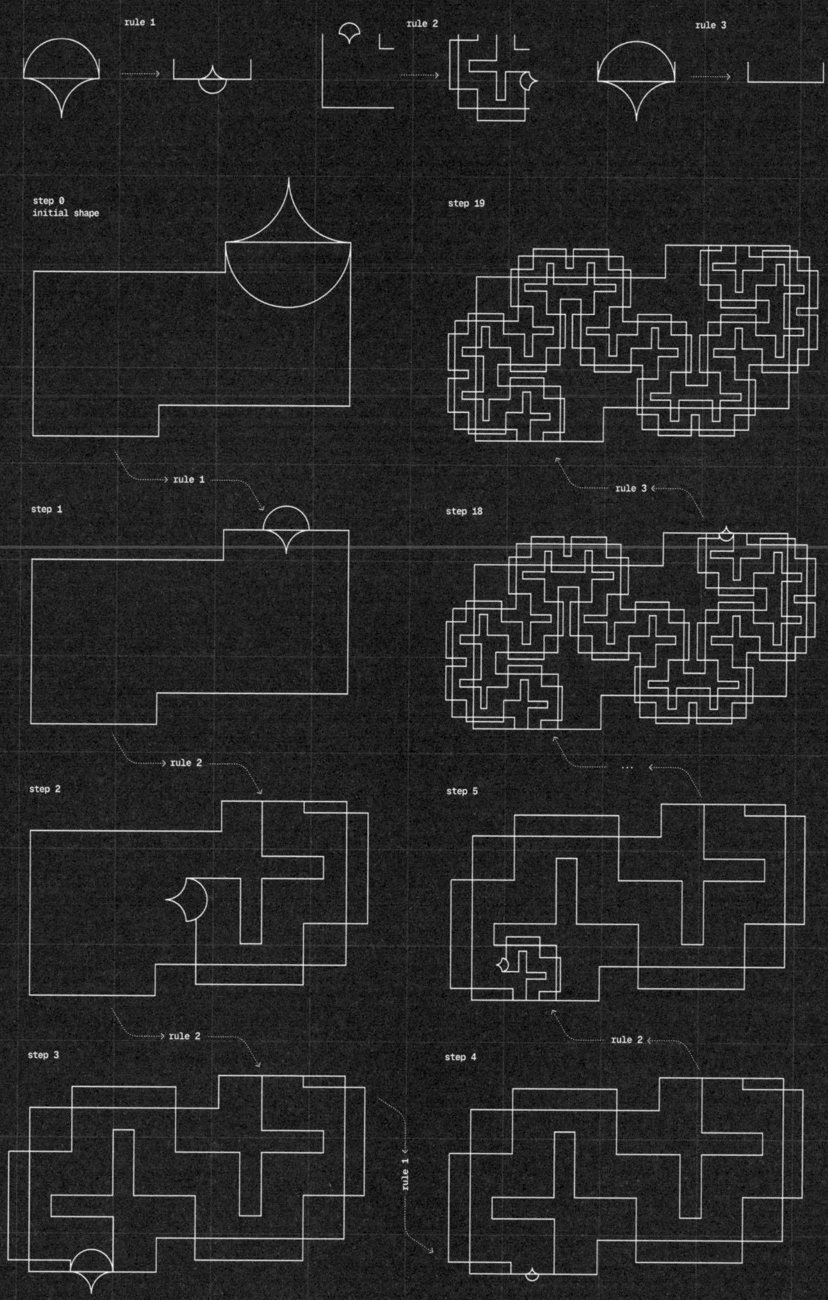

2

Typical shape grammar procedure, by J. Gips and G. Stiny.

Functions and parameters were no longer abstract theoretical constructs but executable commands that guided the form-finding process. This approach reached a critical moment with **Patrik Schumacher's 2008 manifesto** on Parametricism, which reaffirmed the potential of procedural rule sets in architecture. The widespread adoption of parametric workflows — from digital fabrication to generative design — reinforced the notion of architecture as a process increasingly shaped by the encoding of heuristics into computational logic. 7

7 Schumacher, "Parametricism as Style," 2008.

At its core, shape grammar and parametric modeling positioned architectural design as a rule-driven practice, capable of being translated into precise instructions for computers. This period represents a defining chapter in architectural theory and computational research, solidifying the role of rule-based thinking in the discipline. More importantly, this tradition corresponds to a pivotal moment in the broader chronology, where insights from grammatical theory in linguistics were transposed into design methodologies in architecture. It is striking to observe how grammatical conceptions of sentence structure found resonance in the ways architectural theorists of the time conceptualized the logic of building (Fig. 3).

Between Grammar and Semantics

A somewhat parallel trajectory emerged gradually in the second half of the 20th century. With figures such as Christopher Alexander, Bill Hillier, Julienne Hanson, and others, architecture was studied and abstracted using frameworks that marked a pivot away from grammar and toward semantics.

Christopher Alexander's work remains a cornerstone in this transition. His exploration of built forms as patterns — interconnected and nested elements that shape urban and architectural structures — anticipated many of the semantic frameworks that would later emerge in computational design. "**A Pattern Language**" (1977) stands as one of the earliest systematic attempts to categorize architectural forms, mapping their interrelations in a quasi-ontological manner. Throughout Alexander's work, spaces are grouped by typology and scale into collections of patterns, whose relationships he then articulates. His approach laid the groundwork for a more nuanced understanding of architectural systems — one that moved beyond rigid formalism to encompass the deeper logic of spatial organization. 8

8 Alexander et al., A Pattern Language, 1977.

A few years later, Space Syntax, developed by Bill Hillier and Julienne Hanson, advanced similar structural and linguistic ambitions. In "**The Social Logic of Space**" (1984), they proposed that spatial configurations could be studied like language, 9

9 Hillier & Hanson, The Social Logic of Space, 1984.

3

The grammatical decomposition of meaning in linguistics (left) and in architecture (right).

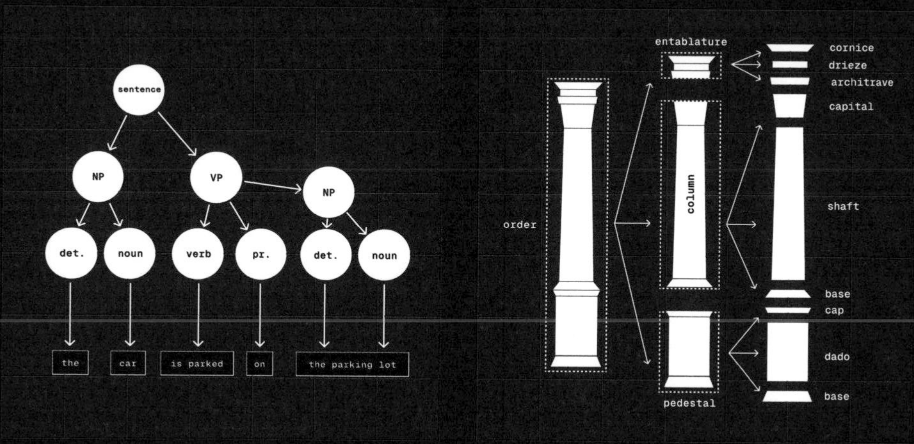

in linguistics

in architecture

4

The semantic decomposition of meaning in linguistics (left) and in architecture (right).

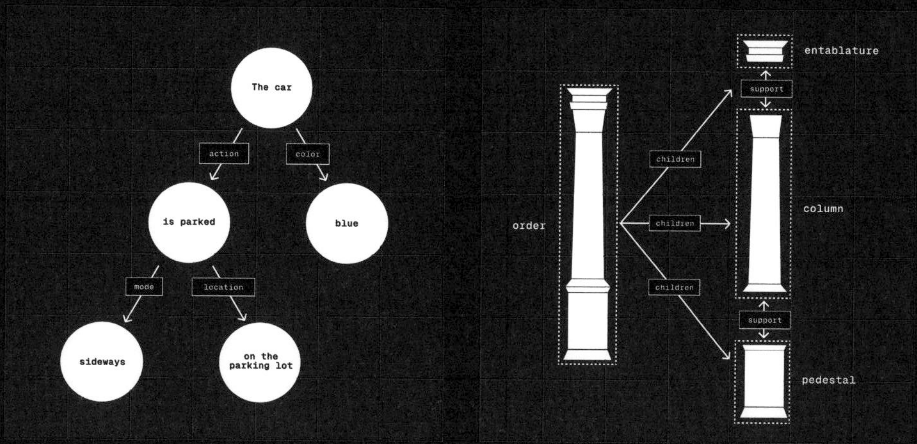

in linguistics

in architecture

broken down into graphs that delineate spatial functions and their interrelationships. The Space Syntax methodology applied statistical analysis to spatial structures to determine their influence on social interaction. With Hillier and Hanson, architecture began its abstraction through semantic graphs: space, understood as a kind of syntax, occupies a conceptual position between grammatical structure and a relational logic akin to the principles of semantic graph theory — principles that would later underpin developments in computational semantics.

In short, these early theorists developed architectural frameworks rooted in concepts from linguistics at the intersection of grammar and semantics. Just as linguists modeled language as relational graphs, architects began to express building systems as networks of entities and relationships. To this day, that parallel remains anything but coincidental (Fig. 4).

Semiotics: The First Semantic Moment

Yet another tradition — semiotics — sought to answer the same question through different means. In architecture, semiotics came to represent the study of how buildings and spaces communicate meaning through signs and symbols. Also rooted in linguistics, particularly in the work of Ferdinand de Saussure and Charles Sanders Peirce, semiotics was transposed into architectural discourse as a way of understanding the built environment as a language that could be read and interpreted. Saussure's concept of the "sign" — comprising a signifier (form) and a signified (meaning) — was adapted by architects and theorists to explore how buildings convey cultural, political, and social messages.

The emergence of semiotics in architecture coincided with a reaction against the perceived sterility and abstraction of Modernism, and the rigidity of its functionalist agenda. Thinkers such as Charles Jencks advocated for a postmodern return to symbolism, pluralism, and layered meaning. In "**The Language of Post-Modern Architecture**" (1977), Jencks argued that architecture should function as a language of signs, capable of communicating with diverse audiences. Umberto Eco, in "**Function and Sign: The Semiotics of Architecture**" (1986), asserted that architecture is "a system of signs," and that buildings should be interpreted as cultural texts.

To capture the essence of this semiotic moment in architecture, a diagram by Jencks might best express the key idea behind the movement (Fig. 5). In an effort to compare the form, function, and technique of various architects' work, **Jencks created what he called "a semantic space."** Each quality mapped to a dimension, and individual

10 Jencks, The Language of Post-Modern Architecture, 1977.

11 Eco, "Function and Sign: The Semiotics of Architecture," 1986.

12 Jencks, "In Semiology and Architecture," 1969.

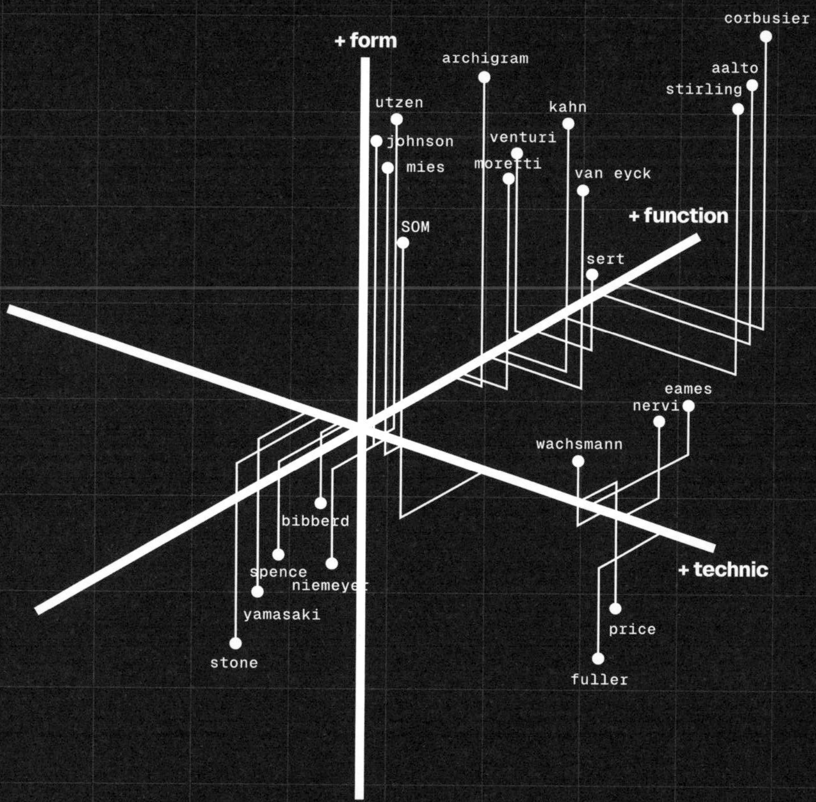

5

“Semantic space” of contemporary architects, by Charles Jencks, 1969.

architects were positioned within this three-dimensional framework. The diagram exemplifies the core premise of semiotics: that architecture is inherently contextual and relational. Architects, positioned along three axes, are defined in relation to others. Jencks's Semantic Map anticipated the abstraction potential of semantic thinking within architecture. One can see a clear continuity between this rather illustrative diagram from the late 1960s and the notion of feature space used in contemporary computational semantics. The tools have changed, but the underlying intuition remains: architectural concepts can be abstracted into semantic space to be compared, classified, or even generated. For the time being, it is enough to note that semiotics gradually made its way into architectural production — not as literal applications of Jencks's or Eco's theories, but in more loosely reframed versions taken up by figures like Peter Eisenmann, Aldo Rossi, and Charles Moore. By the early 2000s, however, its influence had waned, as architectural discourse turned toward other movements, including parametricism and late-stage postmodernism.

If semiotics left a lasting mark on architecture, it is in a set of core convictions that shaped the movement:

- Architecture is a communicative system; space is like a text that can be decoded;
- Form and ornament carry symbolic and ideological weight;
- Meaning is not fixed; it is shaped by users, context, and culture.

These tenets of semiotics continue to inform some of the intuitions behind the new semantic turn currently emerging within our discipline.

Semanticism: A Second Semantic Moment

By now, it is clear that semantics is not foreign to architecture. The second half of the 20th century saw multiple efforts to borrow from its concepts and incorporate them into architectural discourse. In much the same way that computation and deep learning revitalized semantics in linguistics, architecture today stands to benefit again from the analogy. As we have seen, an initial grammatical moment gave rise to successive semantic "waves," leaving the discipline with tools and conceptual models inherited from frameworks that are, in some respects, becoming outdated.

Two realities now coexist in architectural practice. On one hand, the daily work of architects happens within tools — from BIM software to parametric modeling interfaces — where built forms are still defined either manually or procedurally. High-level descriptors such as style, program, atmosphere, and typology remain difficult to communicate programmatically to machines. On the other hand, AI seems to upend this status quo, as its ability to map abstract concepts to tangible geometry improves rapidly. When an abstract prompt can generate a rendering, a 3D mesh, or a set of CAD primitives, a new dialogue begins between the architectural discourse — the realm of words, meanings, and semantics — and the act of architectural production — the realm of design, form, and geometry.

This tension has all the features of a watershed moment, one of those historical junctures where the discipline finds itself at the intersection of radically different technical cultures. This pivotal moment challenges us to anticipate where this evolution is headed and to ask what this new technical culture might ultimately mean for architecture. In short, the increasing permeability between semantic principles and architectural practice marks an important inflection point: a new "semantic moment." Semanticism offers a name for this shift. It positions semantics not only as a descriptive framework for architecture, but also as a generative one. This movement toward Semanticism may represent a natural evolution of the discipline's design culture, one that acknowledges the layered complexity of architectural form and embraces the technologies needed to fully articulate that innate complexity.

Reduced to a few core convictions, Semanticism corresponds to the idea that:

- Architectural forms are conditioned by their signification, such that "form follows meanings."
- As with semantics, studying architecture requires untangling the many layers of meaning embedded in built forms.
- As with semantics, composing new architecture involves crafting forms that best express a given design's intended meanings and context.
- Both the study and generation of the built environment benefit from AI, as models support the translation between semantically rich abstractions and meaningful, context-specific architectural forms.
- The creative use of AI models — through retraining, repurposing, nesting, and recombination — opens up expansive new avenues for architectural and design inquiry.

As with any theory, however, Semanticism comes with both epistemic gains and limitations. Both should be weighed against persistent challenges within the discipline. Beginning with the former, we identify at least three areas where Semanticism offers clear contributions to the architectural agenda, each addressing a key disciplinary concern: distinction, polysemy, and transposition.

Distinction — "The means of architecture is given by our capabilities to make and sense physical distinctions in space." This assertion, which opens **William J. Mitchell's seminal book "The Logic of Architecture,"** captures the importance of our shared ability to recognize and articulate difference in the built environment. Describing and measuring subtle differences among forms speaks directly to the purpose of the architectural discipline. This, too, is a core pursuit of semantics in linguistics: the disambiguation of meaning by untangling overlapping significations. By analogy, Semanticism's first contribution to architecture is to offer a computational framework for differentiating between forms. In this sense, it brings statistical learning into the discipline as a means of documenting variation between built forms and, ultimately, refining inherited architectural categories.

13 Mitchell, "The Logic of Architecture," 1990.

Polysemy — Architecture thrives when the design process is able to acknowledge the sheer diversity of built forms. The same conditions — a brief, a site, a program — can always yield a plurality of valid design responses. This "one-to-many" mapping has a direct analogue in semantics through the notion of polysemy: the idea that a single term can refer to multiple various meanings depending on context. Similarly, Semanticism embraces the possibility of a polysemy of architectural forms, as AI enables design phenomena to be modeled not as singular outcomes but as distributions — that is, wide arrays of potential answers distilled through the latent space of AI models. In other words, when a single semantic abstraction can be translated into entire families of shapes rather than a single form, the design process is enriched with a wealth of relevant options for the architect's immediate benefit.

Transposition — In architecture, it is a given that contextual factors — stylistic, typological, cultural, historical, sociological — have an impact on built form. Similarly, in semantics, words derive their meaning from context. Emulating this principle, AI's latest generative models are increasingly able to synthesize forms while accounting for contextual factors: the aesthetics of a style, the characteristics of a typology, the atmosphere of a place, and so on. Compared to earlier generative grammars, these models represent a significant leap forward. Semanticism sees in this a powerful opportunity for architects to engage with such transpositions. When it becomes feasible to generate forms that register the influence of selected contextual inputs (Fig. 6), architectural design and research begin to draw on an entirely new framework. In other words, at the intersections of known typologies, styles, and programs lie entirely new families of forms — ready to be brought into the world.

Semanticism, however, is not without its limitations. These, too, are important to articulate and examine as we develop a fuller understanding of what lies ahead.

Control — To begin with, Semanticism reconfigures control over the design process. In other words, working with AI means that control must be relinquished in order to be regained, loosened in order to be retightened. The first phase of this paradox stems from how AI systems operate. Neither a "white box" — a fully transparent and controllable algorithm — nor a "black box" — a hermetic model that offers no user agency — AI stands as a "gray box" in the computational landscape. **This framing, as applied to architecture by Andrew Witt**[14], captures the shifting balance that AI strikes between control and complexity. As models become more sophisticated and capable of approximating increasingly complex problems, the legibility and interpretability of their inner workings tend to diminish. Semanticism's reliance on AI thus comes at a price: using it as an alternate computational framework often means initially relinquishing direct control over the design process. However, this control can be gradually reclaimed as tools become "grayer." Models can be retrained and repurposed, and software leveraging AI can help clarify their internal complexity. Still, the mappings constructed

14 Witt, "Grayboxing," 2018.

in a model's latent space are deeply technical, often unpredictable, and sometimes imprecise — if not irrelevant — to the relationships they are intended to represent. In this process, the very notion of meaning can become blurred or distorted. Early semioticians explicitly studied the complexity of architectural meaning, developing methodologies that enabled designers to trace connections between words and forms. In contrast, the automation of such mappings within AI's latent space introduces a new kind of opacity. As a result, the correspondences generated between concepts and built forms may be more quantitative and at times more robust than those produced by earlier methods. At other times, they may be incorrect — or entirely misleading — with little explanation available to the user. In such cases, this automated "making" of meaning risks becoming at times an error-prone procedure that obscures the design process as a whole.

Space — In tandem, Semanticism trades space for its abstractions. Designing with AI requires that we clarify our intent in ways that can be synthetically interpreted by machines. The reduction of architecture into clear yet schematic encodings — text, numerical values, interfaces, etc. — appears to be a precondition for designing with this new technology. For this reason, graphs, diagrams, language, and other abstract media gradually become the tools through which architects communicate their design intent to machines. These "semantically-rich" abstractions condense architecture in order to express its meaning while stripping away other dimensions. If the grammatical turn already introduced a sense of abstraction — by offering procedures, scripts, and schedules to designers — the semantic turn reinforces this tendency by encouraging architects to operate through even higher-level abstractions. As a result, space, in its more grounded and experiential dimension, may become less immediately addressed when working with AI than with earlier frameworks. In other words, when the design of space remains the aim of Semanticism, its relationship to space tends to become more indirect.

Style — Finally, Semanticism is not a style. The oft-quoted motto of the Viennese secession, "To every age its art. To art its freedom," reminds us how deeply style has shaped architectural epochs. Today, however, AI's capacity to emulate, synthesize, and hybridize styles has introduced a new form of eclecticism, fueled by expansive creative freedom. Rather than affirming its own specific style, Semanticism operates as a catalyzing framework from which styles may emerge. A (simplified) account of latent space helps explain this role: as AI models learn, they build compressed representations of the data they ingest, structured as multidimensional spaces that designers can navigate to generate images, texts, and more. Within these "maps," architectural concepts such as styles are assigned specific locations. As designers explore such latent spaces, the outputs they generate may recapture canonical styles or, more interestingly, reveal hybrid blends located between known aesthetics. On the one hand, this capacity to reveal previously vast, untapped fields in between known styles is deeply fascinating for designers. On the other hand, the traditional role of stylistic principles tends to fade away. In this context, the design process seems to unshackle itself from the imperative to abide by the rules of established aesthetics. And while architecture may welcome this sudden absence of constraints, the almost boundless agency it enables can also be overwhelming. Setting aside the anchoring support of stylistic systems leaves designers with many more moving pieces — and, it must be said, with more responsibility, too.

6

Examples of various architectural representations generated with Midjourney using basic textual prompts.

the plan of a european city center, city scape, green and grey, smooth surfaces, urban influences.

an isometric view of a model of a parisian housing block.

a floor plan of a house with two bedrooms.

the living room of a minimalist, modern house, in the daytime, with a view on a landscape.

On Conditions

As AI enters the field, Semanticism appears — at the very least — as a plausible scenario for architecture. Yet for it to develop into a truly useful framework, several conditions must be met in the years ahead.

First and foremost, the transparency and controllability of AI models must improve. A theory focused on meaning cannot realistically rely on the opacity and unpredictability of today's models. In other words, the evolution of network architectures will largely determine whether Semanticism matures or loses momentum. The current "gray box" must become lighter in shade if it is to meaningfully contribute to architectural knowledge. For now, working with AI can sometimes still feel like a "blind" process, where the relationship between input and output remains obscure, limiting its ability to produce structured, useful insight.

Second, the ability of AI to synthesize and operate on modalities of architecture, especially 3D geometry and vector-based representations, will shape Semanticism's prospects. Early prototypes suggest that this capability is advancing rapidly. Still, at present, there is a clear ceiling: AI must eventually align with the formats architects value most.

Finally, Semanticism — or whatever name the discipline may adopt for this shared discourse — will not succeed unless architects seize the opportunity to reflect on what AI could mean for architectural thinking. One thing is certain: beneath the surface, things are shifting, as practitioners increasingly integrate these tools into their workflows. And since theory often takes time to catch up with practice, we hope this new technological culture will be critically addressed by designers, theorists, and researchers in the years to come.

REFERENCES

Latent Architecture: A Semanticist's Perspective
[Article]
Stanislas Chaillou, Architectural Research Quarterly 24.4, 2020

Semanticism: Towards a Semantic Age in Architecture
[Article]
Stanislas Chaillou, Artificial Intelligence and Architecture, 2022

Semanticism: When Form Follows Meaning
[Website]
Author's website

Archinect's Lexicon: "Semanticism"
[Website]
Archinect, 2023

CHAPTER V

Portraits of a Period

A LANDSCAPE ACTORS IN AI TIMES

**Concomitant with its deployment in our field, AI has prompted an increasingly vocal and fragmented discourse around its presence in architecture.
This year's Venice Architecture Biennale testifies to this reality: whereas five years ago the debate was still nascent, today a much broader range of participants is actively engaged.**

In response to this growing echo chamber, the following chapter offers a glimpse of current debates from three distinct perspectives: those of theorists, researchers, and designers. Typically, these categories remain somewhat exclusive, with each group approaching this new technology with markedly different agendas, expectations, and reflections. Together, however, they offer a comprehensive view; collectively, these lenses capture the main facets of AI's emergence in architecture. "Thinking about," "building upon," and "practicing with" represent three distinct ways of envisioning AI that drive the work of these three expert communities today.

As readers explore this gallery of portraits, we hope that certain key aspects of the current landscape become evident, as we have tried to convey them: stakeholders shaping AI's influence on our discipline now operate across traditional divides: between academia and the private sector, within and beyond disciplinary boundaries (as specialists within architecture are increasingly joined by contributors from other fields), and across the full spectrum of our industry, from large-scale firms to smaller, more experimental studios. This diversity underscores the acute pervasiveness of AI today — a stark contrast to the circumstances at the time the first edition of this book appeared, just a few years ago.

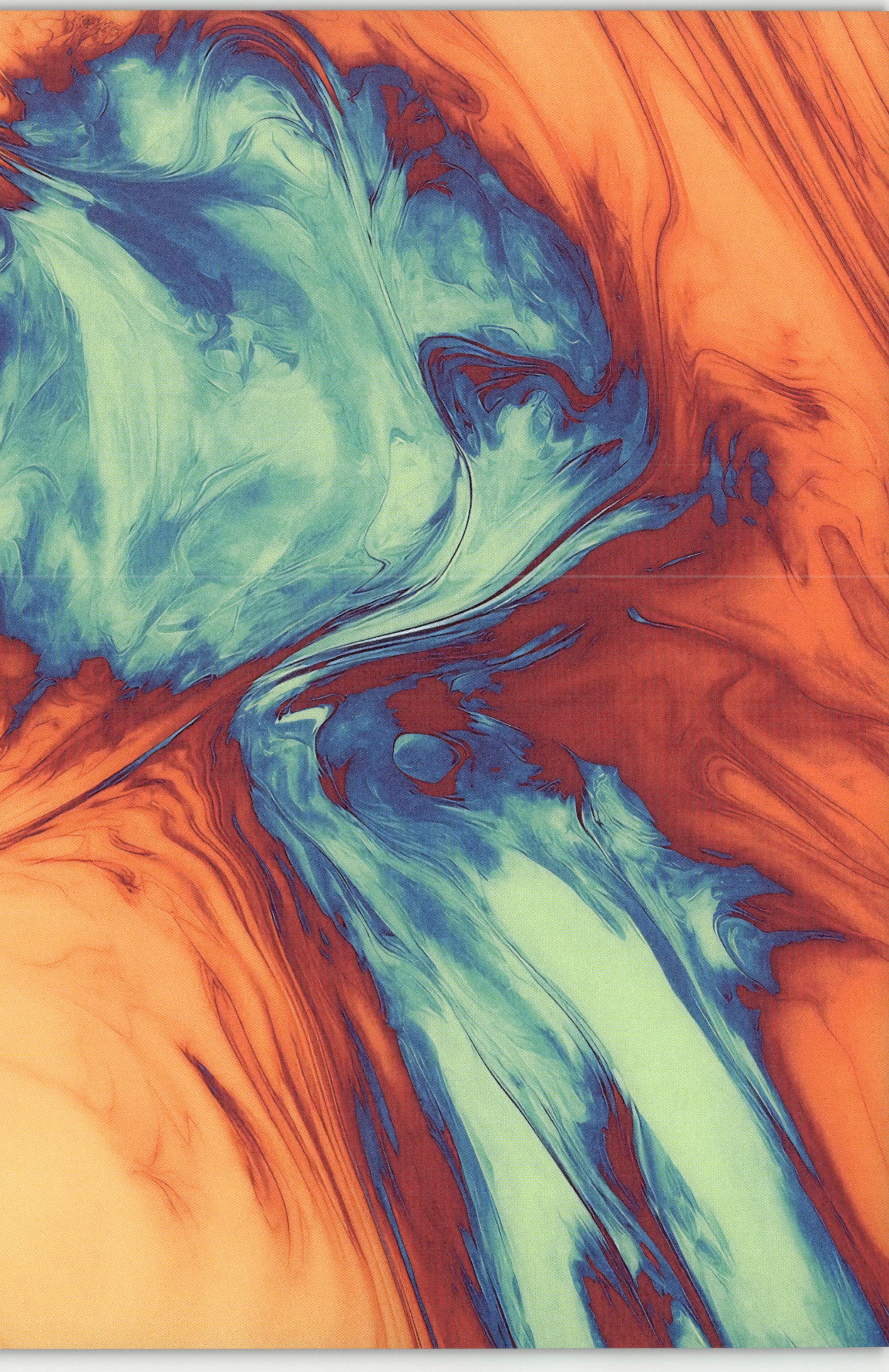

The Theorists

CONTRIBUTIONS – PART I

We begin this chapter by turning our attention to the work of theorists who are shaping and leading today's discourse. In recent years, scholarly debate has shifted from the question of whether AI has a role in architecture to a deeper inquiry into the foundations and consequences of this technological turn.

As AI began to yield meaningful results in the practice, theoretical inquiry followed the path of the adage: "If it works in practice, does it work in theory?" In this chapter, three scholars each trace a distinct thread within the ongoing debate.

With Mario Carpo, we adopt the lens of the design critic and explore one facet of the current discussion: the central importance of datasets in the age of AI, and with them, the resurgence of references, and through them, a renewed focus on history and tradition in architecture. For Carpo, since "every dataset is a canon, [and] every canon is a dataset," AI ushers in a revived relationship with the past for our discipline. **With Phillip Bernstein**, we strike a more pragmatic tone, examining the contrast between the promise of this new technology and its actual contribution to architectural practice. Bernstein's reflections revolve around the tension between "what is" and "what could be," weighing the real outcomes of AI against its theoretical potential and the dynamics of our industry's culture. **With Andrew Witt**, the inquiry takes an experimental turn. Drawing on his work with Certain Measures, Witt investigates the role of nonsense, the construction of meaning, and the potential of AI in our discipline, not only as a generator of form but also as a tool for analyzing architecture's deeper meaning.

MARIO CARPO — Mario Carpo is an architectural historian and critic. He is the Reyner Banham Professor of Architectural History and Theory at the Bartlett School of Architecture, University College London, and Professor Emeritus of Architectural Theory at the Institute of Architecture at the University of Applied Arts Vienna (die Angewandte), where he held a professorship until the end of 2023. His research and publications focus on the history of early modern architecture and the theory and criticism of contemporary design and digital technologies.

PHILLIP BERNSTEIN — Phillip Bernstein is Deputy Dean and Adjunct Professor at the Yale School of Architecture. He was formerly a vice president at Autodesk, where he led the company's vision and strategy for architecture, engineering, and construction (AEC) technologies. He is also the author of several books on architectural practice and technology, including "Architecture | Design | Data – Practice Competency in the Era of Computation" (Birkhäuser, 2018) and "Machine Learning: Architectural Futures in the Era of Artificial Intelligence" (RIBA, 2022).

ANDREW WITT — Andrew Witt is Associate Professor in Practice of Architecture at the Harvard Graduate School of Design. His teaching and research examine the relationship between geometry, machines, perception, design, construction, and culture. He is also co-founder of Certain Measures, a design and technology studio based in Boston and Berlin.

Show Me Your Dataset and I Shall Tell You Who You Are

AN ARTICLE BY MARIO CARPO
PROFESSOR AT THE BARTLETT, UCL

As we all know, since the summer of 2022 everyone has been obsessed with generative AI. First, because with few exceptions, nobody had seen it coming — I didn't, for one; so, when it came it was a shock. Second, because some find it promising, and some frightening, never mind that for the time being what generative AI can do amounts to, practically, almost nothing. But before we try to come to terms with what generative AI can do for, or against, the design professions, we must clear up what kind of artificial intelligence we are talking about — as there are many artificial intelligences, often confused under the same name.

A branch of computer science called "artificial intelligence" has been around since 1956. In 1960 Marvin Minsky famously defined artificial intelligence (at the time, not capitalized) as a "general problem-solving machine"; a definition that held good until very recently, and possibly still does. Yet since those distant times, the discipline has already risen and fallen, and reinvented itself many times. Artificial intelligence was very popular in the 1960s, including among architects (see, for example, the groundbreaking book by Nicholas Negroponte, "The Architecture Machine," first published in 1970); this was the time when many thought that computers could do almost everything. As of the mid-1970s, however, it appeared that computers of that time could do little more than nothing; so both cybernetics (Norbert Wiener's new science of "control and communication in the animal and the machine," born in 1948 and partly overlapping with early computer science), and AI itself, were quickly forgotten and relegated to the dustbin of technical history — and of design history.

The digital turn that changed the history of architecture in the 1990s was driven by small computers used as drawing machines, not by big computers used as thinking machines. Computers in the '90s made drawings — including some very special kinds of drawings we could not have drawn without computers; but in the 1990s nobody even tried to use computers to solve design problems, and the precedents of Wiener, Minsky, and even Negroponte were more than forgotten — they were entirely removed from living memory, and they did not play any role in the rise of CAD-CAM, digitally intelligent design, spline modeling, BIM, or parametricism.

Things are changing now because artificial intelligence — seen again, as in the 1960s, as a general problem-solving machine — is back, and this time around it actually kind of works. The recent revival of artificial intelligence came from a branch of computer science that had been tested in the 1960s, then abandoned in the 1970s, based on so-called neural networks; this mode of computation used to be known as "connectionist," and today it is better known as machine learning. Building on that, the second coming of AI in the visual arts — after its first coming, in the 1960s — is due to a new kind of neural network, called generative adversarial networks, or GANs, which turned out to be very good at processing images. GANs, and StyleGANs in particular, have been known since 2014–2016 and have been used by artists and designers since at least 2018. However, the recent hullabaloo over generative AI was due to the release of new, user-friendly text-to-image applications, such as Midjourney , and DALL·E, by OpenAI, in the spring and summer of 2022. And of course, everyone has been mesmerized by generative AI since the release of ChatGPT in the fall of 2022.

Old GANs, which artists and designers have been experimenting with for almost ten years, and today's generative AI, are based on a similar technical logic, and this is where it is capital for us, in the design professions, to make certain that we understand the spirit of the game — to find out how these technologies work, what they can do, and what we could try to do with them.

The technical logic of generative AI is by now well known. GAN artists must first gather a corpus of related images that are pertinent to their project; this corpus, called a "dataset," is then fed into machine-learning algorithms that ferret out what these images have in common. The result of this inductive process is a mathematical matrix that computer scientists call a "latent space," and that roughly corresponds to what philosophers would call the definition, idea, formula, or quintessence of the original dataset. So, for example, if we feed the system a dataset of images of dogs, the "latent space" will be the definition of an ideal dog. This definition, which today is neither verbal nor visual but mathematical, can in turn be applied to different tasks: first, analytic (showing the system a new picture, and asking: "Is this a dog?"); second, generative (asking the system to produce realistic images of dogs that do not exist, or fake dogs); third, combinatory (asking the system to merge two or more datasets in given proportions, producing, for example, pictures of a canine quadruped that looks 80% dog and 20% coyote).

Now, there is an interesting variation of this combinatory mode, where generative algorithms are asked to apply some general aspects of a dataset not to a set but to a single individual — thus transforming this individual into a new one that still looks recognizably similar to the exemplar from which it derives, but at the same time shows some features of an external dataset, to which it is being assimilated. The general traits that define a visual set and are common to all its individuals, but pertain to none in particular, are akin to what western classical artists, starting in the Renaissance, used to call a "manner" or a "style"; not surprisingly, the computer scientists who first developed these processes of transformation and assimilation between an individual and a set decided to call this operation a "style transfer." The term has stuck and is now in current use.

The wave of generative AI that has swept the planet since the spring of 2022 has not significantly altered this conceptual framework, — except that the new chatbots, meant for the general public, are not based on specific, purpose-built datasets, but on huge and generic archives of labeled images (text-and-image pairs) scraped from the internet, called large language models. Evidently, due to their provenance, large language models can only reflect what the internet has already gathered. Cross-modal image generators based on large language models function by the retrieval, aggregation, and averaging of precedent; and, as the precedent from which they derive is a crowdsourced collection of images, generative AI is in this instance a machine that automates the imitation of visual commonplaces.

For example: if I type the prompt "Switzerland" into the latest version of ChatGPT, what I get is in fact an automated, visual opinion poll, showing what Switzerland looks like in the mind of most people (Fig. 1). This may be of some interest to sociologists, or help a tourist office to design a new website, but that would appear, prima facie, of very limited practical interest to the design professions. This is the wisdom of crowds, or the opinion of most, translated into one synthetic picture that is in turn dependent in full, and exclusively, on the dataset from which it derives. Conversely, what is of interest to designers, I would suggest, is the potential of a machine that has long last acquired a capacity to successfully automate imitation. Regardless of the way the original dataset has been put together, generative AI can produce new images that are similar to, but different from, all the images in the original dataset. Generative AI imitates the dataset it was trained on — meaning, the datasets we fed into it. Until recently, creative imitation was seen as a privilege of the human mind. No longer. This is truly a major technical breakthrough, and one with vast epistemological, philosophical, and scientific implications.

But what's the use of it in design? Do today's designers need a machine to imitate a model, a set of models, or some abstract features common to an entire set of models —

for example, to imitate an artistic style? Which designers would need someone else's intelligence, never mind if artificial, to imitate someone else's style — or even their own style? Yet, oddly, many well-known design offices around the world are doing just that, right now. And there may be a logic in it. Because this is what AI does; this is the way artificial intelligence works, and this should give us pause, and make us think.

Generative AI does not create images out of thin air. Instead, it imitates a carefully curated dataset of images we have fed into the machine, and generates new images based on some criteria or parameters of imitation we have set. Is this not what human intelligence always did and still does? Artificial intelligence is here to remind us that there is no creation without imitation, no invention without convention, no design without a tradition, no expression without a language, no project without sources. Artificial intelligence is here to remind us that the first step of each creative process is the awareness, then the acknowledgement, of precedent — of a precedent we relate to, never mind if we like it or not. Every dataset is a canon, every canon is a dataset, and every dataset is a collection of models that someone, at some point, must have chosen (Fig. 2). And regardless of the technology we use, every canon is by definition exclusionary: every time we define a canon — every time we build a dataset — we put something in, and we kick someone out. We may not like that, but that's the way it is — and it always was, long before the invention of generative AI. And today, generative AI is here to remind us that the first step in every creative process is the invocation and selection of a dataset, and that there can be no creation without some precedent of reference — and without some reference to precedent. Precedent is that canon of our own choosing that gives meaning to our voice — for better or worse. Generative AI is here to remind us that we cannot escape precedent — but we can at least try to make it clear that we know there is one, even when we don't like it.

1

Image generated by the latest version of ChatGPT, with the prompt "Switzerland."

Again, many would argue that many cognitive theories, and many art theories, Western and not Western, have always said the same — or at least acknowledged that. And that is true, but with a difference. Humans can be unaware of the sources of their inspiration; they often are. Humans can also forget and even deliberately hide, or obfuscate, the references — the histories, the traditions, the conventions — they have in mind. In short, humans can be dumb, or cheat. Generative AI is brutally transparent. Art created with AI always starts with a dataset. If generative AI works, it is because someone, somewhere, has made a dataset, and chosen a canon. There can be no anxiety of influence when we design with AI. Show me your dataset, and I shall tell you who you are.

As a design critic, I do not necessarily embrace this transparency. But I am glad that the rise of generative AI is forcing us to confront, once again, the role of precedent, tradition, and history in all creative and artistic expressions. This is, in my opinion, the main contribution of generative AI to contemporary design, and to design theory.

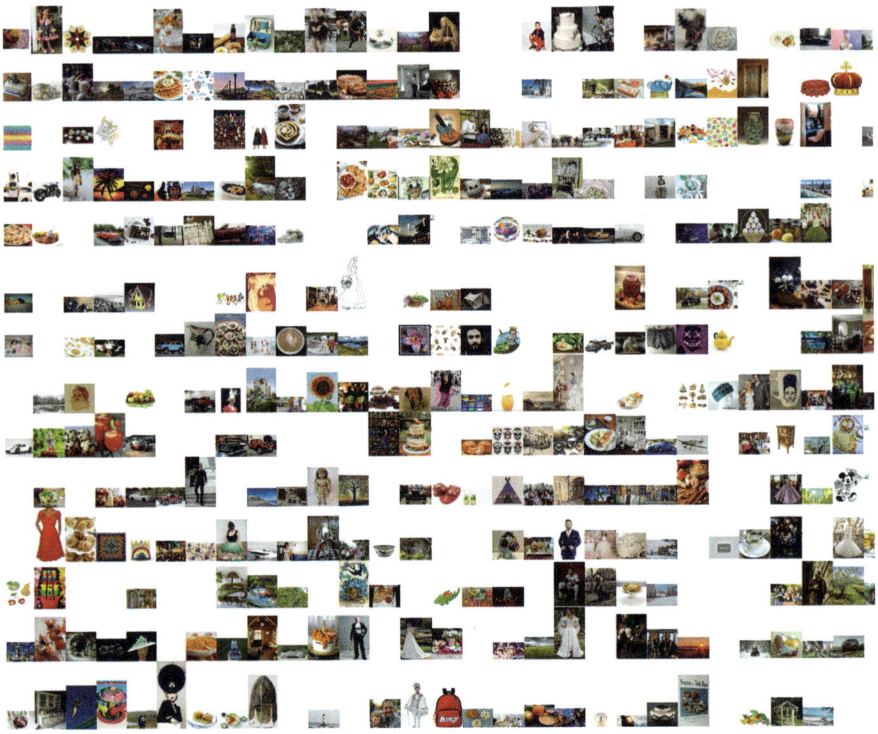

2

Extract from the LAION database, a dataset of 2 billion images underpinning recent advances in image generation.

REFERENCES & BIBLIOGRAPHY

Generative AI, Imitation, Style, and the Eternal Return of Precedent
[Video]
Lecture, Mario Carpo, Harvard GSD, 2024

The Second Digital Turn
[Video]
Mario Carpo, Talks at Google, 2017

Beyond Digital: Design and Automation at the End of Modernity
[Book]
Mario Carpo, MIT Press, 2023

Generative AI, Imitation Learning, and the Automation of Tacit Knowledge
[Website]
Mario Carpo, A+U 646, July 2024

Carpo, Mario. "Every Dataset is a Canon," Architectural Design 94, no. 3 (June 2024), 14–19.

"Formal Analysis, Generative AI and the Eternal Return of Precedent," Log, no. 58 (October 2023): 133–139.

"Imitation Games: Mario Carpo on the New Humanism," Artforum 61, no. 10 (Summer 2023): 184–188.

del Campo, Matias, ed. Diffusions in Architecture: Artificial Intelligence and Image Generators. Hoboken, NJ: Wiley, 2024.

Provocation, Prediction, and Progress

AN ARTICLE BY PHILLIP BERNSTEIN
PROFESSOR AT YALE UNIVERSITY

In his fascinating exploration of the history of the instruments of design, **Andrew Witt draws a distinction** between two types of architectural knowledge (emphasis added): [1]

> *As new machines like ellipsographs, conchoidographs, and planimeters began to encode the knowledge required to perform certain architectural drawing procedures, an epistemological distinction between design knowledge and instrumental knowledge emerged. On the one hand, we might define design knowledge as the architect's trained intuition of formal organization principles such as the relationship of parts to a whole, the ranges of material effects, and the appropriate use of geometry (while) Instrumental knowledge is the narrower understanding of the procedures to successfully manipulate a certain type of technique or technology, which would include the ability to operate an instrument, a device, a machine, a process, or a software to intended effect...In addition to its expedient use to accomplish a particular design, instrumental knowledge facilitates the creation of systems of interrelated technologies to systematically realize design agendas.*

Architects also function as agents in delivery systems of interrelated contributors — clients, designers, builders — necessary to translate a design agenda into a completed building. Those systems are connected by networks of information, risk, materials, labor, and money, but ultimately driven by exchanges of value: the willingness of a given player to accept the contribution of another for transactional benefit. For the architect, design knowledge and instrumental knowledge are tools that generate this value for themselves and the others in the delivery network.

1 Witt, Formulations: Architecture, Mathematics, Culture, 2021.

2 See references to the “Data Interstice” in Phil Bernstein, Bernstein, Machine Learning: Architecture in the Age of Artificial Intelligence, 2022.

As the building industry has digitized, the arsenal of software tools (Fig. 1) and their resulting **datasets have exploded**. Modern programs imbue design knowledge within the computer code itself (consider the data structures and parametric rules within BIM, for example), making the instrumental knowledge necessary to control these tools vast, often exceeding that of the operators’ design knowledge and blurring the distinction between the two. Translating design knowledge into working solutions now requires the architect to master not just this array of tools, but their data structures, relationships, and connections (or lack thereof). Our digital instruments are varied, complex, and hard to use; data is heterogeneous, poorly organized, and siloed in projects and firms rather in common knowledge bases; and architecture lacks any semblance of an approach to “systematically realize design agendas” save ultimately reducing every thought or transaction to paper.

1 This diagram of the 40-odd tools in use at the firm Hart & Howerton signals the struggle to understand how and where the instruments of practice are deployed, and in what relationship.

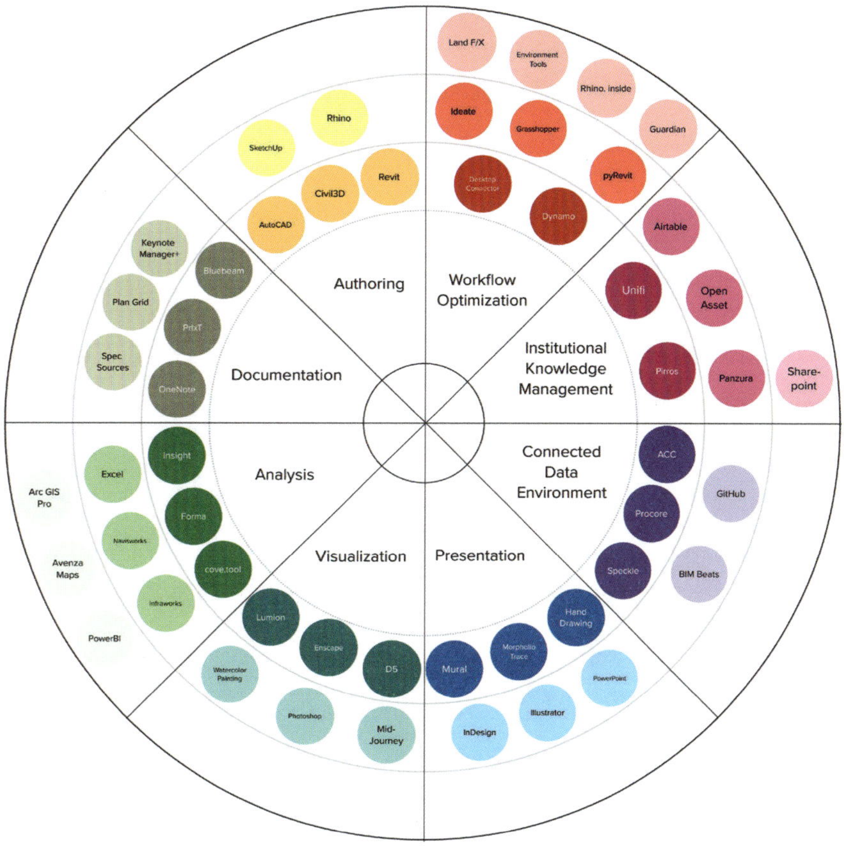

A

Original image of Rudolph Hall, Yale University.

The uploaded image shows a large, brutalist-style building. It is characterized by its raw concrete exterior and geometric design typical of brutal- ist architecture. The structure features angular shapes, with prominent vertical and horizontal lines that define the overall form. There are large, rectangular windows, some recessed into the concrete facade, giving the building a sense of depth and texture. The building has multiple levels and sections, creating a tiered appearance. A banner on the side advertises an archaeology-related event or exhibit. It is located at an intersection, and the surrounding environment includes urban elements such as a traffic light, streetlamp, and adjacent buildings with more traditional brick architecture. A white truck with the name "Infoshred" is parked in front of the building, and a few pedestrians and cyclists can be seen in the scene. The sky is clear and blue, suggesting the photo was taken on a sunny day.

B

Firefly

The uploaded image showcases a large, brutalist-style building. This architectural style is characterized by its raw concrete construction, geometric and modular forms, and an emphasis on functionality. The building features a series of stacked and offset rectangular blocks, creat- ing a rugged, industrial aesthetic. The facade includes large exposed concrete surfaces with some areas showing signs of wear and weathering, adding to its gritty appearance. There are windows embedded in some sections, framed by the massive concrete structure, and balconies or overhangs jutting out at irregular angles. The surrounding environment suggests an urban setting with paved roads, sparse vegetation, and nearby modern buildings in the background. The atmosphere appears slightly subdued, contributing to the starkness of the structure.

C

DALL•E via Chat-GPT

The image shows a large, Brutalist-style building characterized by its raw concrete exterior and geometric, angula design. The structure features prominer vertical and horizontal elements, creating a blocky, modular appearance. It has an industrial and bold aesthetic typical of Brutalist architecture, with deeply recessed windows and protrudin sections that give it a sculptural quality. The building is located at a street intersection, with adjacent buildings of a more traditional style, such as brick facades with decorative elements. On the street level, there is some signage, including one that reads "INFOSHRED," possibly on a truck, and another banner that suggests an event or organization. The street is populated with vehicles, bicycles, and some pedestrians, contributing to an urban setting. The scene is lit by soft daylight, giving the architecture a stark yet dynamic appearance.

2

ChatGPT-4o was asked to describe a photograph of Rudolph Hall at Yale University (A). The resulting text was fed into four image generators to see how they might interpret it (B to E).

D

Stable Diffusion XL

The image depicts a modern, minimalist, three-story building with a clean, geometric design. It has a light gray facade, large rectangular windows, and prominent balconies. The structure is surrounded by neatly landscaped greenery, including bushes, grass, and trees. The setting appears to be in a suburban or urban environment on a bright day with a clear sky. Two people are visible near the building: one walking on the sidewalk in the foreground and another near the building's entrance.

E

Flux

The image shows a striking example of Brutalist architecture, characterized by its use of raw, unadorned concrete and block-like geometric forms. The structure appears to consist of massive rectangular and cubic shapes stacked in a seemingly chaotic but carefully balanced arrangement. The building's heavy and monumental appearance contrasts with the more traditional brick buildings surrounding it. The scene is set in an urban environment, with pedestrians and cars visible, suggesting it is part of a bustling city. The architectural style emphasizes functionality and the raw aesthetic of concrete.

Into the instrumental breach steps artificial intelligence, the advent of autonomous algorithms that by virtue of their ability to absorb vast, disorganized expanses of digital information purport to make sense of the world. In fact, as described by Mario Carpo **"computers can deal with the most overwhelming, meaningless mess... due to their sheer memory, speed, and processing power."** The widespread development and enthusiasm about machine learning tools offers architects two important opportunities: rationalizing digital design knowledge and using the predictive and analytic capabilities that result to improve both the quality and the value of the work.

3 Carpo, Beyond Digital: Design and Automation at the End of Modernity, 2023.

Yet early returns on investment for this opportunity are not promising. Much of the energy, enthusiasm, and engagement in first-generation AI tools for architects has been, much like the case with Witt's antique drawing tools, deployed in the service of form-making and image generation, as the profession yields to its consistent initial instincts to use any new technology in service of aesthetic rather than other more practical and potentially valuable ends. Today's image generators are skilled creators and manipulators of constellations of pixels, much as today's large language models are deft assemblers of word fragments. They recognize, and can maneuver, collections of pixels in arrangements that imply an understanding of buildings and context, but the results, like many interactions with AI, is a hallucination. Despite their apparent precision, language and image generation platforms "understand" nothing about the complex, three-dimensional, technically performative nature of architecture. And what is "known" (as instantiated in their diffusion models) has been culled from the expanses of the internet without regard to provenance, accuracy, or completeness, hardly the basis upon which to build, or professionally rely (Fig. 2).

While image generators are stimulating if imprecise design provocateurs, our collective attention as a discipline would be better spent exploring how machine learning might address more pressing problems of data integration, analysis, simulation, and performance prediction. The building industry is famously inefficient, design and construction risky, and both construction and building operation are major contributors to climate change. The building supply chain is distended, opaque, and challenged by labor exploitation; seemingly banal failures to manage this chain **have resulted in catastrophe**. The easy fascination with image is a distraction from the possibilities of marshalling the next generation of technologies toward more important, constructive, meaningful, and valuable ends.

4 The negligent management and control of the supply and delivery chain was the cause of the disastrous Grenfell Tower fire in 2017. See Grenfell Tower Inquiry, 2024.

But where to start? In a recent economic analysis of the AI boom, Goldman Sach's Kash Rangan described the progression of every computing innovation **as comprised of three elements: infrastructure, platforms, then applications**. AI infrastructure has been created by what Goldman calls "hyperscalers" (Google, Meta, Microsoft, and

5 Nathan, "Gen AI: Too Much Spend, Too Little Benefit?," Top of Mind, 2024.

the like) by creating massive compute and storage. First-generation platforms — ChatGPT, DALL·E, or Flux, or open-source code bases like Meta Llama or Mistral — underly a **flurry of AI startups**. Many of those applications are designed to drive short-term productivity gains rather than profound innovation in the design agenda, and this is not surprising given the overall productivity challenges of **the building industry itself**. But incremental productivity gains yield little value across the entire delivery chain, and tend to disappear as they are widely adopted, suggesting that any profound impacts of these first-generation applications will be short-lived. But since first-generation platforms have little useful "knowledge" of architecture — and given that they are unlikely to wholesale replace architects, as **"it is very difficult to imagine that an LLM will have the same cognitive abilities as humans to pose questions, develop solutions, then test those solutions and adopt them to new circumstances"** — architecture should press toward the development of second-generation platforms while taking advantage of episodic opportunities to improve productivity. Whether these new applications could be built using diffusion models alone — rather than augmented by rules-based knowledge known as neuro-symbolics — is the subject of another exploration. But for AI to be a truly useful instrument it must instantiate design and building knowledge more specifically, reason spatially, and work within the more complex context of the interrelated technologies that comprise building.

6 The website "AI in AEC" purports to follow every AI-based tool for the building industry market. It currently lists almost 1,500 such applications. See Mikulić, AI in AEC - AEC AI Hub, 2024.

7 The construction industry has a longstanding reputation for diminishing productivity. For an interesting study of the underlying statistics, Goolsbee and Syverson, "The Strange and Awful Path of Productivity in the U.S. Construction Sector," 2023.

8 As described by MIT's Daron Acemoglu, in Nathan, "Gen AI: Too Much Spend, Too Little Benefit?," 2024.

There are preliminary but promising experiments in this realm. The technology startup SKEMA, founded by some of the original developers of building information modeling (BIM), take such an approach, combining the "innate" knowledge of componentized design and construction, overlaying machine learning strategies for layout and integration, and then connecting the resulting design output to a more detailed BIM in Revit (Fig. 3). Tools like SKEMA are the nascent signals of such emergent industry-specific architectural foundation platforms. An array of seemingly prosaic but profoundly useful tools could be built from such origins, starting with algorithms that could integrate the disparate representations of a project that reside in various programs and file servers of a typical project team. Rather than create a more potent **"lowest common denominator" file format or standard**, a properly trained AI might know how to find all representations of a given building element across various data domains, or even reason about its material, performance, or location. Broader predictive tools could identify construction logic errors or conflicts, coordinate trade labor, identify life safety or material performance issues, even help with the eternal challenge of accurate construction cost estimating. Training next-generation platforms requires our discipline to overcome an even more daunting obstacle: data cooperation. First-generation models have been trained on billions of items — words fragments and pixels — easily scraped from the internet. AEC (architecture, engineering, and construction) data, in the form of drawings, models, correspondence, construction administration records, reality-capture telemetry

9 In the CAD era, AutoCAD's DWG file format served this role. Today, the Industry Foundation Classes (IFCs) move geometry and limited metadata between various applications. See buildingSMART, "Industry Foundation Classes," 2024.

from construction sites, cost estimates — the list is endless — are neither coherently organized nor consistently structured. Even if they were, propriety project data is zealously guarded as intellectual property by the firms that created it. All of which is to suggest that the industry must find a means to collect, anonymize, immunize from liability, curate, and store as much of its data as possible as training material for its machine learning tools. Such a "data trust" would involve a degree of cross-disciplinary integration and cooperation that has no precedent in the modern design and construction economy.

But if we can solve our internal conflicts around the organization and sharing of data as the basis of next-generation machine learning systems, there are tremendous gains to be had. Instrumental knowledge is a means to an end: the deployment of machine-based design knowledge in the service of innovative, useful, and beautiful architecture. Architects and their collaborators are in the business, in part, of anticipating the future and creating the built conditions to meet that future. Yesterday's ellipsograph, necessary to draw a conical line on a piece of paper, gives way to today's building information model, perhaps augmented by tomorrow's predictive algorithm trained on the world's shared AEC data. That algorithm supports the architect in creating more robust, sustainable, functional, and cost-effective buildings driven by design knowledge and skill that can only be deployed by humans who can see and understand the comprehensive solution that is a superb design. If those algorithms can both free the human designer to spend more time resolving that design while improving its ultimate behavior through the predictive and analytical power of algorithms, machine learning will have found its real potential for architecture.

3

The SKEMA application uses a combination of machine learning, modular plan optimization from a catalogue of parts, and BIM insight to allow rapid planning of projects with repetitive parts. The conceptual plan (left), once generated by the algorithm and refined by the architect, can be converted easily into a building information model (right). Image courtesy of SKEMA Inc.

REFERENCES & BIBLIOGRAPHY

Who Is the Architect? Understanding Professional Agency in the Emergent Era of AI
[Video]
Lecture, Phillip Bernstein, Ball State University, 2024

Machine Learning: Architecture in the Age of Artificial Intelligence
[Book]
Philipp Bernstein, Routledge, 2022

Industry-Changing Tech
[Article]
Interview, Phillip Bernstein, AIA, 2023

The Future of Making Buildings
[Video]
Lecture, Phillip Bernstein, TEDxYale, 2017

Bernstein, Phil. Machine Learning: Architecture in the Age of Artificial Intelligence. London: RIBA Publishing, 2022.

Carpo, Mario. Beyond Digital: Design and Automation at the End of Modernity. Cambridge, MA: MIT Press, 2023.

Goolsbee, Austan, and Chad Syverson. "The Strange and Awful Path of Productivity in the U.S. Construction Sector." National Bureau of Economic Research, 2023.

Nathan, Allison. "Gen AI: Too Much Spend, Too Little Benefit?" Top of Mind. New York: Goldman Sachs Group, Inc., 2024.

Witt, Andrew. Formulations: Architecture, Mathematics, Culture. Writing Architecture Series. Cambridge, MA: MIT Press, 2021.

Nonsense, Noise, and Machinic Meaning

AN ARTICLE BY ANDREW WITT
ASSOCIATE PROFESSOR AT
HARVARD UNIVERSITY

Nonsense is a curious concept in discussions of artificial intelligence. When it appears as the output of AI systems, nonsense — most emblematically, machine hallucinations — is taken as evidence of flawed processes in need of rectification and repair. Yet as an input or prompt to AI systems, nonsense becomes an extreme test of AI's ability to create coherent associations from enigmatic starting points, to untangle nonsense into something meaningful. Far from being incidental or vestigial, nonsense is a gauge for the surprising hermeneutic capacity of machine intelligence to infer meaning, a kind of Turing Test for extreme sensemaking. Can exquisitely sensitive neural nets that exceed human capacity to perceive also exceed human capacity to interpret meaning?

AI is a vast combinatorial machine composed of staggering matrices of numeric weights and biases, and its highly multidimensional statistical tuning endows it with phenomenally capable sensemaking abilities. Because neural networks are mathematical functions — that is, they are rules for mapping one space onto another — as long as the inputs of a neural net conform to some minimal rules, the network will guarantee some form of output, often surprisingly lucid. To test the phenomenal capacity of AI sensemaking, one need only provide gibberish prompts to a favorite neural image generator. The prompt itself is nonsense, noise. Yet the results are almost invariably self-consistent and coherent. AI thus acts as a kind of translation machine from nonsense to coherence in the face of inhuman complexity or obscurity.

In comparison to the oracle-like sensemaking of AI, the human capacity to make sense of cryptic and enigmatic inputs is more modest and limited. Staring into the static noise of a television has long been a popular trope of insanity. Yet, paradoxically, noise is also necessary for human perception, as variants of noise suffuse and animate the electrical apparatus of our nervous systems. Thus, noise is both a strange, irradicable defect and an essential catalyst — for AI and for human cognition itself.

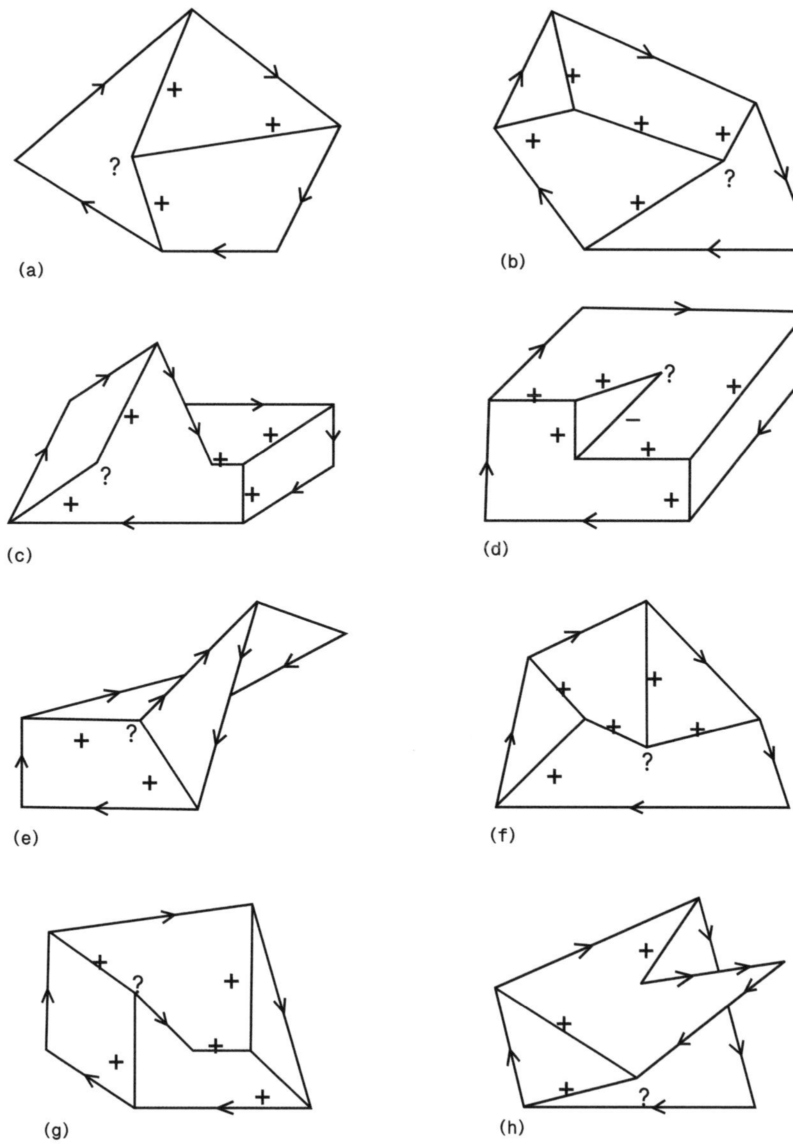

1

After the diagram "Picture of objects for which there is no labelling [possible]," in D. A. Huffman, Impossible Objects as Nonsense Sentences, 1971.

This paper unpacks the uses of enigmatic images of nonsense and noise in systems of artificial intelligence, both as prompts and products. They reveal an uncomfortably close boundary between hallucinations and rational coherence that is straddled by modern AI. The interpretation of visual enigmas reveals clues about how machines — and humans — might construct meaning.

Nonsense Drawings

In 1971, American mathematician D. A. Huffman published "Impossible Objects as Nonsense Sentences" in the journal "Machine Intelligence" (Fig. 1). Building on earlier work by the psychiatrist Lionel Penrose and mathematician Roger Penrose, Huffman posed several challenges of "picture analysis," and proposed early artificial intelligence methods for resolving these issues. In particular, he offered syntactic rules for the interpretation of diagrammatic drawings of polyhedral geometries to determine whether the drawings in question were actually possible to construct with planar faces, or if, in fact, they represented "impossible objects." In effect, Huffman proposed one of the first tests of AI's capacity for spatial reasoning.

Though his paper considered visual and spatial questions, Huffman's allusion to nonsense sentences — a specifically linguistic construction — was no accident. In effect, he was asserting a syntactic structure for both drawings and visual perception that paralleled language itself. Since intelligence and reasoning must be syntactically based, Huffman's impossible objects presented a curious conundrum: they were syntactically coherent, yet they frustrated meaningful interpretation. For Huffman, it was the interpretation of such unusual images that revealed rationality in both human and machine. Huffman's and the Penroses' nonsense sentences owe much to the earlier investigations of linguist Noam Chomsky. In his 1957 book "**Syntactic Structures**," Chomsky explores grammatically illogical but poetically evocative nonsense sentences such as "colorless green ideas sleep furiously." Chomsky constructed such sentences to distinguish what is syntactical and grammatical from what is meaningful. In so doing, he suggested that at least some sentences could not, in fact, be made meaningful.

1 Chomsky, Syntactic Structures, 1957.

A few years after Chomsky's paper, in 1961, a curiously enigmatic book made its appearance on the shelves of Parisian bookstores. Upon opening it, the intrigued browser would be greeted with what appeared to be shredded pages that, when variously recombined, created a combinatorial factory for nonsense sentences. The book, Raymond Queneau's "Cent Mille Milliards des Poemes," was a mix-and-match flipbook, a simple device that allowed near-endless recombination. Though every possible poem adhered to a certain syntax — conforming to the structure of a sonnet, rhyming in turn — many were distinctly enigmatic. The book demonstrated the capacity to create poetry, even beauty, in nonsense. It made tangible and beautiful the vast combinatorial space of linguistic syntax. Novel as it may have seemed, "Cent Mille Milliards des Poemes" recalled not only Chomsky's work and the well-known "exquisite corpse" technique of surrealism, but also an unusual calculational precedent. An equally curious mathematical text, published nearly a century earlier, shared the same combinatorial flipbook mechanics: "Automatic Arithmetic: A New System for Multiplicarion and Division without Manual Labor." Published by John Sawyer, a British accountant who patented his method in the US in 1878, "Automatic Arithmetic" had a strikingly similar structure to "Cent Mille Milliards des Poemes": a series of flipbook-style strips, recombinant with certain rules, producing syntactically consistent results. The inventive format of Sawyer's and Queneau's books essentially blackboxed specific syntactic operations in the physical-mechanical artifact of the book.

Combinatorial methods such as Queneau's offer a way to endlessly produce sentences or constructions that have a syntactic regularity yet frustrate meaningful interpretation. They pose a specific challenge to contemporary AI systems: could AI infer meaning where there is none, or where a human cannot initially see it? Nonsense sentences, generated from combinatorial processes that ensure both their syntactic regularity and semantic obscurity, are thus an intriguing way to test the limits of possible coherence. Despite the intention for such sentences to be purely formal constructs devoid of meaning, suitably trained neural nets are remarkably adept at wresting meaning from nonsense sentences. Using the logic of a linguistic combinatorial engine similar to Queneau's, we can probe the limits of AI's ability to construct meaning. Recently, our design office, Certain Measures, put that sensemaking capacity to the test with a project inspired by the work of Chomsky, Huffman, and the Penroses on the generation of syntactically rigorous impossible objects. "Twilight Crystalline Models Hunt Wistfully" (Fig. 2, 3) is a multichannel video project that tests models and language as entangled modes of architectural representation. In particular, it contorts multimodal artificial intelligence models to create images, or perhaps meanings, of sentences akin to Huffman's "impossible objects."

The project originated as a purely combinatorial exercise in the creation of hundreds of strange, cryptic, or indecipherable descriptions of models. The video triptych consists of three screens: a series of text descriptions of contradictory, paradoxical, or improbable architectural models; an AI-generated image of an associated architectural model; and a map of the internal workings of the AI as it processes these paradoxes. The project foregrounds the indispensable but hackable role of language in the description, reading, criticism, and formulation of architecture. One subtle but important part of the piece is the activation map, which shows the machinic view of the image. This view is noisy — it is the state in between the flawless, human-readable image and the underlying weights of the neural network itself. There is also a purely mechanic representation of the model, a visualization of the underlying weights. It's an image that is almost a Gerhard Richter version of noise, evidently stochastic but evolving in a smooth and almost serene way.

Noise Images

If nonsense sentences and drawings adopt consistent syntax but illusory semantics, noise images defy syntax altogether in a blizzard of visual entropy. Noise images are the corruption of the representational medium itself, a scrambling of pixels and exploding of coherence. The mathematical definition of noise was laid out by Claude Shannon in his "Mathematical Theory of Communication," where he quantified a theoretical signal-to-noise ratio limit that is still in use today. For Shannon, noise was a perturbance that degraded and confused an underlying signal. Noise is thus a characteristic of any signal propagation — of communication, information, and therefore meaning — that has somehow gone awry. Noise arises as a byproduct or degraded version of a signal propagated through a transmission system, an imperfect replica of something that has come before.

Designers have long been fascinated by corrupted replicas as a creative rejoinder to the rigid uniformity of mass production. The process of iterative electromechanical copying was used generatively by the designer-artist Bruno Munari for his "Xerographie" series, in which he dragged various images and objects across a photocopier mid-scan to create strange shifts and textures — an almost haptically generated noise. The connection between copying and noisemaking becomes even more interesting when we consider automatic and digital transformations of copying and transcription, particularly the copying of dynamic entities, which channels some of the slippage and blurring of Munari's "Xerographies." The concept of "generation loss" is particularly relevant to this entropic view of noise as a degradation through reproduction. Generation loss is the progressive degradation that can occur through iteratively copying — normally afflicting analogue media like photographs, cassettes, records, and films. It is a very particular kind of cybernetic feedback involving duplication, replication, and genetic drift.

AI copymaking or deepfaking, though vastly more sophisticated, occasionally betrays the artifacts of signalized generation loss. In particular, early dynamic deepfakes, such as those from Karol Majek, Gene Kogan, or Dat Tran, literally came apart at the seams. They almost appeared as if the faces of the deepfakes were noisily melting away, losing coherence to the entropic degradation. There is a feeling of generation loss happening in real time.

Despite their status as ciphers or defects, noise images are foundational to virtually all modern implementations of AI. Although the image, sound, and video products of generative AI feel marvelously and vividly specific, the seed of these products is an initial state of vertiginous noise. These images are little more than matrices of random values, an arbitrary point. Indeed, it is only through exhaustive iteration, from stochastic initial conditions to gradually more coherent images, that neural networks converge toward their refined and marvelous products.

There are parallels in human vision, where empirical tests confirm that even surprisingly noisy pictures can be the basis of coherent perceptual images. Experimental aspects of the psychology of perception were also radically expanded by computers like the IBM 7090, and automated stereodrawing provided a remarkable tool to develop significantly more complex visuals. Bela Julesz, a researcher at Bell Labs, laid out a range of surprisingly complex autonomic perceptual behaviors that he explored through his random-dot stereograms in his 1971 book "Foundations of Cyclopean Perception." These stereograms are composed of two views with have no apparent relationship to each other — one often displaying some modest axial symmetry, the other appearing completely random. When viewed as a stereopair, they reveal complex volumetric objects — extruded volumes or hyperboloids of revolution, for example. Julesz argued that such dissonance between the evident noise of a single image and the clarity of the paired stereoscopic viewing suggested an intricate physiological process for stereo fusion, revealing a deeper logic of perception beyond illusion.

2

"Twilight Crystalline Models Hunt Wistfully," installation view. Courtesy of Certain Measures.

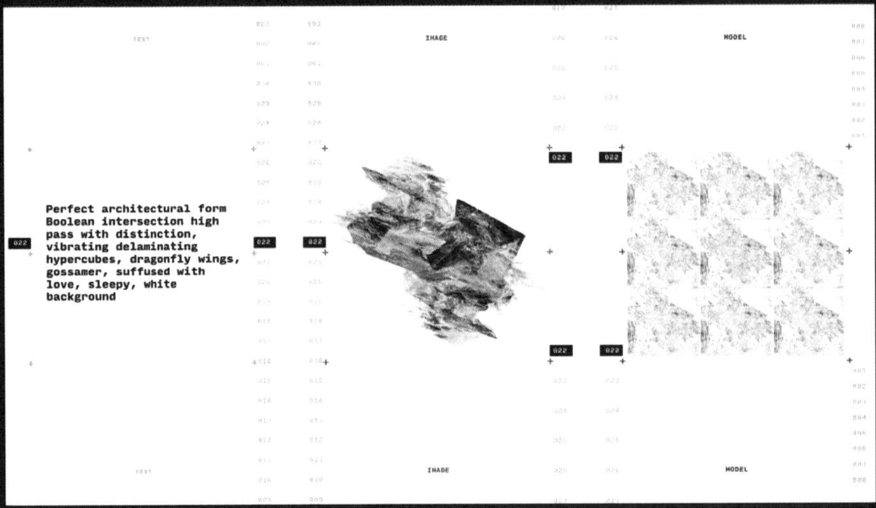

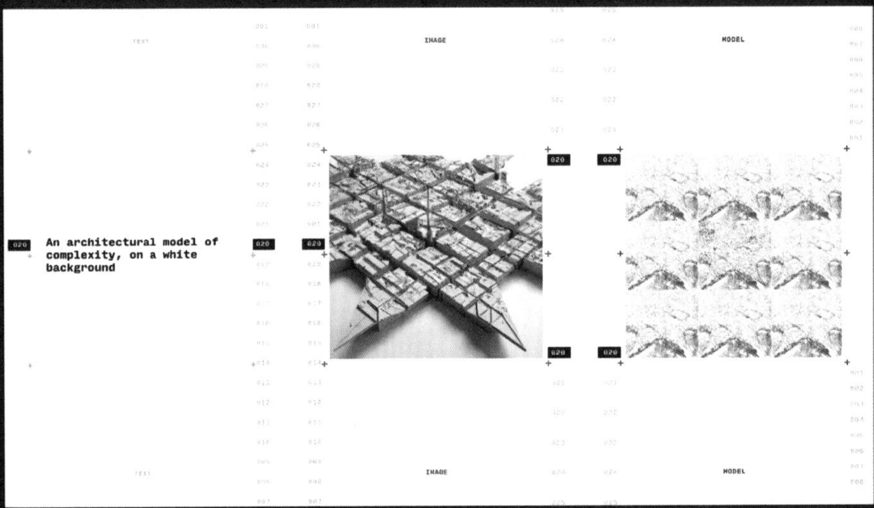

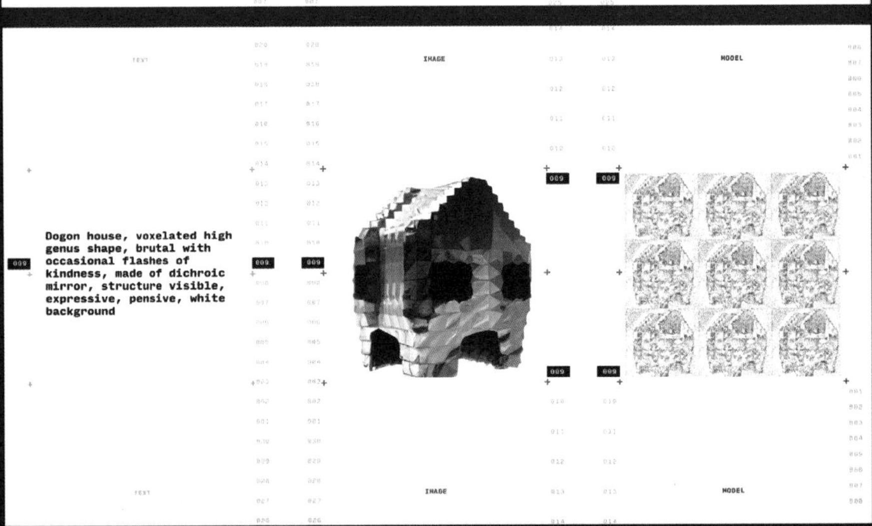

3

“Twilight Crystalline Models Hunt Wistfully,” still. Courtesy of Certain Measures.

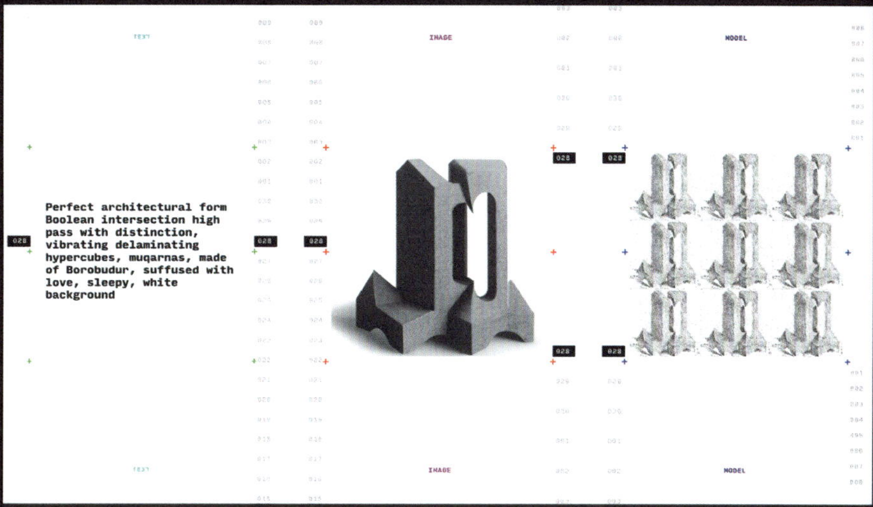
TEXT
IMAGE
MODEL
028
Perfect architectural form Boolean intersection high pass with distinction, vibrating delaminating hypercubes, muqarnas, made of Borobudur, suffused with love, sleepy, white background
028
TEXT
IMAGE
MODEL

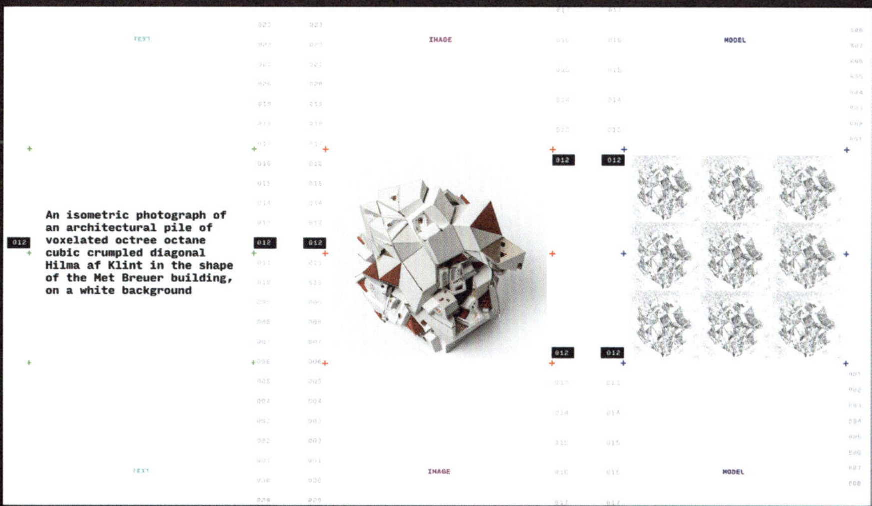
TEXT
IMAGE
MODEL
012
An isometric photograph of an architectural pile of voxelated octree octane cubic crumpled diagonal Hilma af Klint in the shape of the Met Breuer building, on a white background
012
TEXT
IMAGE
MODEL

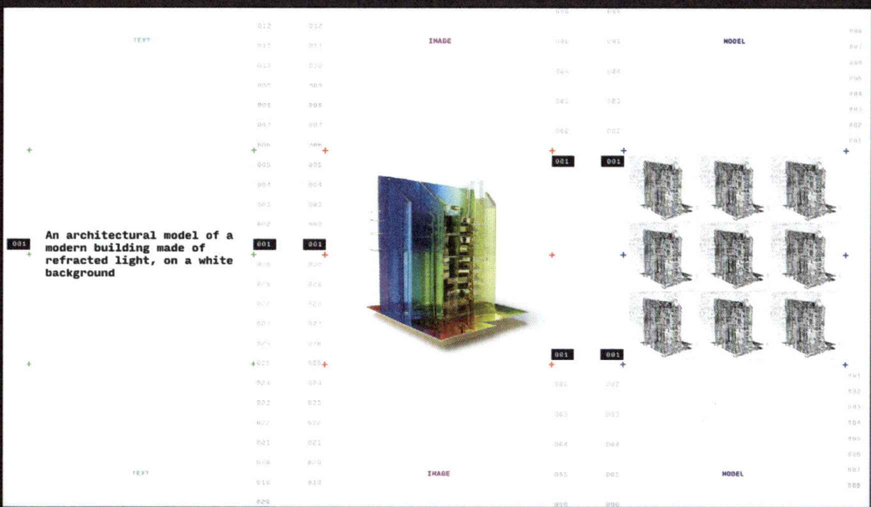
TEXT
IMAGE
MODEL
001
An architectural model of a modern building made of refracted light, on a white background
001
TEXT
IMAGE
MODEL

AI and the Making of Meaning

What is the meaning of noise and nonsense in discussions of AI? Noise images and nonsense drawings are confounding cousins, differing in their particulars but sharing certain enigmatic and inscrutable quality. For both humans and machines, they pose challenges to coherence and stretch the limits of perception and cognition. Yet British philosopher of noise Ray Brassier argues that there is a **"tension between the negative characterization of noise as form-destroying entropy and the positive aesthetic valorization of noise as form-generating novelty...[an] irreconcilable tension between the destruction and generation of form."** This tension is at the heart of the generative mechanism of AI, which harnesses entropy as an engine of creation.

2 Brassier, foreword to An Epistemology of Noise, 2013.

Noise images, in their role as seeds and input to AI processes, are the germ of AI hallucinations and dream images. In this sense, they echo the random, noise-like firing of neurons that accompanies human dreaming. In fact, physiologists Aldo Faisal, Luc Selen, and Daniel Wolpert argue that **"noise permeates every level of the nervous system, from the perception of sensory signals to the generation of motor responses, and poses a fundamental problem for information processing. In recent years the extent to which noise is present and how noise shapes the structure and function of nervous systems have been studied."** It is ambiguous in some cases whether noise is a degradation of function or an active requirement, a kind of precondition for cognitive function.

3 Faisal, Selen, and Wolpert, "Noise in the Nervous System," 2008.

The almost oracular potential of AI to read the meaning in noise points to a key divergence in machinic and human reading. The capacity of AI to make meaning, or at least to propose and map a universe of possible meanings, may also be a power to help make meaning where meaning is difficult, obscure, and challenging. AI may be a key not only to generate architecture, but to reveal, more fundamentally, what the meaning of architecture is.

REFERENCES

Formulations
[Book]

Andrew Witt, MIT Press, 2022

Spolia, Data, and Charting a Relational Architecture
[Video]

Lecture, Andrew Witt, Playing Models, 2024

Through a Machine Lens
[Article]

Andrew Witt, Loci Communes 1.2, 2022

Formulations, Mathematical Design, and Writing
[Video]

Interview, Andrew Witt, Getting Simple Podcast, 2022

The Researchers
CONTRIBUTIONS – PART II

The past five years have profoundly impacted the research landscape. As a handful of tech companies continue to release increasingly powerful foundation models, this new generation of AI tools has begun to permeate academic discourse.

While this top-down dynamic unfolds, researchers — both from within and beyond the field — have been reconfiguring their work in response to this new wave of models. As this momentum builds, their research begins to fuel both academia and the tech industry. In this chapter, we turn to three researchers whose work is poised to leave a lasting mark on our discipline, whether directly or indirectly.

With Anastasis Germanidis, we revisit the early days of Runway, now one of the most influential GenAI-powered creative platforms. The research led by Germanidis and his team resulted in of the first truly effective AI-driven video generators and now offers a glimpse of AI's potential in 3D generation. Our conversation touches on the importance of large world models and speculates on what may be coming next for the field. **With Immanuel Koh**, we return to in-field research. Koh's stream of projects and investigations provides a timely illustration of current advances in AI-enabled architecture, engineering, and construction (AEC). He underscores the importance of encoding, and the need for research to engage with the formats that shape our discipline. **With Aaron Hertzmann**, we delve into the later stages of this current phase. Hertzmann is one of those early pioneers who, long before the term "GenAI" entered circulation, helped lay the intellectual groundwork for understanding computer-generated art. He shares insights from his work at Adobe Research and reflects on his personal journey through topics that lie at the intersection of creation and computation.

ANASTASIS GERMANIDIS — Anastasis Germanidis is Co-Founder and Chief Technology Officer of Runway, one of world's leading companies applying deep learning techniques to audiovisual content for the art, creativity, and design industries. In addition to his role at Runway, Germanidis is a machine learning researcher, trained at New York University, with a background in both engineering and interactive art.

IMMANUEL KOH — Immanuel Koh holds a joint appointment as Assistant Professor in Architecture and Sustainable Design (ASD) and Design and Artificial Intelligence (DAI) at the Singapore University of Technology and Design, where he also directs Artificial-Architecture. He earned his PhD at the École polytechnique fédérale de Lausanne (EPFL), conducting research at both the School of Computer and Communication Sciences and the Institute of Architecture.

AARON HERTZMANN — Aaron Hertzmann is a Principal Scientist at Adobe Research and Affiliate Faculty at the University of Washington. He is widely recognized for his contributions to computer vision and machine learning, as well as for his theoretical work at the intersection of computer science and visual art. He spent ten years as a professor at the University of Toronto and has worked at Pixar Animation Studios, Microsoft Research, the Mitsubishi Electric Research Laboratories, and Interval Research Corporation.

Towards World Modeling with AI

AN INTERVIEW WITH ANASTASIS GERMANIDIS CTO AT RUNWAY

Generative AI has become a pervasive phenomenon, and platforms like Runway have become the go-to place for creative people to use this technology. Could you give us a sense of your background and what Runway does today?

AG — My name is Anastasis Germanidis; I am the CTO of Runway. We are building creative tools that use AI. We are also an applied research company, in the sense that we are both building AI models for image and video generation, as well as creating the tools wrapped around those models. We see ourselves as being present across this entire stack, from the conception of AI models to crafting the sandbox that allows people to work with them.

When we started out, generative models were used in a few different ways, but that was nowhere near the level of adoption we see today. It has been a long journey. Our goal today is to identify ways how these models can augment creative processes and help people bring their ideas to life faster. For instance, **our most well-known model is called Gen-3** (Fig. 1, 2, 3, 4). It is the third generation of models that allows you to generate short videos using a text prompt, a starting image, or an existing video. We see this tool being used in a variety of ways: short clips, entire films, architecture, etc.

1 Germanidis, "Introducing Gen-3 Alpha: A New Frontier for Video Generation," 2024.

With Runway, you chose to build an editor — a sandbox that not only allows for the generation of images and videos, but also for their repurposing and editing. Why did you choose to position Runway at this intersection?

AG — One approach to generative AI is to think that from a single text prompt, creatives will soon be able to synthesize entire movies. That is not our vision. We believe that AI models can amplify and increase the number of choices you have when working on a project. Those choices take different forms: you might start from a prompt or an image, get a video out of that, and then move on to other formats, other mediums. It really is a multi-step process, and in order to support this kind of work, you need to build not only generative components but also editing components. So our goal is not to create single-step workflows, but rather to empower a more iterative approach to the creative process.

"Control," therefore, seems to be an important topic to discuss. What is your design philosophy when it comes to providing control to your users?

AG — Indeed, control is key. In fact, there are two ways to think about these types of AI models. One way is to think about them through the lens of the agent-based approach, where the user gives some initial instruction and the agent performs a sequence of actions with limited human input. We tend to prefer the other way: the idea of AI models as "thought partners," where you are provided with choices at each step of the way, allowing you to move faster through creative iterations. You usually figure out where you are going as you are designing — AI helps in that discovery process. "Control," therefore, translates for us into the exploration potential these models give you. They represent a greater level of control over the design space, and, conversely, allow users to explore it more quickly.

That is also why a large portion of our team is working on new modes of control. For instance, we were the first to introduce the idea of "motion control," where the user can start from an initial frame, pick the type of objects to be included in the scene, and specify where these objects might move in the scene or how the camera might fly through the scene. This way, the user can start thinking more like a director, rather than focusing solely on what the scene contains semantically. In other words, matters of composition, expression, etc. can also be addressed in Runway.

If you had to map out the main kinds of conditioning you can apply with Runway, which would you list?

AG — Motion control is one. But I think we can do even better: the way characters interact or express themselves in videos is definitely an area we want to explore further. More precise character expressions, movement, etc., are areas where we can still grow in precision. Consistency — of characters, of environments — is also a key topic for us, and something further on the horizon. To give an example: if a user wants to tell a story in a specific location, that place needs to be represented consistently, in the same way, throughout the generated story. Disjointed sets of shots, which can occur with some generative models, are what models need to solve in order to provide creatives with more reliable solutions.

There is a paper you co-authored that has become a reference in the literature — "Structure and content-guided video synthesis with diffusion models." Can you walk us through its significance?

AG — This paper is the one that led to Gen-1. **With Gen-1, you had to provide a driving video, a reference image, or a prompt.** The model would then capture the structure of the driving video by converting it into a depth map and use that conditioning depth map video with the reference image provided to create a new, synthetic video. This led to many different use cases, one of which was style transfer. With style transfer, the core idea was to disentangle the structure of the scene from its aesthetics. Another use case was to take an untextured 3D scene and add a photorealistic overlay onto it. It is essentially using AI as a new type of rendering engine — one you can control intuitively through image reference or text prompts.

2 Runway, "Introducing Gen-1: The Next Step Forward for Generative AI," 2023.

When working with models trained to apply styling — and with the notion of style being something obviously very subjective — how do you come up with objective, quantifiable methodologies to guide model performance? In other words, how can we drive models to mimic something as subjective and relative as style? What is Runway's approach to this topic?

AG — "Evaluation" is the operative word here, and maybe one of the most challenging things in our field. Evaluation methods help us understand how models perform as they get trained. There are, in fact, metrics you can use: measures of temporal consistency, for instance, where you take subsequent frames and compare their similarity to evaluate how smoothly they transition. That same principle can be applied to other things, like 3D consistency, geometrical consistency, etc. So that as you move through a generated scene, you can evaluate how well the model maintains the continuity of the scene's features all along the generated sequence.

When it comes to style, it is indeed difficult to assess performance. One way in the literature has been to use preference studies: you compare outputs from two different models and ask users which they prefer, then aggregate those user responses. In our case, what we really focus on is creative feedback. At Runway, creatives are involved from day one of model development. One example: the captions we provide models during training are key. Making sure we provide the right terms, the right details, is essential, and working with filmmakers helped us get that right.

With film generation, architects started paying even more attention to generative AI, as 3D generation seemed to be closer to reaching maturity. AI seems finally able to generate movement through space while respecting some persistence and basic physics. To what extent are these notions of scene persistence, physics, etc., truly happening in generated scenes from Runway?

AG — This touches on a well-known discussion: the difference between simulation, which runs on more traditional algorithmic techniques, and learning those same rules through deep learning. I see them as different means towards the same goal.

What we see with video generation models is that as you scale them — using more compute and data — their 3D understanding improves in a predictable way, which can be measured through metrics like geometric consistency and other methods mentioned before. Let's take the notion of occlusion to explain that point. Occlusion is when an object briefly passes between the camera and another object further in the distance, and then the background object gets hidden (occluded) and then reappears. The model's ability to maintain consistency in the details of this object that disappears and reappears is one way to benchmark its implicit grasp of real-world behavior. Using occlusion, it became quite clear that there was a drastic improvement between Gen-1 and Gen-3 Alpha.

It's the same with models' increasing capacity in recent years to mimic fluid dynamics, gravity, etc. I think there is still room for improvement, of course, but seeing so much progress in so little time is very exciting.

Let's touch on 3D: how far are we from translating these generative video universes into actual, tangible geometry — Nurbs, NeRFs, voxels, point clouds — that designers can manipulate?

AG — It is definitely possible today, to some extent. There is some work being done along those lines, using pre-trained diffusion models to generate actual geometry. It's being studied today not just for objects, but for entire scenes, spaces. It's not our main area of focus, since our work focuses on video generation, but, yes, there are ways to leverage pre-trained models to create 3D outputs.

1 Snapshots of Gen-3 generated videos, prompt: "A giant humanoid, made of fluffy blue cotton candy, stomping on the ground, and roaring to the sky, clear blue sky behind them."

2 Snapshots of Gen-3 generated videos, prompt: "An ultra-wide shot of a giant stone hand reaching out of a pile of rocks at the base of a mountain."

3 Snapshots of Gen-3 generated videos, prompt: "An aerial view of the ocean. a maelstrom forms in the water swirling around until it reveals the fiery depths below."

4 Snapshots of Gen-3 generated videos, prompt: "An empty warehouse where flowers start blooming from the concrete."

runway

We have spoken about the path to progress and how models might improve in the future. Will the change come from a new generation of models, or from scaling current frameworks?

AG — I believe that the current generation of models can be scaled much further — more data, more compute — rather than jumping immediately to a new generation of models. The underlying framework between Gen-2 and Gen-3 Alpha, for instance, is not massively different. There is some difference in model architecture, of course, but the overall framework is very similar. The amount of compute is really the main difference. And scaling these models further can be done fairly reliably in the near future.

In that respect, there is a **general principle called the "scaling law."** It allows you to roughly determine how big your model needs to be to utilize a given amount of compute and data. It also helps you figure out how to optimally scale compute and data. Depending on the final task you are trying to achieve, the scaling factors might vary, of course. Also, as you scale, you will bump against many limits — physical factors like power constraints, etc. — that will limit you in your ability to push along the scaling law. At the end of the day, it is always a trade-off: one should always consider the incremental improvement gained by scaling a model, and decide whether continuing to scale is worthwhile. Tiny improvements are not always worth the cost and effort of scaling certain models.

3 Wikipedia, "Neural Scaling Law," 2025.

Let's conclude this interview on the notion of space: there seems to be an increasing ability to represent space among the latest generation of AI models. What could be the long-term technological unlocks for GenAI?

AG — What I see as a very interesting path forward is **the idea of more universal simulations**. Right now, models are trained on human-generated data — text, films, etc. But you could imagine models trained on many different scales of observational data. Being able to develop models that can learn across those scales could have all sorts of advantages, like helping us on scientific discoveries, for instance. That is why I see GenAI moving in the direction of universal modeling, where models will be trained to grasp more and more aspects of the universe as a whole, at different scales of representation. "General world models" are a manifestation of that type of new model. **At Runway, we are, in fact, already working on things along that line. We might even have something published on the topic by the time this book comes out...**

4 Germanidis, "Introducing General World Models," 2023.

5 Since our interview with Anastasis, Runway released Gen-4. See Runway, "Introducing Runway Gen-4," 2025.

REFERENCES

A Brief History of Video Generation
[Video]

Lecture, Anastasis Germanidis, Ray Summit 2024

Introducing General World Model
[Video]

Short Clip, Runway ML

Structure and Content-Guided Video Synthesis With Diffusion Models
[Article]

Paper, Esser et al., 2023

Towards Universal Simulation
[Website]

Manifesto, A. Germanidis Website

The Architecture of 3D Encodings

AN ARTICLE BY IMMANUEL KOH
ASSISTANT PROFESSOR AT SUTD

What makes architecture difficult for artificial intelligence (AI) is its representability, and thus its computability. Or more specifically, the complexity of converting architecture into sparse or dense vectors (i.e., numerical representations) for deep neural networks to process, learn, generate, and even reason about architectural designs, whether in the configuration of spaces or the perception of forms. This process of "converting" (or vectorizing) is called "encoding." In deep learning, "embedding" is sometimes used interchangeably with "encoding," especially when used in the context of autoencoding models, which aim to learn a representation (encoding) for a given dataset by reducing its dimensionality. In computing, the verb "**encode**" means "to change information into a form that can be processed by a computer." In layman's terms, it can also be understood as "**digitize**." In the case of character encodings, to encode is to assign or map numbers to graphical character symbols such as the letters of the English alphabet.

1 Oxford Learner's Dictionaries, "Encode," 2025.

2 Oxford Learner's Dictionaries, "Digitize," 2025.

As an illustration, it is worth starting with the most familiar character encoding of the internet at the turn of the 21st century: ASCII (American Standard Code for Information Interchange), published as a standard back in 1963. ASCII is defined by 7 bits — 128 binary sequences (string identifiers) — onto which 128 characters are mapped. So, the word "Hello" is encoded as "1001000 1100101 1101100 1101100 1101111" in 7-bit binary, or "01001000 01100101 01101100 01101100 01101111" in 8-bit binary, or "48 65 6C 6C 6F" in hexadecimal — all formats a computer can process. Today, UTF-8 (Unicode Transformation Format – 8-bit), as defined by the Unicode Standard, is the default character set on most webpages and extends ASCII to encode as many as 1,112,064 characters, thus finally resolving the earlier issues around international character support.

In AI, there are several different encodings using sparse vectors, such as one-hot encoding, ordinal encoding, and binary encoding. Could architecture form be encoded in a similar way? One of the earliest attempts in architecture is by the architect and mathematician Lionel March, who demonstrated that the built form of Ludwig Mies van der Rohe's 1958 Seagram Building can, in fact, be encoded in binary as "0001 0000 0000 1000 0011 1110 1111 1110 0000 1111 0000 0000" or in hexadecimal as "10083EFE0F00" (March 1976). Using a 3×5×3 voxel model, each voxel is encoded either as 1 or 0 to represent "mass" and "void," respectively. However, unlike the computing constraints in the available number of bits reflected in the encodings of ASCII or UTF-8, March's code length is not fixed but dependent on the complexity of the chosen built form, whereby the positioning of 0s and 1s has no real significance (Steadman, 2001). For example, while the 12-digit hexadecimal (or 48-bit binary) code of the Seagram Building refers to a 3D massing, the longer 18-digit hexadecimal code "F2803F71280EFE032F" (72-bit binary) of Le Corbusier's Maison Minimum refers to a 9×8 2D plan. March's attempt to formulate an "architecture of form" is essentially that of an "architecture of encoding."

What March started half a century ago in formulating a disciplinary encoding of form (albeit an imperfect one) has become all the more important today if architects are to have a stake in the design and development of future deep learning models that might better "represent" or "re-represent" architecture and even set the path toward a new architecture. An "architecture of encoding," as used here, is not simply a predetermined one-to-one mapping between forms and numbers, as in standardized ASCII or in March's unstandardized case. It is fundamentally about transforming architectural data into a meaningful and learned architectural representation — one that can be ingested by and is effective for the training of deep neural networks. Apart from the curation of the architectural training dataset and its modality, disciplinary knowledge is also embedded in the design of the encoding itself. Encoders compress data to its most salient features as latent space, which decoders then decompress or reconstruct. Encoders are either part of an autoencoder model architecture or an encoder-decoder model architecture. Autoencoders are trained via unsupervised or self-supervised learning, typically for reconstruction tasks where inputs and outputs are the same. Encoder-decoder models, by contrast, are trained via supervised learning, with inputs and outputs that are typically different. For example, a variant of the autoencoder — the denoising autoencoder — and the text encoder of the pre-trained CLIP model (Radford et al., 2021) are both important components in today's most powerful image-to-text generation models, such as Stable Diffusion (Rombach et al., 2022). In most GPT-style large language models (LLMs), a decoder-only transformer model is common. Through selected research projects conducted at the Artificial-Architecture research group based at the Singapore University of Technology and Design (SUTD), this paper discusses insights into what might constitute an "architecture of 3D-encodings." Each project illustrates the design, development, implementation, and results of a particular 3D-encoding for architecture.

Auto-Encoding Architecture

Could Building Information Modelling (BIM) be AI-encoded? BIM data is an important source of detailed and structured information in the AEC (Architecture, Engineering, and Construction) industry. However, without a formal "BIM" encoding, it remains unusable for the training of any deep neural network models. This challenge has led to research into novel BIM encodings, such as Graph-BIM Encoding (Fig. 1).

Crucial to the formulation of Graph-BIM encoding is the ease of accessing and extracting discrete architectural entities from BIM as graph representations, which in turn allows for a novel adaptation of the variational graph autoencoder (VGAE) model architecture originally used in other domains (Kipf and Welling, 2016). By conceptualizing every building as an undirected graph in a three-dimensional grid, each graph node is encoded either as a column or an endpoint of a wall, and each graph edge is encoded as a wall. Node features include spatial locations and boundary relations, while edge features include spatial extents, boundary conditions, wall types, opening types, and room types.

In one of the initial proof-of-concept studies (Liang, Zhong and Koh, 2024), a VGAE model utilizing a variant of a graph neural network (GNN) encoder was trained on approximately 3,000 floor plans from the House-GAN dataset (Nauata et al., 2020). As a reconstructive VGAE model, it calculates loss between the input's original graph adjacency matrix and the output's reconstructed one. As a generative VGAE model, the training uses the same dataset — except that some of the internal edges (i.e., inner walls) are masked, retaining only the external edges (i.e., outermost walls) and nodes (i.e., columns or endpoints of a wall). The results demonstrate that the VGAE can indeed reconstruct BIM 3D models with high accuracy, generate (and potentially reason) entire spatial layouts — either conditioned or unconditioned with partial layout information — and even perform latent interpolation of novel designs between different BIM models.

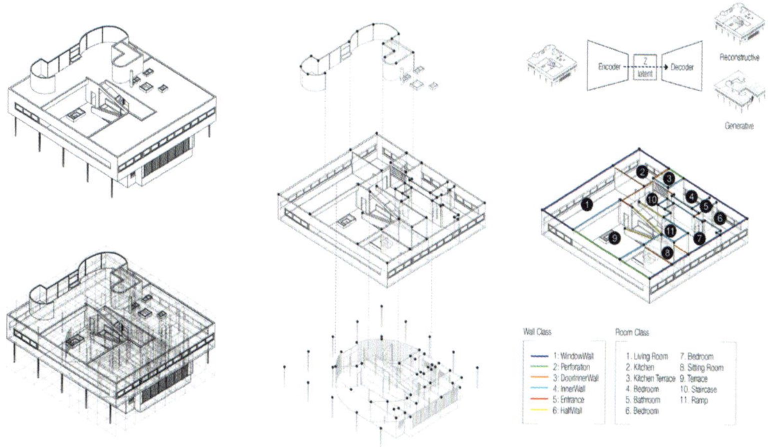

1

Graph-BIM Encoding, 2024. Left: Each building is encoded as graph within an adaptive three-dimensional grid. Center: Each graph node is encoded as either a column or the endpoint of a wall. Right: Each graph edge is encoded as a wall of a specific class, and each zone is encoded as a room of a specific class. The trained VGAE models are capable of reconstructing existing BIM models with or without partial input and of generating novel BIM models by sampling or interpolating in the learned latent space.

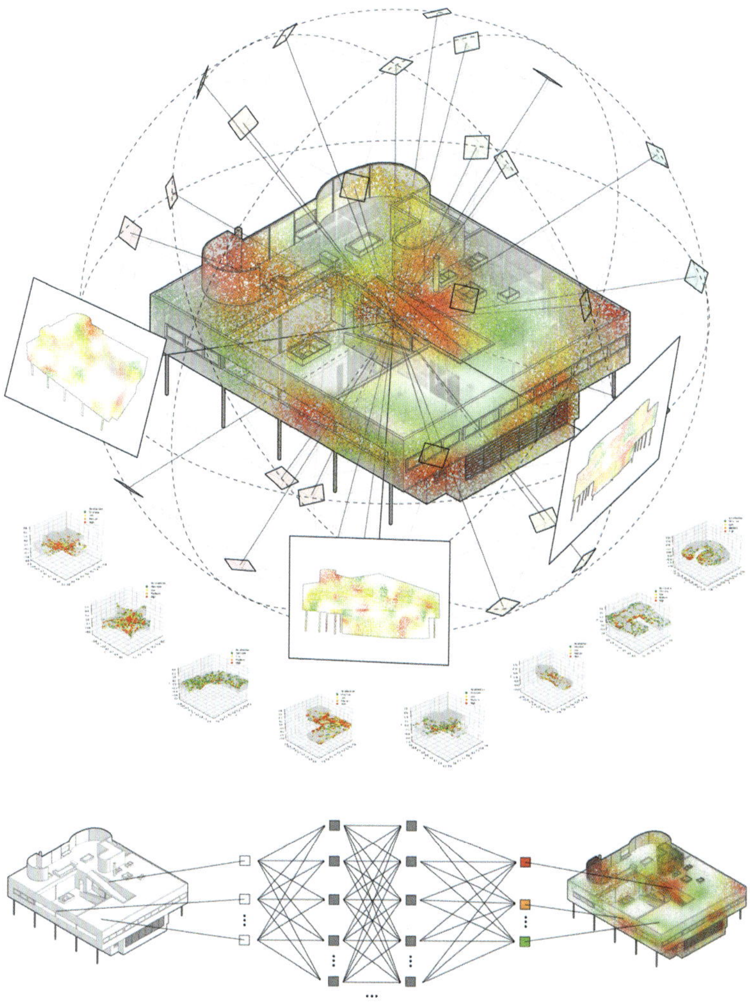

2

Brain-Perception Encoding, 2024. Top: EEG and eye-tracking signals triggered when observing a 3D architectural model in VR/AR are processed in parallel to generate a corresponding 3D saliency point cloud, where red to green = high to low saliency, and transparent = no saliency. Center: Sample plots of 3D saliency point clouds generated at SUTD using original 3D CAD models provided by HKS, Inc. Bottom: The trained DGCNN model predicts likely personal preferences and attention distributions for any unseen 3D CAD model in the form of a 3D saliency point cloud.

Auto-Encoding Brain

Could perception be AI-encoded? More specifically, could AI learn an internal model (i.e., representation or encoding) of our brain's preference and our eyes' attention to architectural forms? While current text-to-image generation models such as Midjourney and Stable Diffusion have become increasingly prevalent among architecture schools and architecture practices for early-stage design, other non-linguistic design inputs that architects use may be at risk of being reduced or lost in such AI workflows.

Rather than an input with a text prompt that returns an output of a 2D rendered image, the Brain-Perception Encoding project (Fig. 2) uses a combination of electroencephalogram (EEG) and eye-tracking signals to return 3D saliency point cloud outputs. These biometric sensors capture how one might interactively perceive 3D architectural models of diverse geometric diversity in virtual or augmented reality (VR/AR). In doing so, unconscious yet personal inputs could be taken into consideration when designing or experiencing architecture in space and time. For the EEG task, Enobio 8 is used alongside custom algorithms for effective filtering of EEG noise signals. For the eye-tracking task, Microsoft HoloLens 2 and Unity's Mixed Reality Toolkit (MRTK) are used alongside a custom raycasting algorithm for the user's gaze. A saliency score is formulated based on eye-tracki metrics (e.g., 0 = no attention, 1 = maximum attention) and EEG event-related potentials (ERPs) (e.g., -1 = rejection, 0 = neutral, 1 = approach) aggregated across any 3D points on the surface of the architectural model that fall within the gaze's area of interests (AOIs) during a given time duration. Once the data is encoded, a variant of a graph neural network (GNN) called a dynamic graph convolutional neural network (DGCNN) model (Wang et al., 2019) is adapted and implemented. Different personal DGCNN models are trained using the data of individual human subjects interacting with multiple 3D CAD architectural models. Each trained AI model thus becomes a personalized brain-perception encoding model capable of simulating (or predicting) a 3D saliency point cloud for any given 3D form. This project builds on earlier research at Artificial-Architecture (Koh and Chen, 2023) and has been supported by HKS, Inc. through their initial provision of 3D CAD models.

3

Neural Artefact Black, 2023. Top to bottom: Each row shows one of five different 3D camera views of the final design. Left to right: Each column shows the same 3D camera view of the final design as it progressively converges from noise during the 3D diffusion process of the custom fine-tuned text-to-3D model. The emergent "Janus" effect is visible in the "doubling" of frontality on the back elevation of the bench, resulting in an unexpected formal bifurcation at the leftmost end of the bench.

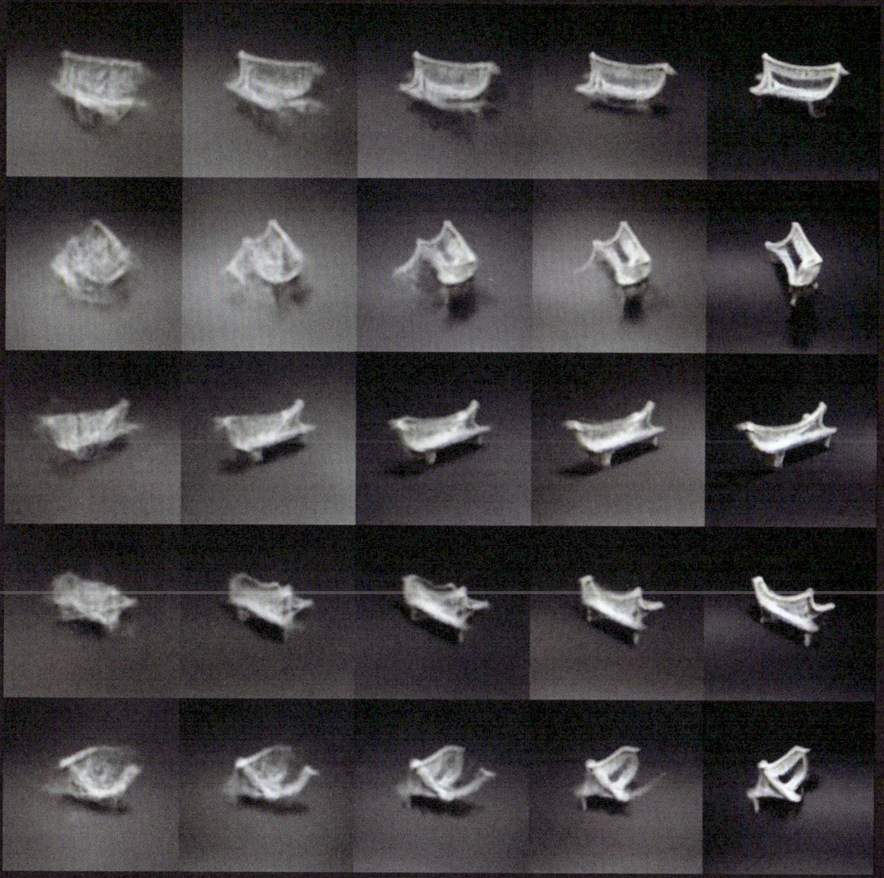

4

Neural Artefact Black, 2023. Medium: Partially charred teak. Dimensions: 220 x 108 x 121 cm. The "Janus" effect inherent to current non-3D aware text-to-3D diffusion models is apparent in the formal ambiguity of the bench design itself. 1 Express Place, Singapore. Photograph courtesy of Arts House Limited.

“Weird” Encodings

As reflected in the previous projects, the “what” and “how” of encoding play a critical role in the disciplinary use of deep neural networks in architecture — from the choice of architectural features and data modalities to the design of encoder architectures and loss functions. There are theoretically infinite ways of 3D-encoding architecture, and each differs in its semantic and algorithmic effectiveness. However, assuming that architectural knowledge should only be injected (rather than discovered) through a precisely defined encoding risks missing the serendipitous value of unorthodox or weird (Fisher, 2017) encodings from those approaching the discipline of architecture from the outside in. One such interesting example is neural radiance fields (NeRF), an implicit representation of 3D scenes via training a multilayer perceptron (MLP) on set of images, based on the concept of inverse rendering (Mildenhall et al., 2020).

The NeRF paradigm may sound paradoxical to architects, whose workflow typically begins by modelling geometry in 3D, then applying textures and materials, setting up virtual cameras and lighting, rendering as 2D images, and finally saving or exporting the 3D model (e.g. as mesh, voxels, or point cloud) in a standard file format. The project Neural Artefact Black (2023) deliberately amplifies the architectural consequences of such non-3D-aware, “weird” 3D encoding. Neural Artefact Black is the world’s first built physical public art bench generated directly in 3D with a custom fine-tuned text-to-3D model (Fig. 3) and fabricated in an artisanal way with 100% upcycled wood (Fig. 4). It deliberately embraces the unresolved “Janus problem” in AI as a creative aesthetic opportunity. The “Janus” effect is a commonly generated AI artifact whereby an object’s canonical view (e.g., front view) appears in its other, non-canonical views, resulting in a 3D-generated object with multiple fronts or faces.

Whether conceptualized as an inside-out disciplinary formulation or a weird outside-in one, the architecture of form is fundamentally an architecture of encoding. It is fundamental because it holds the key not only to developing a more architectural form of AI, but also to creating a potentially new form of architecture.

REFERENCES & BIBLIOGRAPHY

AI Sampling: On Plasticity and Form
[Video]
Lecture, Immanuel Koh, 2021

Architectonics from Artificial Minds
[Video]
Lecture, Immanuel Koh, 2024

Image Synthesis from Layout With Locality-Aware Mask Adaption
[Article]
Paper, Li et al., 2021

Artificial & Architectural Intelligence in Design
[Book]
Immanuel Koh, Asiapac Books, 2020

Fisher, Mark. The Weird and the Eerie. London: Watkins Media Limited, 2017.

Kipf, Thomas N., and Max Welling. "Variational Graph Auto-Encoders." arXiv:1611.07308 (2016).

Koh, Immanuel, and Ashley Chen. "Your Memory Palace in the Metaverse with AI." Proceedings of the AAAI Symposium Series, 1, no. 1 (2023): 19–22. https://doi.org/10.1609/aaaiss.v1i1.27469.

Liang, Jiadong, Ximing Zhong, and Immanuel Koh. "Bridging BIM and AI: A Graph-BIM Encoding Approach for Detailed 3D Layout Generation Using Variational Graph Autoencoder." In Accelerated Design.

Proceedings of the 29th CAADRIA Conference, edited by Nicole Gardner et al., 221–30. Singapore: CAADRIA, 2024. https://doi.org/10.52842/conf.caadria.2024.1.221.

March, Lionel. "A Boolean Description of a Class of Built Forms." In The Architecture of Form, edited by Lionel March, 41–73. Cambridge: Cambridge University Press, 1976.

Mildenhall, Ben, Pratul P. Srinivasan, Matthew Tancik, Jonathan T. Barron, Ravi Ramamoorthi, and Ren Ng. "NeRF: Representing Scenes as Neural Radiance Fields for View Synthesis." arXiv:2003.08934 (2020).

Nauata, Nelson, Kai-Hung Chang, Chin-Yi Cheng, Greg Mori, and Yasutaka Furukawa. "House-GAN: Relational Generative Adversarial Networks for Graph-Constrained House Layout Generation." arXiv:2003.06988 (2020).

Radford, Alec, Jong Wook Kim, Chris Hallacy, Aditya Ramesh, Gabriel Goh, Sandhini Agarwal, Girish Sastry, Amanda Askell, Pamela Mishkin, Jack Clark, Gretchen Krueger, and Ilya Sutskever. "Learning Transferable Visual Models from Natural Language Supervision." arXiv:2103.00020 (2021).

Rombach, Robin, Andreas Blattmann, Dominik Lorenz, Patrick Esser, and Björn Ommer. "High-Resolution Image Synthesis with Latent Diffusion Models." arXiv:2112.10752 (2022).

Steadman, Philip. "Binary Encoding of a Class of Rectangular Built Forms." In Proceedings of the 3rd International Space Syntax Symposium, edited by John Peponis, Jeffery Wineman, and Sonit Bafna, 09.1–09.16. Atlanta: Georgia Institute of Technology; Ann Arbor: A. Alfred Taubman College of Architecture and Urban Planning, University of Michigan, 2001 https://discovery.ucl.ac.uk/id/eprint/13221/.

Wang, Yue, Yongbin Sun, Ziwei Liu, Sanjay E. Sarma, Michael M. Bronstein, and Justin M. Solomon. "Dynamic Graph CNN for Learning on Point Clouds." arXiv:1801.07829 (2019).

30 Years in the Field of Generative Art

AN INTERVIEW WITH AARON HERTZMANN PRINCIPAL SCIENTIST AT ADOBE RESEARCH

We are witnessing a new dawn in the creative field, propelled by a new generation of AI models. Your own career started decades before the current generative AI boom. How did you come to this intersection of computer graphics, machine learning, and art — well before "genAI" was even a thing?

AH — It was a lot through serendipity! I studied both art and computer science in college; that was essentially four years of writing code and painting pictures. Then, when I had to pick a PhD topic, I chose computer graphics, at a time when there was some interest around making images look like paintings. **My PhD then revolved around that topic**, using computer graphics techniques to generate paintings (Fig. 1) and drawings from images and 3D models. A few years ago, considerable interest emerged around applying AI to making art. By that point, I had many decades of experience in that topic, as well as the shared experience of the computer graphics community, so I felt that maybe I could contribute to this new discussion.

1 Hertzmann, Algorithms for Rendering in Artistic Styles, 2001.

We are living in odd times: this AI revolution seems to put on the same level of importance the input from true experts like yourself and that of the "dabblers" or tech enthusiasts, who do not necessarily contribute at the same fundamental level as scientists and machine learning (ML) engineers do. To help us bring back some contrast to this rather flattened landscape of opinions, can you help us better grasp the significance of your contribution?

AH — Let's start with the PhD thesis I just mentioned: this work was about writing code that makes paintings. As I started working on this thesis, it became very clear

that writing rules to explicitly account for what the act of painting is seemed very hard. That's when I started thinking that there was this new "thing" called "machine learning," that people were using in very obscure ways, that maybe could be useful. I worked at that point on applying ML to transferring style, in a paper from 2001 titled
2 "**Image Analogies**." It also lets you generate photographic images where you could control the layout of generated images.

2 Hertzmann et al., "Image Analogies," 2001.

This research was part of a trend of techniques that used textural models of photos to make new photos. The first texture synthesis algorithm was impressive at the time, but not controllable. A lot of interesting work followed soon after to make texture synthesis controllable and effective, applying this method to many other use cases (hole-filling in images, etc.), as well as the Content-Aware Fill technique that became very popular in Photoshop (Fig. 2). When Generative adversarial networks (GANs) were invented a decade ago, we saw the same spread of these techniques to a whole array of use cases, allowing artists to repurpose GANs for many different creative tasks. Same thing when diffusers came along in 2022.

All these different waves went through the same trend as in the early 2000s: first, an impressive new image synthesis algorithm is invented. It's very exciting and cool, but not useful to artists because it doesn't offer any control. But then there quickly follows a wave of research that makes it controllable and useful. This happened with texture synthesis, with GANs, and it's happening again now.

There have always been new tools coming; however, control seems "loose" this time around. Do you think that's intrinsic to this technology, or something that is bound to change, the same way control was brought to many other technological tools that creatives embraced?

AH — I think there will be much control in the future, it is just a matter of time. At its core, it remains a trade-off between predictability and creativity; if you are in the early stage of ideation, you value some types of serendipity. The most interesting aspects of these new systems are maybe when you get unexpected outputs. It is, in fact, when things become more controllable that they become less dramatic and more useful.

Still, the lack of control seems to penalize AI as soon as creative people — architects, photographers, etc. — leave the early steps, the ideation stage, and move to

the next stage, where ideas need to be condensed into controlled forms. Do you think AI can remain relevant at these steps?

AH — To answer this question, I like to turn to how previous generations of technologies for creatives — prior to the current AI trend — have been turned into useful, controllable tools, and how this rise in controllability has served the entire design process, not just the ideation stage. After all, all these methods, be it AI or not, are different mathematical formulations of "how to make images." Controlling them takes time but happens soon after each new generation gets released. A good example is diffusers: since they came out in the literature in 2022, so many papers have been published showing how to control this type of model, to personalize them, tune them to your own style, etc. This blossoming of control techniques in the literature speaks to the fact that even the more recent families of models will become controllable eventually, as previous generations did.

Where do you see limitations for these technologies? Is there a "technical glass ceiling" of sorts?

AH — It is hard to predict; one view is that we will never have enough data to capture all the phenomena of the world. And although we can build systems to account for some of the missing variability, grasping the full breadth of the world's phenomena appears to be the most obvious limit. But even so, it is hard to tell until we have explored the full boundaries of this new technology. Each of our current approaches has reached natural limits but then got replaced with a new paradigm that didn't have those limits, so it's hard to make predictions about technological limitations.

Your sensibility is also that of an art critic. Let us turn to that facet of your personality and ask: Why is Generative AI exciting for the arts today?

AH — I have always been excited about the way technology changes the way we understand art and how it enables artists to make new things. Architecture certainly has this tradition of new building techniques, new styles, etc. To me, it was initially the visceral excitement of feeling that there is something new. Around 2018 and 2020, for instance, with GANs, we saw models that were able to produce images that looked both weird and different. **I like the term used by Robert Pepperell: "indeterminate."** It connected the AI-based production at the time to older traditions within modern

3 Ishai, Fairhall, and Pepperell, "Perception, Memory and Aesthetics of Indeterminate Art," 2007.

art history, where images that look like they ought to be real would not add up once scrutinized further. At a deeper level, this notion of indeterminacy has something to do with how human vision works.

As another example, **DeepDream** (Fig. 3) was very interesting for a few reasons: this model came about as some engineers from Google were trying to figure out how a certain type of image classification method worked. They took images, and increased some network's activation function, and in doing so created some hallucinatory images. Despite the general consistency of the image from afar, dogs and cats were woven all across the image pattern, creating this type of indeterminate representation described by Pepperell. These images revealed visual biases in the ImageNet dataset (Fig. 4), which was created long before DeepDream ever existed, and the peculiar historical reasons why the ImageNet challenge set happened to heavily focus on dog breed classification. It is interesting to see how technological choices made a while ago ended up having a significant impact on the artistic production that came out much later.

4 Mordvintsev, Olah, and Tyka, "DeepDream - A Code Example for Visualizing Neural Networks," 2015.

As this genAI wave was happening in tech, did you see the art world on the West Coast evolve with it?

AH — The mainstream art scene did not really embrace it until it was in the news; and even then, there has been some resistance to this technology. There are, however, separate art scenes: some communities came online, or some smaller galleries focused on technology showcase AI artists — but truly, where I thought things were happening was more in the interstitial space of social media.

Let's talk about the notion of authorship. You have worked on this topic in the past and even published papers on the subject. Attribution seems to be a burning question in genAI times. It is easy to venture an opinion, but much harder to have it be informed by a deep understanding of this technology. That is why I turn to you for an answer. How do you think about authorship in AI times?

AH — When a person uses some technology to make pictures, that person is the author. This has been true in the age of photography and in the past 60 years of computer art, even though people were often confused by authorship. Sometimes works are collaborations, sometimes many people contribute to a work in many different ways,

1

A mapping from one style to another is first modeled (“modeled mapping”), then applied to a given image to produce a new image with the modeled style applied (“generated mapping”). Ima from Hertzmann thesis “Algorithms fo Rendering in Artistic Style (2001).

2

Application of Photoshop's Content-Aware Fill, a tool based on Hertzmann's research at Adobe.

3

Result from DeepDream applied to the Mona Lisa; DeepDream enhances patterns in images to create a dream-like appearance.

4

Sample images taken from the ImageNet dataset.

but that doesn't change our main notion of authorship. An artist — or a creator in general — has agency and societal membership in a way no computer ever does.

In terms of attributing training data, it is very hard to do attribution with these large models. Despite a few papers published in recent years on the topic, no one really knows how this attribution problem could be solved. One way to think about it is to say: "Suppose I had to remove an image from a dataset and retrain the model — would I still be able to generate this one image?" If the answer is "no," then you could say that the removed picture was somehow responsible for the model's output. That is one way to approach attribution in these types of models. But it seems never truly to be the case that removing a certain image really affects the outcome. There is, in fact, so much redundancy in the visual world that it is hard to pinpoint the exact contribution of one or multiple images. It is often overestimated how much attribution can actually be computed within AI models. In that respect, there is a very interesting paper by Ren and Materzynska et al. at MIT, showing that if you train a model on photographs, and you then want to train it on different artistic styles, you really need only a few examples to do it. What that says is that when it comes to modeling artistic styles, so much of it comes from the real world. It makes the notion of style a simple manipulation of real-world visual imagery, rather than something that exists in a vacuum. It takes us back to this quote from Leonardo da Vinci: "Painting is the grandchild of Nature."

One question remains: How will art evolve in AI's presence?

AH — Yes, that's indeed a good place to end our discussion. I think AI will actually cut both ways. Like many previous technologies, AI has both harms and benefits. Two of these are that more people will be able to produce boring, standardized visuals, while at the same time more people will be able to express provocative, exciting, brilliant ideas. It is this simple duality — with very complex impacts, benefits, and threats — that makes this technology both extremely exciting and a massive challenge to the cultural production of the decades to come.

REFERENCES

My Journey in Art and Computing
[Video]
SIGGRAPH 2024 Award Talk

Can Computers Create Art?
[Video]
Lecture, Aaron Hertzmann, 2022

Art and the Science of Generative AI: A Deeper Dive
[Website]
Paper, Epstein et al., 2024

Generative Models for the Psychology of Art and Aesthetics
[Website]
Aaron Hertzmann, Empirical Studies of the Arts 43.1, 2024

The Designers

CONTRIBUTIONS – PART III

If previous chapters have shown how extensively AI has already permeated the architect's toolkit, this chapter explores the diverse ways practitioners have begun to approach this technology in their daily practice.

Here, we have gathered impressions and reflections on how architects are choosing to embrace and frame this new technological moment. At stake in the following contributions is the role of AI in contemporary design process and its implications for architectural practice today.

With Carlo Ratti, AI moves to the center of architectural discourse. The 2025 Venice Biennale, "Intelligens. Natural. Artificial. Collective." curated by Ratti is itself a declaration of the technology's significance for the field. Ratti sketches out the potential of AI for architecture's future and sets the tone for this Biennale's engagement with the topic. **With the Foster + Partners Applied Research and Development (R+D) team**, we unpack how the firm has embedded AI throughout its practice. From early-stage adoption to the integration of AI-enabled solutions across design workflows, the evolution of the Applied R+D team exemplifies how leading firms have navigated the rise of AI over the past five years. **We close the chapter with Coop Himmel(l)au**, where a technology driven practice has shifted its focus away from parametric design toward pioneering AI-based methodologies for the discipline at large.

CARLO RATTI — Carlo Ratti is an architect, urbanist, and professor at the Massachusetts Institute of Technology, where he directs the Senseable City Lab. His work investigates intelligent systems at the convergence of natural and artificial environments. Ratti was appointed curator of the 19th International Architecture Exhibition of La Biennale di Venezia (2025), titled "Intelligens. Natural. Artificial. Collective." Among other things, the exhibition explores the presence of AI in architecture.

FOSTER + PARTNERS APPLIED R+D TEAM — The Applied Research and Development Team at Foster + Partners is a multidisciplinary group of architects and engineers. Its expertise spans art, aerospace engineering, computer science, landscape architecture, structural engineering, and applied mathematics.

COOP HIMMELB(L)AU — Coop Himmel(l)au is an architecture studio founded in 1968 in Vienna by Wolf D. Prix, Helmut Swiczinsky, and Michael Holzer. Under Prix's leadership, the firm became the first in the world to develop an in-house architectural AI, Deep Himmelblau, launched in 2017. Partner and Head of Research Karolin Schmidbaur and computer specialist Daniel Bolojan lead the development of the project.

Architecture of Multiple Intelligences

AN ARTICLE BY CARLO RATTI
CURATOR OF THE 2025 ARCHITECTURE BIENNALE

Sudden transformations sparked by abrupt technological leaps have punctuated the history of architecture. During the mid-1400s, in the context of a craft-based architectural convention, Leon Battista Alberti presented a mathematical method of graphic representation. In so doing, Alberti paved the way for Renaissance classicism: architecture focused on precision and representation through drafting rather than inexact construction by artisans. Four centuries later, steel and glass helped engineers like Isambard Kingdom Brunel, Sir Joseph Paxton, and Gustave Eiffel to design daring and visionary structures and break through the limits of what could be built.

Technological advancements have fostered a new aesthetic that merges architecture and engineering, resulting in remarkable achievements. An epoch later, at the crest of the mechanical era, Le Corbusier appropriated the tools and forms of mass production, concluding that the house is a machine for living in. Architecture was optimized not only from the perspectives of design and structural engineering but also from the perspectives of mass production and social functionality.

The driving force behind architectural improvements is technological integration. Le Corbusier dreamt of "realiz[ing], harmonically, the city that is an expression of our machinist civilization" (Le Corbusier and O'Byrne Orozco, 2010). Yet our societies have transitioned in the last few decades from mechanization to computation and automation (Ratti and Claudel 2016).

Since the 1990s, computation and the convergence of bits and atoms have been probably the most disruptive force in the built environment. Artificial intelligence sits at the center of it, being the latest protagonist of this history. In other words, the best way to see AI in architecture is not as a new development — rather, as the culmination of decades of technological advancements that have gradually transformed how we think, design, and ultimately live the built environment.

From the earliest days of computing, multiple practitioners have sought ways to integrate digital tools into the design process. AI can be seen as the natural progression of this trajectory. It allows us to process data — it is always useful to remember that there is no AI without data to train it — to better address the urban environment.

Moreover, so much has changed in the popular perception of AI since the first edition of this book appeared roughly three years ago. What happened, in technological terms, has been the equivalent of 2007's "iPhone moment." Similarly to how the launch of Apple's first smartphone turned the Internet of Things from a theoretical concept into a mass reality — ushering in the possibility for architects and planners to have an unprecedented look at people's movements in cities and buildings — the deployment of LLMs (large language models) in late 2022 has turned AI into an all-too-present reality (not to say a journalistic obsession) for millions of people, including countless architects.

How are our ways of designing, building, and ultimately living the built environment changing at the time of increasingly powerful LLMs? In other words, paraphrasing Cedric Price: AI is the answer to the future of architecture; but what was the question? Quite often, when using LLMs, we have the impression of dealing with some kind of "idiot savant." These systems know everything about every subject and can answer our questions by regurgitating their knowledge. But they are absolutely baffled by questions that are still unanswered — which are then the most important ones in life. Moreover, it is well known how AI responds to the prompts we give it, and if we train it with our biases and limitations, the answers will reflect those same flaws. Unoriginality and prejudices — not the best recipe for innovation, I would say.

In the field of design visuals, the consequences of this approach are manifest. Try asking these systems for a wooden cottage surrounded by nature and near a waterway. Within seconds they will provide an admirable synthesis of Frank Lloyd Wright's Fallingwater, Mies van der Rohe's Farnsworth House, perhaps a Baumschlager Eberle-esque wooden facade, and an interior from Matteo Thun. Plus, millions of other visual references that you will have difficulty discerning.

This is the main shortcoming of AI as of today. To tell it differently, we can retrieve a quote from one of the protagonists of European architecture criticism in the second half of the 20th century, Bruno Zevi, who said the following while commenting on various streams of modern architecture creators: "After all, there is no reason to be surprised. In every era, there has been plagiarism, imitation, and 'false modernity.' Authentic artists, creators of language, have always been very few; they are surrounded by a group of 'literati,' up-to-date professionals who build correctly, with a vague touch of inspiration, but in prose, not in poetry; then follows the tide of plagiarists; among these, the presumptuous and rhetorical ones confuse the great with the gross. Ignoring the lexicon, grammar, and syntax of modernity, they build in 'modern style,' that is, at best, without communicating anything." (Zevi trans. Rykwert 1978, 7)

Here, I think AI may sweep away the seconds and thirds that Zevi referred to, but not the firsts — at least for the time being. Based on the above, we could then explore key areas of development that architects might want to pursue to make the use of LLMs in tune with the present challenges of the urban world.

Today, AI has arrived at the text-to-image level, that is, from text description to an image. But it will only take a few years, with the right training sets, to get to text-to-BIM. That is, from textual description to the actual project. Text-to-BIM technology could enable architects to create detailed 3D models — encompassing construction specifications, safety information, and other metadata — from text prompts, making the design process automated. This could leave them more space for creative solutions, while more practical matters can be delegated to AI. With virtual simulations, designers and engineers can test hypotheses, identify potential errors, and provide creative and effective solutions before breaking ground. Beyond generating visual models, text-to-BIM can incorporate construction specifications, safety information, and other essential metadata into the model. This opens up new possibilities for sustainable design, as AI can identify inefficiencies and waste in the building process. By using AI to generate building models directly from written descriptions, architects can avoid the tedious "bookkeeping" (Chaillou 2022, 120) and often the error-prone task of manually translating ideas into detailed plans.

Will this be the "death of the architect"? Certainly, many aspects of our profession will die — those that are more repetitive and low on the synthesis of preconceived ideas. But there will always remain one aspect that no AI can scratch yet, as it does not belong to any training set: inventing what is not yet there. The key to successfully integrating AI into architecture lies in how we use it: as a complement to, rather than a replacement for, all forms of ingenuity. This is also what we will explore at the Biennale Architettura 2025 in Venice under the theme "Intelligens. Natural. Artificial. Collective."

In short, architectural design is an evolving, participatory process in which diverse forms of intelligence come together to shape the built environment. AI is a powerful force, but it is just one part of a larger ecosystem — where humans will continue playing a key role in the foreseeable future.

REFERENCES & BIBLIOGRAPHY

Biennale Architettura 2025
[Video]
Presentation, Carlo Ratti

AI & City Safety
[Video]
Carlo Ratti on the Urbanistica Podcast, 2022

Future Cities
[Video]
Carlo Ratti and Andrian Kreye, DLD Conference, 2022

Designing Natural-Artificial Cities
[Article]
Interview, Carlo Ratti, CityChanger, 2022

Portions of this text's introduction were adapted from Carlo Ratti and Matthew Claudel's The City of Tomorrow (Yale University Press, 2016).

Chaillou, Stanislas. Artificial Intelligence and Architecture: From Research to Practice. Vienna: Birkhäuser Verlag, 2022.

Le Corbusier, and María Cecilia O'Byrne Orozco. "Elaboration du Plan Régulateur de Bogotá." In Le Corbusier en Bogotá, edited by María Cecilia O'Byrne Orozco. Bogotá: Universidad de Los Andes, Facultad de Arquitectura y Diseño, 2010.

Ratti, Carlo, and Matthew Claudel. The City of Tomorrow: Sensors, Networks, Hackers, and the Future of Urban Life. New Haven: Yale University Press, 2016.

Zevi, Bruno. The Modern Language of Architecture. Translated by Joseph Rykwert. Cambridge, MA: MIT Press, 1978.

Reimagining Architectural Practice

THE AI-NATIVE FUTURE OF DESIGN AND OPERATIONS

MARTHA TSIGKARI AND SHERIF TARABISHY, FOSTER + PARTNERS APPLIED R+D TEAM

Foster + Partners is a renowned global studio founded in 1967 by Norman Foster, specializing in sustainable architecture, urbanism, engineering, and design. Known for its integrated approach, the practice unites experts from various disciplines to develop innovative and holistic design solutions that emphasize sustainability and energy efficiency. The Applied Research + Development (R+D) team operates as an in-house consultancy and embodies this ethos through a multidisciplinary collaboration of architects, engineers, and expert programmers. Our diverse expertise spans art, architecture, computer science, landscape architecture, structural engineering, and applied mathematics. Focused on cutting-edge research and development, the team addresses complex design challenges by merging the latest advancements with practical architectural and engineering applications. Our proficiency in computational design, performance analysis, optimization, fabrication, and interaction design is complemented by expertise in emerging technologies such as augmented reality, machine learning, and real-time simulation. This approach allows us to combine human intuition with computational precision, contributing significantly to the studio's groundbreaking work in machine learning and beyond.

The past few years — since the previous issue — have been a transformative journey for us as we transitioned from exploring the potential of machine learning (ML) in architecture to embedding AI deeply within the fabric of our practice. Instead of incrementally integrating AI into existing tools, we adopted a bottom-up approach to reimagine workflows entirely, leveraging modern AI technologies. This shift — from the challenge of top-down data restructuring to building AI-native systems — has yielded profound insights and exciting results.

Rewriting Processes from the Ground Up

Our initial attempts to address data challenges through centralized, top-down restructuring faced significant hurdles. Legacy systems, inconsistent formats, and deeply ingrained workflows made systemic change challenging. Recognizing this, we pivoted to a bottom-up approach, where we analyze and map individual processes across the design and operational sides of the business, reimagining them from scratch to fully leverage the capabilities of AI. A key aspect of this strategy is ensuring that reimagined workflows are data-ready from inception — not by forcing ML additions onto legacy systems but by rethinking workflows from first principles. If this succeeds, what does it mean to have a business where data flows seamlessly, knowledge is democratized, and processes are continuously optimized? While we don't claim to have all the answers, we believe that defining what it means to be an AI-native business is key. If there is any parallel, it must be the mid-1990s emergence of "internet-native" businesses like Amazon and eBay. These companies fundamentally built their business models around what the internet could do, rather than adapting traditional business models to it. The most pressing question back then was, "What is your internet strategy?" Merely a decade later, such a question became as redundant as asking, "What is your electricity strategy?" With the pace of AI advancements, a decade may soon feel like a lifetime.

Collaborative Design with Generative AI

On the design side, we identified critical gaps in existing image-based generative tools: many models lacked compliance with the legal and infrastructure requirements of our business, and there was no effective way to audit or trace ML contributions to specific projects. Furthermore, we recognized a need for better integration of ML into the broader design workflow to ensure its potential was fully realized.

To address these challenges, we developed our proprietary AI Portal (Fig. 1) to integrate generative image-based ML models directly into the early stages of the design process.

The objective was to enable designers to augment their designs with AI-generated suggestions to foster new levels of creativity. The AI Portal was developed as a collaborative platform. It enables team members to view and interact with designs generated by their colleagues through the system. This platform promotes cross-pollination of ideas and a spirit of collaboration. It's not about showcasing AI-generated images but about fueling the initial spark of an idea, inviting others to contribute, and watching the design evolve. What we're trying to provide is not just a tool to "generate designs" but a space to stimulate dynamic exchanges of ideas, track progress, and encourage creativity.

The platform integrates directly with Rhino, ensuring that any creation from Rhino is shared instantly with the entire team, enabling others to build upon it. Additionally, all models used within the AI Portal comply with legal and infrastructure security constraints. Submitted jobs through the system are processed on on-premises GPU servers, and depending on demand, we scale out to our cloud infrastructure. This ensures robustness during peak demand while maintaining cost efficiency. This shift from isolated workflows to collaborative, AI-augmented design highlights the power of inclusivity through technology in driving better outcomes and fostering innovation.

Knowledge Extraction and Dissemination: Democratizing Expertise

One of our most impactful projects revolved around addressing the fragmentation of expertise accumulated over decades. Knowledge trapped in dense technical documents or in the minds of long-serving employees posed a significant bottleneck for new and experienced staff alike. How should knowledge be captured, shared, and used today?

Using large language models (LLMs), we developed a search engine that allows employees to ask questions in natural language and receive specific, actionable answers (Fig. 2). By highlighting source documents and page numbers, the system bridges the gap between static records and dynamic, accessible knowledge. Employees at all experience levels should have easy access to decades of accumulated insights. Beyond the tools themselves, we've focused on building trust between domain experts and users of these systems. Features like asynchronous verification of ML-provided answers and mechanisms to flag better responses ensure accuracy and encourage specificity in user queries. This also allows us to monitor and refine the data provided to designers, creating a feedback loop for continual improvement. This democratization of expertise empowers employees to perform effectively, ensuring a new kind of business sustainability — one where institutional knowledge is not siloed but actively shared, built upon, and transferred effectively across generations. Cross-generational knowledge transfer, previously unattainable at scale, is now within reach.

Expanding Beyond Design: AI in Operations

Recognizing the untapped potential of AI in operational workflows, we extended our efforts to areas beyond design. Below are two prototypes we developed with various colleagues:

> **Resource prediction models**: By analyzing past data, we built a probabilistic model to help us more accurately predict resources for future projects. The objective is not only to streamline the issuance of proposals — saving time and resources — but also to enhance project conversion rates. Additionally, it empowers newly hired employees to quickly integrate their workflows into our processes, without needing decades of in-house experience to understand how internal resources work. While it doesn't replace the invaluable expertise of veteran team members, it provides newer employees with enough autonomy to operate effectively and ask the right questions.
>
> **Lead identification workflow:** Our experimental automated system for screening project leads globally pairs in-house expertise — based on historical records — with potential projects intelligently. This shift from manual workflows to automated, insight-driven processes underscores the untapped value of AI in business operations.

Towards Proactive Systems

By systematically recording the experiences of employees and embedding this knowledge into AI systems, we are creating a fairer, more accessible environment for new employees to excel. This eliminates the steep learning curve traditionally associated with joining a large practice, ensuring that the expertise of past generations is readily available to the next. Yet a recurring theme across our projects is the vision of a system that not only captures knowledge but also proactively disseminates it. While most of our current efforts have centered on collecting data and waiting for users to ask the right questions, our next milestone is to make those systems capable of anticipating needs. By incorporating contextual information and intelligently surfacing relevant data at the right moment, we aim to help users navigate complex workflows without requiring them to articulate specific queries. This shift — from reactive to proactive systems — will represent a significant leap toward making AI an indispensable partner in architectural practice. The potential of this approach extends beyond efficiency — it represents a redefinition of business sustainability, where knowledge is the backbone of growth and resilience.

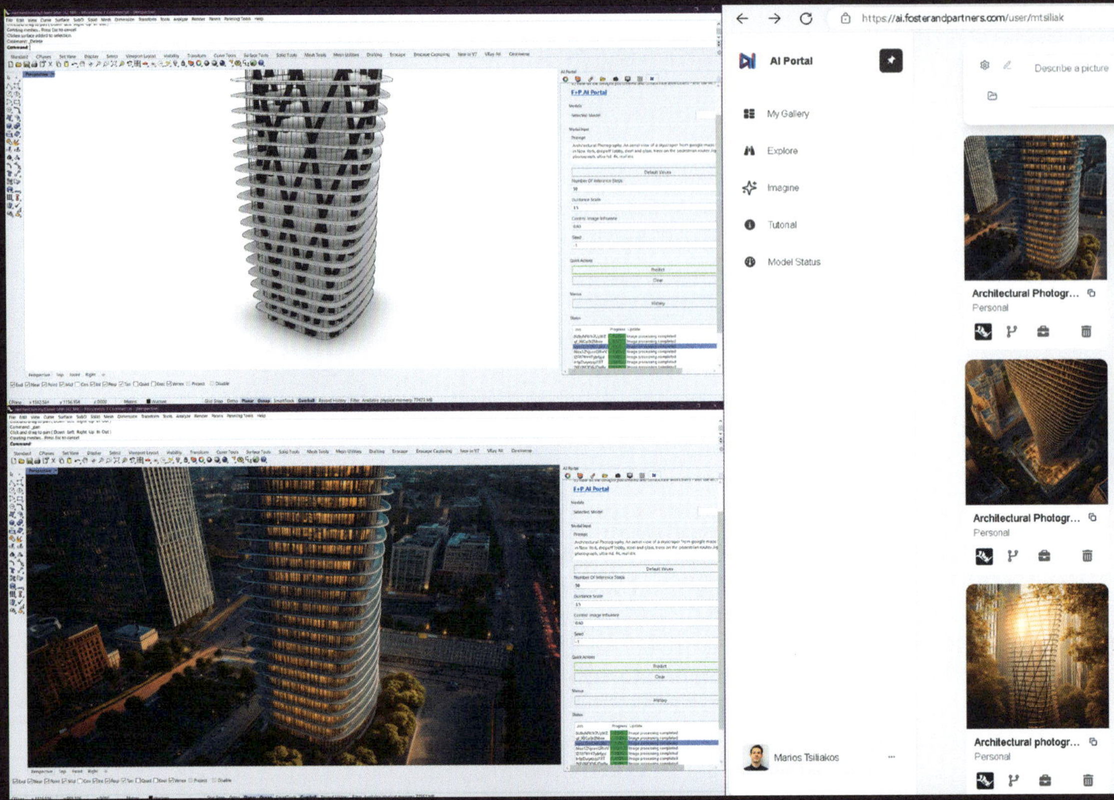

1

Snapshot of Foster + Partners AI Portal's Rhino plugin and web app.

2

Snapshot of Foster + Partners Ask Portal.

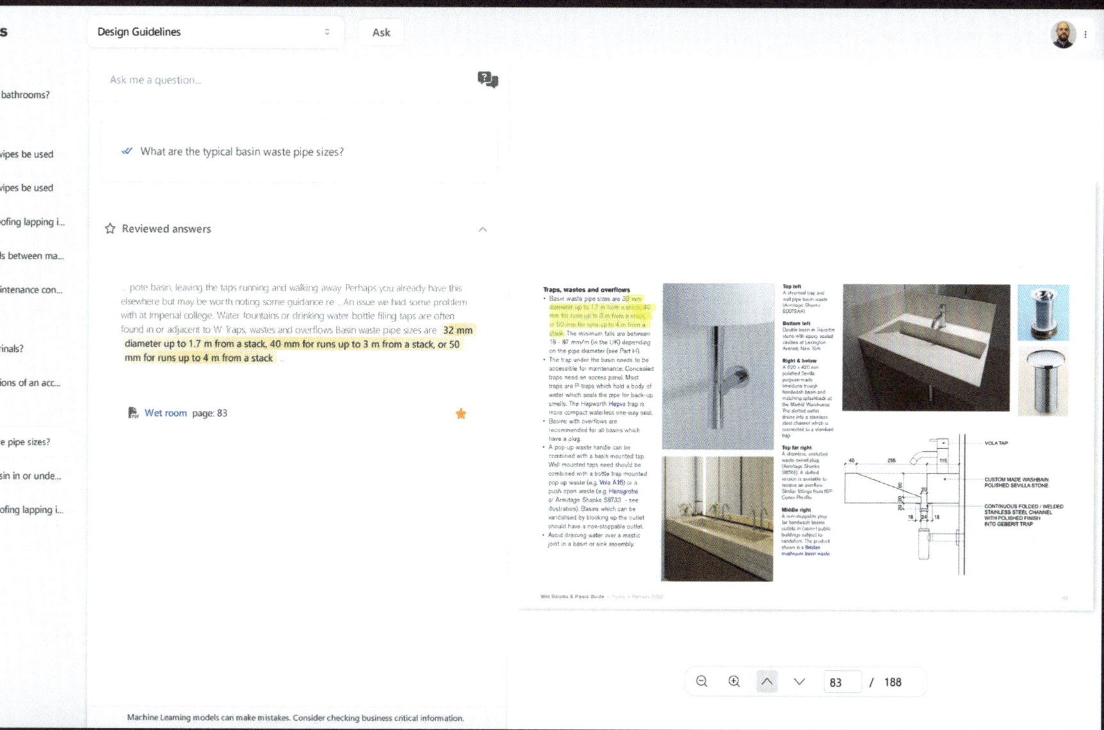

An AI-Native Practice as the New Norm

The journey from experimenting with ML to embedding AI at the core of our operations will continue to fundamentally reshape how we work. Our vision for an AI-native business is not just about adopting the latest technologies but about creating a new culture where data, knowledge, and innovation flow seamlessly across all aspects of the practice. This approach promises not only to optimize processes but also to redefine what it means to collaborate, design, and operate in the built environment.

We believe the future of architectural practice, and businesses in general, lies in the AI-native paradigm. Knowledge-driven systems have the potential to empower designers, foster inclusivity, and build a foundation for sustainable growth. Framing the future of business as how well we can answer the question, "What does it mean to be an AI-native business?" places a profound responsibility on business owners and practitioners to rethink their services from first principles. Rather than waiting for vendor-driven solutions or old tools and methodologies dressed up with AI labels, it's essential for us to question how our service can be delivered in a fundamentally better way. This requires reimagining not just what we do, but how we do it — leveraging AI to create workflows, systems, and experiences that are truly transformative for our designers, clients, and the built environment.

REFERENCES

Martha Tsigkari and Francis Aish
[Video]
Lecture, NXTBLD, 2021

Architectural Frontiers
[Article]
Interview, Martha Tsigkari, Disrupt Magazine, 2024

Foster + Partners at AECtech
[Website]
Lecture, Martha Tsigkari, 2022

Data-Driven
[Website]
M. Tsigkari, S. Tarabishi, and A. Davis, NXTBLD 2024

AI, Deep Himmelblau, Architecture, etc.

AN INTERVIEW WITH COOP HIMMELB(L)AU

WOLF D. PRIX, KAROLINA SCHMIDBAUR, DANIEL BOLOJAN

The importance of digital tools for architecture has perhaps been most vividly demonstrated over the past decades by Coop Himmelb(l)au. As our discipline stands at a new crossroads, with AI introducing an entirely new paradigm, many of us turn once again to your practice to understand how the field might evolve. The experiments developed in your office — as well as your contribution to the ongoing discourse around AI — give you a certain authority in this conversation. That is also why we hope this interview will offer practitioners some insight into what might be coming for our industry in the decades ahead. Let's dive in.

Coop Himmelb(l)au was among the few firms to lead the parametric turn in architecture. How has your practice approached the transition to AI — both in operational terms (the implementation of new software, the restructuring of workflows) and theoretically (the development of a discourse around this technological shift)?

CH — Coop Himmelb(l)au's transition to artificial intelligence (AI) reflects a natural evolution of our longstanding design philosophy rather than an abrupt shift driven by technological trends.

In our opinion, our engagement with innovative tools predates and transcends the parametric era. Our history of integrating technology demonstrates an openness to experimentation that has been integral to our practice since the beginning. Parametric design, for us, was never the defining paradigm, but rather one of many tools assimilated into a broader, more dynamic approach to architecture.

From an operational standpoint, our integration of AI builds on this legacy. Rather than relying on a single, all-encompassing AI model, we employ a node-based framework that mirrors the complexity of architectural design and the tools at hand. This approach involves discrete yet interconnected processes — some deterministic, such as optimizing facade rationalization, and others generative, fostering speculative and exploratory outcomes. For example, early experiments allowed us to translate sketchy, intuitive concepts into formal explorations, a process that aligns seamlessly with our tradition of converting abstract ideas into tangible architectural propositions. These tools are not end-to-end solutions but components within a collaborative ecosystem where human agency remains central. Designers interrogate, negotiate, and critically engage with AI outputs, ensuring that technology enhances, rather than overrides, the creative intent.

This operational strategy is deeply tied to what we call an "open process." A design philosophy that rejects linear, parameter-driven workflows in favor of a multilayered, iterative dialogue between diverse strategies and models. AI in this context becomes a partner in addressing this complexity and allows us to oscillate between intuitive leaps and analytical precision — a rhythm that has long defined our work. AI provides a new medium for exploration, offering inputs that we refine through critical evaluation.

From a formal standpoint, how would you describe the forms your practice has produced using AI tools, compared to the parametric aesthetics you engaged with decades ago?

CH — Coop Himmelb(l)au's use of AI does not mark a departure from or evolution of a parametric aesthetic, as we never fully embraced that paradigm. Our forms, whether shaped by parametric tools or AI, reflect a process-driven ethos where technology serves the architectural idea, not the other way around.

Our association with parametricism often stems from our use of tools like Grasshopper. But our use of parametric tools has always been technical rather than stylistic, a means to address specific challenges like facade rationalization or structural optimization, rather than a top-down imposition of an aesthetic agenda.

Form, in our practice, emerges not from a predetermined aesthetic but from a dynamic synthesis of a project's content with its architectural expression. This process, far from being tool-driven, is a negotiation between top-down and bottom-up strategies, a reciprocity that has defined our work long before and beyond the parametric moment. Top-down approaches, such as those often linked to parametricism, imply a preconceived form broken into buildable parts, constrained by a priori parameters. In contrast, our method oscillates between rational constraints and intuitive exploration, allowing unexpected solutions to challenge initial assumptions. As Wolf dPrix has articulated, this stems from a resistance to "obedience in advance" — the tendency to limit creativity by over-rationalizing too early in the process.

The introduction of AI tools has not shifted this fundamental approach or produced a distinct "AI aesthetic" in our work. Instead, AI integrates into our existing framework as a collaborator, informing and enriching the process without dictating its outcome. This interplay ensures that our architecture remains alive, avoiding the rigidity that can stifle creativity when tools overly constrain the design.

Compared to the parametric tools of decades past, AI offers greater flexibility and generative potential, but it does not redefine our formal language. Parametric models, by their nature, encode a finite set of possibilities upfront, limiting outputs to what is predefined within the system. AI, conversely, introduces a broader speculative capacity, producing outputs that can surprise and provoke, which we then refine through critical synthesis. Yet, the resulting forms are not dictated by AI any more than they were by Grasshopper; they are the product of our ongoing dialogue between concept and realization, intuition and pragmatism.

Deep Himmelblau is the name your practice has given to your in-house AI research and experimentation. What does this work entail?

CH — The term originated as a wordplay, blending "deep learning," the foundational technology driving our explorations, with "Deep Blue," IBM's famous chess-playing AI, while riffing on our own identity as Himmelb(l)au.

The work under **Deep Himmelblau** began modestly with early experiments around 2017 (Fig. 1). Initially, we explored how these models could interpret and extrapolate from sketches or abstract inputs. What started as a curiosity evolved over time into a structured initiative, growing in scope and sophistication as AI techniques and models matured and our understanding of their potential deepened. Today, Deep Himmelblau encompasses a range of experiments aimed at integrating AI into our design process, not as a standalone solution but as a dynamic collaborator within our broader "open process" philosophy.

1 Coop Himmelb(l)au, "Deep Himmelblau Presentation," 2025.

At its core, this work entails developing and testing AI tools tailored to the multifaceted nature of architectural design. Rather than pursuing a singular, all-encompassing model, we focus on a modular system that addresses distinct aspects of the process. Some efforts involve generative models that produce speculative forms or configurations, offering provocative starting points that challenge conventional thinking. Others focus on deterministic applications, such as optimizing structural systems or rationalizing complex geometries for construction. A key example from our early work was using deep learning to translate rough sketches into facade proposals, bridging the gap between conceptual freedom and practical realization. Over time, this has expanded to include explorations with GANs, autoencoders, diffusion models, and many other deep learning architectures, allowing us to synthesize diverse inputs into coherent architectural propositions.

Data is a central concern when working with AI. How does your practice approach this? Do you build your own datasets? How do you select, curate, or exclude information fed into your models?

CH — Data is indeed a central concern in our AI endeavors at Coop Himmelb(l)au, and our approach reflects both the richness of our nearly 60-year archive and the deliberate strategies we employ to harness it effectively. The foundation of our data work lies in the extensive documentation accumulated over decades spanning sketches, physical models, digital renderings, parametric models, and detailed project records. This vast repository, a living record of our practice, provides a unique resource that we are actively working to leverage. However, beyond simply tapping into this archive, we also build bespoke datasets tailored to specific research goals, ensuring that our AI tools align with our architectural vision and priorities.

Yes, we do build our own datasets — a process that combines the reuse of historical material with the creation of new, structured data. For instance, we've compiled comprehensive datasets for a select group of significant projects, around 12 buildings handpicked by Wolf dPrix for their importance to our legacy. These include detailed 3D models, 360-degree renders, and layered information such as materiality, depth maps, and structural details. For our text-based models, whether for text queries or text-to-image generation, we engage in a cross-office effort where all designers in the office help develop a very structured dataset of annotations and textual descriptors of our work.

Curating these datasets involves identifying recurring themes across our portfolio that define Coop Himmelb(l)au's DNA. This isn't a matter of dumping everything into a dataset and letting the AI sort it out; it requires critical judgment to balance the inputs. For instance, early training runs might reveal an overreliance on specific features, like the double-cone geometry of a particular project, prompting us to adjust weights or retrain the model to achieve more flexibility and diversity in outputs. This process is part manual and part automated, as we refine the model through trial-and-error iterations. Over multiple training cycles, we test and tweak until the results strike a balance that feels true

A

Deep Himmelblau sample output based on geomorphological samples and CHBL project samples. Each node network learns the semantic representation and the underlying compositional rules of the architectural and non-architectural domains in order to perform coherent network-to-network cross-resolution blends and cross-layer feature combinations.

C

Latent space algorithmic explorations. The latent space of the Deep Himmelblau network can be explored using an algorithmic approach that allows for a strategic search through different techniques designed to enable intuitive navigation.

1

Snapshots from early iterations of DeepHimmelb(l)au.

B

Latent space algorithmic explorations define the design path through strategic navigation of the Deep Himmelblau network. Using an algorithmic approach, we trace sequences within the latent space by identifying clusters of semantically related nodes – each step simulating a possible progression in composition. One network node guides the evolution of the form, while another injects features characteristic of the Coop Himmelb(l)au design language, enabling semantic transfer and reinterpretation within the generated architectural outputs.

D

Latent space architectural interpolation generated through representational learning and domain transfer techniques. This image illustrates a hybrid architectural composition produced by navigating the latent space of the Deep Himmelblau network. The form results from algorithmic blending layers across various networks, simulating a stylistic transition between abstract design vocabularies and learned representations from the Coop Himmelb(l)au archive.

to our identity. Our approach to data is both pragmatic and philosophical. Practically, it ensures our AI tools are fed high-quality, relevant information that reflects our history and aspirations. Philosophically, it mirrors our design process: a dialogue between intention and discovery, where human agency shapes the raw material into something meaningful.

Daniel Bolojan often speaks about the importance of modular networks — AI models conceived as building blocks that can be endlessly recombined to tackle specific tasks in the design process. How does this work, and how have you used it to develop tools for architecture?

CH — At Coop Himmelb(l)au, our advocacy for network modularity (a node-based system) — conceiving AI models as recombinable building blocks tailored to specific tasks — stems from a deep alignment with the Coop Himmelb(l)au design philosophy and a pragmatic understanding of architecture's complexity. This approach, which Daniel has often emphasized in talks, rejects the notion of a singular, all-encompassing AI model in favor of a flexible, node-based modular system that mirrors the multifaceted nature of the design process. It allows us to maintain creative control, adapt to diverse project needs, and integrate AI seamlessly into our open framework.

The rationale for modularity is twofold. Philosophically, it preserves the freedom inherent in our approach to design. We've always resisted prescriptive workflows — whether starting with a sketch, a scanned model, or a conceptual provocation, the process must remain fluid and open to reinterpretation. A monolithic AI model risks imposing a rigid, a priori structure, where outcomes are constrained by predefined parameters. By contrast, a node-based system lets us assemble and reconfigure AI components as needed — say, beginning with a generative model to explore forms, then linking it to a deterministic model for structural optimization. This flexibility ensures that the tools serve the designer's intent rather than dictating it, embedding opportunities for serendipity or, as Karolin puts it, "building in the accident."

Practically, modularity reflects the diverse demands of architectural design, which no single model can fully address. Architecture requires both breadth and depth — generalist capabilities for ideation and specialist precision for tasks like facade rationalization or budget analysis. It also spans deterministic needs (e.g., predictive optimization) and generative exploration (e.g., conceptual brainstorming). A single AI, no matter how advanced, cannot excel in everything simultaneously. Drawing from **Jeff Hawkin's "A Thousand Brains"** theory of intelligence — where intelligence emerges from multiple, specialized neural processes or "models" — we've designed our Deep Himmelblau

2 Hawkins, A Thousand Brains: A New Theory of Intelligence, 2021.

system as a network of discrete nodes. Each node tackles a specific task, and their outputs are synthesized through human oversight and/or computational processes, much like how we combine physical models, sketches, and digital simulations in our traditional workflow. This modularity also positions us for the future, as AI evolves toward more agentic systems — models capable of autonomous task execution.

One area of research that has caught researchers' attention is federated learning, a topic you have also investigated. What is it, and what relevance does it have for architecture?

CH — Unlike traditional methods where data is centralized in one location for training, federated learning allows a model to learn from distributed datasets without ever sharing the raw data itself. Instead, local models process data on a local machine, extract insights (e.g., patterns or updates), and send only those updates to a central network, which aggregates them to improve the global model.

For architecture, federated learning offers a compelling solution to two key challenges: data privacy and process integration. Architecturally significant data is often proprietary, tied to confidentiality agreements making it impractical to pool into a massive, shared dataset. Publicly available AI models, trained within generic image libraries, lack the depth and specificity of real project data, limiting their utility for our field. Federated learning could sidestep this by enabling a model to learn from rich, private datasets across an office or even the profession without compromising ownership. The central network evolves by aggregating anonymized updates, not the data itself, creating a collective intelligence that respects individual boundaries.

We like to think of this aligning with our philosophy, flipping the typical top-down imposition of a pre-trained model into a bottom-up, collaborative system. Rather than deploying a static AI that dictates outcomes, federated learning could allow designers' inputs — say, the screenshots, sketches, or iterative outputs they generate daily — to trickle up and shape the tool. Imagine a folder where each designer saves progress shots of their work: a local model could analyze these, identify patterns or preferences, and send distilled updates to the main network. Over time, the network learns from the office's collective output. This creates a feedback loop where the tool grows with us, rather than imposing a rigid framework we must conform to.

Beyond the office, federated learning holds broader potential for architecture as a profession. Its promise lies in fostering a symbiotic relationship — where tools and architects grow together, preserving the bottom-up creativity that defines our work.

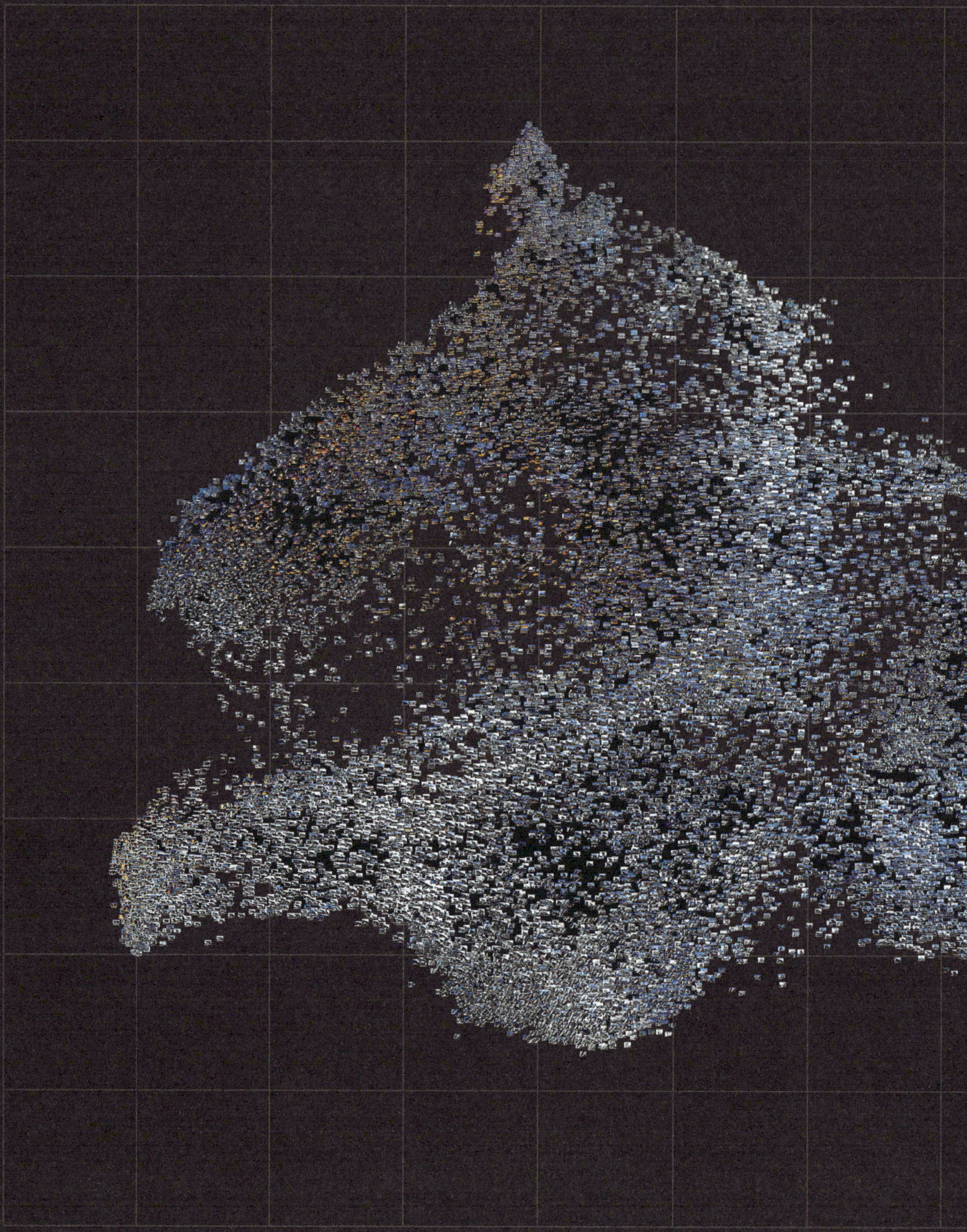

2

Snapshot of the latent space of the Deep Himmelblau network, a universe of design possibilities. Through a web-based interface, the system enables designers to engage with the Deep Himmelblau network in a very intuitive manner.

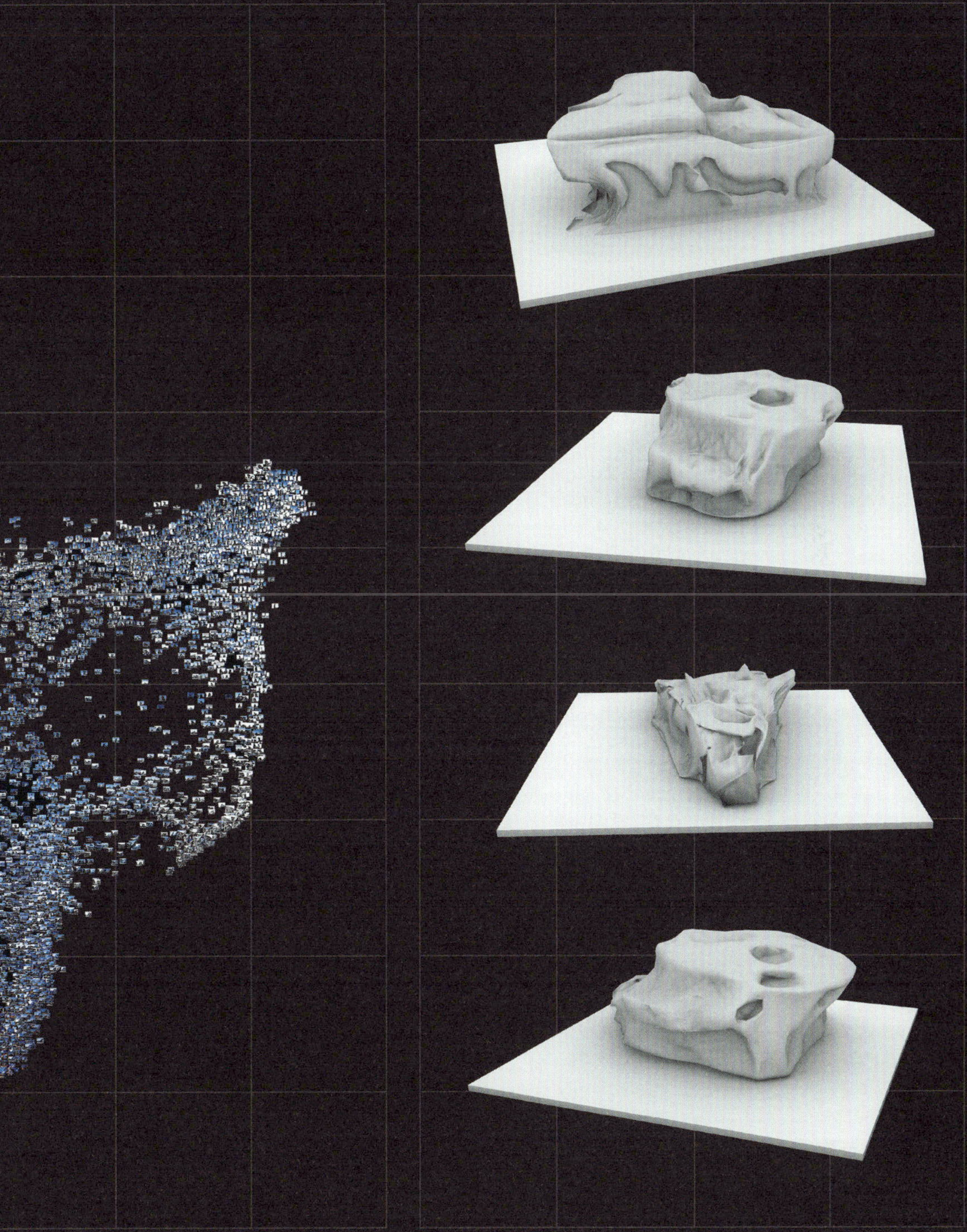

3

Geometry-based latent space snapshot. The novel 3D Deep Himmelblau network node recognizes projects in three dimensions and allows for formal interpolations. Not only is the network capable of generating high-quality 3D design samples, but it also gives users control over the produced samples at different design stages by adjusting the style of latent vectors and noise.

AI is also used in your practice to address environmental performance. How exactly?

CH — We have found a way to leverage AI to enhance our approach to environmental performance, particularly by integrating it into the early stages of design where rapid, informed decision-making can have a significant impact. One specific way we've applied AI is by developing tools that provide quick, rough environmental simulations based on minimal inputs, such as a physical model or a sketch. Traditionally, analyzing a design's environmental performance — say, solar exposure, wind flow, or energy efficiency — requires a precise, digitized or parametric model, a process that can take time to set up. Our aim with AI is to collapse that timeline, delivering immediate, approximate feedback that designers can use to guide conceptual development without disrupting creative flow.

As AI has matured over the past ten years, how has Deep Himmelblau evolved and improved? What challenges have you encountered along the way?

CH — Over the past decade, Deep Himmelblau has evolved from a nascent exploration into a sophisticated, integral part of our design process. This evolution mirrors the broader advancements in AI, particularly the emergence of powerful tools like GANs and stable diffusion models, which we've progressively integrated into our workflow. As AI capabilities expand, so do our applications. This growth reflects our ability to adapt cutting-edge technologies to our needs, expanding the scope and depth of what Deep Himmelblau can achieve. Improvements have been both technical and conceptual. Technologically, we've refined our tools to leverage newer models, such as GANs, which offer richer generative potential, and stable diffusion, which enhances accessibility through intuitive outputs. Conceptually, we've honed our modular approach, building a network of recombinable nodes that address specific design tasks — from rough environmental simulations to detailed structural refinements. Interestingly, progress hasn't always meant adopting the latest models outright. We've found that some earlier AI systems, with their less polished, more abstract outputs, preserve an openness of interpretation that aligns better with our exploratory ethos than the hyper-realistic results of newer models. This selective adoption keeps the process dynamic and avoids overreliance on realism at the expense of creativity.

Despite these advancements, significant challenges have persisted, particularly around accessibility and democratization within the office. Developing user-friendly interfaces and fostering AI literacy across the office are critical hurdles we continue to address, aiming to empower all designers to leverage Deep Himmelblau independently.

Another challenge has been balancing innovation with relevance. The rapid pace of AI development tempts one to chase the latest breakthroughs, but we've learned to evaluate each advancement critically — asking how it fits the bigger vision rather than adopting it for novelty's sake. This discernment ensures that Deep Himmelblau evolves in step with our practice, not ahead of it, preserving the synergy between tool and designer.

What is AI still missing in terms of supporting your design process? Given the central role of 3D in Coop Himmelb(l)au's work, where do current AI tools still fall short? Your office has experimented with 3D latent spaces — have those experiments proven fruitful?

CH — Our experiments with 3D latent spaces and generating point clouds from 2D images have shown promise as a generative tool. For instance, we've trained models to interpret a sketch and produce thousands of 3D interpretations, offering a wealth of formal possibilities in a point-cloud format. These experiments have been fruitful for early-stage ideation, providing rapid, abstract 3D (Fig. 3) extrapolations that spark creative dialogue. However, the results often remain too speculative or "fake," lacking the coherence and precision needed for practical application. For quick renderings in acquisition projects, this imprecision can be a hindrance, producing visuals that don't hold up under scrutiny. More critically, in our real design work, jumping straight from an image to a 3D model risks bypassing essential steps that we meticulously develop through iterative processes.

The push for 3D capabilities sometimes feels like a desire for instant objects, sidestepping the intellectual and creative labor that defines practice. We often find ourselves wary of this fixation on 3D, as it can reduce design to a superficial deliverable — a shiny model — rather than a reasoned solution. Current AI excels at "System 1" tasks (to borrow from **Kahneman's book "Thinking, Fast and Slow"**), offering instinctive responses based on past data, like interpolating historical forms. Yet, it lacks the "System 2" capacity for slow, intentional reasoning through novel problems — crucial for navigating the third dimension in a way that respects process. Without this, AI struggles to move beyond generative novelty to support the full spectrum of design, from concept to realization. It lacks the ability to fully engage the third dimension with depth and to reason through our process demands. Our 3D latent space experiments have been a fruitful step, enriching ideation, but they fall short of replacing the hands-on synthesis we rely on. As AI matures particularly toward agentic, reasoning-capable systems, we anticipate it will better support our node-based system and 3D-centric workflow, enhancing rather than shortcutting the complexity that defines architecture.

3 Kahneman, Thinking, Fast and Slow, 2011.

Finally, looking ahead: Coop Himmelb(l)au has often anticipated how architecture would evolve in response to past waves of technological change. As AI continues to scale, what new traits do you think architecture will inherit from it?

CH — Rather than focusing solely on visible formal changes, we envision AI ushering in deeper, systemic qualities: agency, differentiation, and a redefined creative partnership that will fundamentally alter how architecture is conceived and practiced.

One prominent trait will be agency, propelled by the rise of agentic AI — systems capable of reasoning and acting with intentionality. To date, AI has largely augmented our process, enhancing ideation or optimization as a tool under human direction. As it matures into a co-creator, architecture will inherit a dynamic where AI actively participates in decision-making.

Another trait will be differentiation, amplifying the divide between innovative and generic architecture. AI's accessibility risks homogenizing design in uninformed hands. Conversely, other practices, rooted in exploration and criticality, will leverage AI to push boundaries further. The gap between these paths will widen: AI as a commodity will streamline routine building, while AI as a creative partner will empower bold, context-specific work. For Coop Himmelb(l)au, this means sharper clarity in what architecture can be. Less a product of rote automation, more a synthesis of human vision and machine insight, amplifying our legacy of innovation.

A third trait could be process fluidity, redefining how architecture evolves from concept to realization. With AI deployed at scale, the discipline might inherit a seamless integration of ideation, analysis, and execution — blurring traditional phases. Our experiments with rapid environmental simulations or 3D latent spaces hint at this, collapsing timelines and embedding performance into early sketches. As AI gains agency, this fluidity could extend further, enabling real-time adaptation to site, client, or material shifts, making architecture more responsive and alive. Scaled AI could elevate techniques of openness and flexibility into a near-instinctive dialogue between designer, tool, and context. We speak and the building reverberates. Looking ahead, architecture will inherit duality: a tool for efficiency in the mainstream, and a catalyst for unprecedented creativity among the visionary.

REFERENCES

From Sketch to AI
[Video]

K. Schmidbaur and E. Baseta, IAAC Lecture Series, 2022

From Decon to AI
[Video]

Wolf D. Prix and Dragoş Bolojan with Thom Mayne, 2020

Deep Himmelblau
[Website]

AI at Coop Himmelb(l)au

Sequence by Deep Himmelblau
[Video]

Work by Coop Himmelb(l)au, 2020

Closing Remarks

It is increasingly evident that the exploratory phase of the early 2020s — a period marked by rapid experimentation and speculative engagement with AI — now lies behind us. We have entered what may be more aptly described as the adoption phase of AI within architecture.

Where once we saw isolated prototypes and early proofs-of-concept, we now witness fully integrated tools supplanting them. Experimental workflows have matured into standardized practices, and the early community of pioneers and tinkerers has given way to a much broader and more diverse body of adopters, ranging from practitioners and educators to commercial developers and institutional stakeholders.

It is within this evolved context that we conclude this second edition not with finality, but with a set of convictions that we believe are essential for the immediate future of our field.

First and foremost, AI remains in flux. Despite speculation about the onset of an "AI winter" — a period of stagnation or diminishing returns — the short-term trajectory of this technology remains decidedly dynamic. AI does not seem to have reached a stable endpoint just yet; rather, it continues to evolve rapidly. In the near term, we can expect further technological refinements that will reshape both the capabilities of AI itself and its modes of application in architecture. In other words, the dust has not settled yet, and our discipline stands to witness a host of additional contributions — technical, conceptual, and operational — in the coming years.

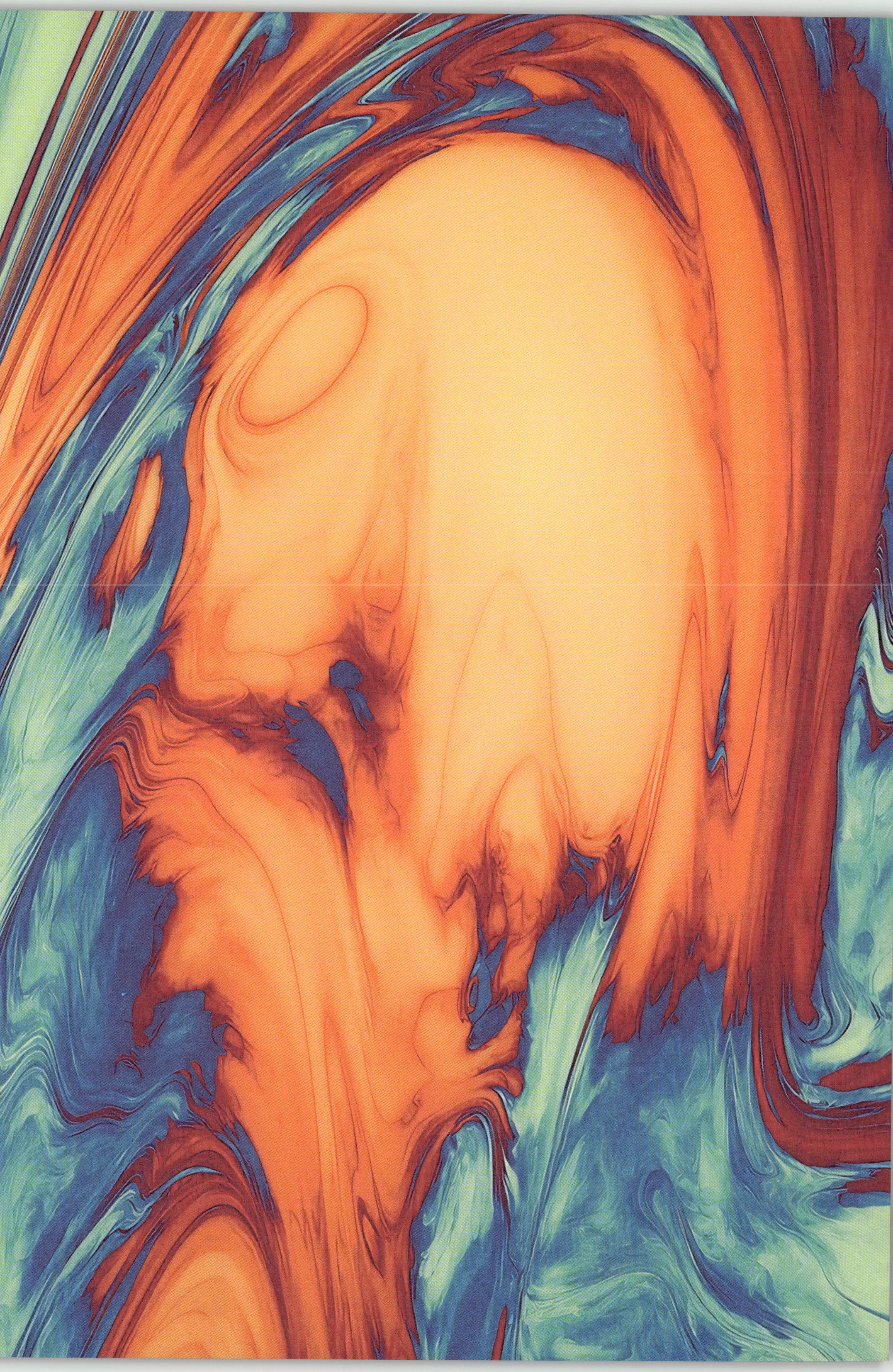

Second, a critical inflection point looms on the horizon: the capacity of AI to natively generate three-dimensional content and vector-based outputs. Achieving this milestone will be pivotal in determining the relevance and depth of AI integration into architectural practice. Surpassing this threshold is not merely a technical achievement but a fundamental requirement if AI is to meaningfully engage with the spatial and formal complexities inherent to architectural design. Reaching this goal will likely define a new chapter in the field's relationship with computational technologies.

Third — and perhaps most crucially — we are beginning to observe a deeper shift in focus. As AI becomes increasingly commoditized, the emphasis is shifting from raw generative capabilities toward control, refinement, and precision. The next wave of innovation in architecture will hinge upon the development of interfaces and workflows that bridge the gap between the rough, unstructured outputs of current AI models and the nuanced, deliberate articulations required by architectural designers. In this light, the pressing task for technologists and developers is clear: to build workflows and interfaces that level up the controllability of AI models, so as to better serve the design process. This imperative constitutes today a new frontier for technological innovation within our industry.

Beyond these short-term trends, it is essential to understand AI within the broader epistemic transformation it heralds for our discipline. The revolution we are witnessing is not solely defined by the adoption of novel tools or methodologies; it reflects a deeper shift in architectural thinking. At the core of this transformation lies AI's growing capacity to construct statistical mappings across domains that were previously unconnected — linking disparate mediums, scales, typologies, and levels of abstraction in unprecedented ways.

This capability marks the emergence of a significant new moment in architecture, one that echoes similar upheavals in other creative disciplines. As argued a few years back and again here, this broader shift can be encapsulated by the term "Semanticism": a conceptual framework that foregrounds the renewed importance of the semantic dimension in architectural production. Semanticism offers a name for this era — a moment in which meaning, interpretation, and symbolic intention regain centrality, catalyzed by AI's distinctive ability to operate across multiple registers and domains.

Thus, this paradigm invites practitioners to critically engage with the epistemic underpinnings of this technological turn, while also inspiring them to harness AI's potential with intentionality, rigor, and creativity. This new period is more than a mere trend — it is one of epistemic reorientation, signaling new directions for how architecture might be conceived, practiced, and understood in the decades to come.

Finally, we hope this book will help architects in situating themselves, helping them understand their place within this ongoing revolution across creative fields and guiding their approach to these times of change. If anything, this second edition aspires to serve as a provisional map for practitioners in navigating the seemingly messy and unstructured AI scene of the decade. Though it may soon become outdated as AI rapidly matures, it will hopefully serve, for a time, as a valuable entry point into this fast-moving technological landscape.

Index

Contributors

Andrew Witt

Andrew Witt is Associate Professor in Practice of Architecture at the Harvard Graduate School of Design.
His teaching and research examine the relationship between geometry, machines, perception, design, construction, and culture. He is also co-founder of Certain Measures, a design and technology studio based in Boston and Berlin.

Carlo Ratti

Carlo Ratti is an architect, urbanist, and professor at the Massachusetts Institute of Technology where he directs the Senseable City Lab. His work investigates intelligent systems at the convergence of natural and artificial environments. Ratti was appointed curator of the 19th International Architecture Exhibition of La Biennale di Venezia (2025), titled "Intelligens. Natural. Artificial. Collective." The exhibition explores the presence of AI in architecture.

Mario Carpo

Mario Carpo is an architectural historian and critic. He is the Reyner Banham Professor of Architectural History and Theory at the Bartlett School of Architecture, University College London, and Professor Emeritus of Architectural Theory at the Institute of Architecture of the University of Applied Arts Vienna (die Angewandte), where he held a professorship until the end of 2023. His research and publications focus on the history of early modern architecture and the theory and criticism of contemporary design and digital technologies.

Phillip Bernstein

Phillip Bernstein is Deputy Dean and Adjunct Professor at the Yale School of Architecture. He was formerly a vice president at Autodesk, where he led the company's vision and strategy for architecture, engineering, and construction technologies. He is the author of several books on architectural practice and technology, including "Architecture | Design | Data – Practice Competency in the Era of Computation" (Birkhäuser, 2018) and "Machine Learning: Architectural Futures in the Era of Artificial Intelligence" (RIBA, 2022).

Foster + Partners Applied R+D Team

The Applied Research and Development (R+D) Team at Foster + Partners is a multidisciplinary group of architects and engineers. Its expertise spans art, aerospace engineering, computer science, landscape architecture, structural engineering, and applied mathematics.

Immanuel Koh

Immanuel Koh holds a joint appointment as Assistant Professor in Architecture & Sustainable Design (ASD) and Design & Artificial Intelligence (DAI) at the Singapore University of Technology and Design, where he also directs Artificial-Architecture. He earned his PhD at the École polytechnique fédérale de Lausanne (EPFL), conducting research at both the School of Computer and Communication Sciences and the Institute of Architecture.

Aaron Hertzmann

Aaron Hertzmann is a Principal Scientist at Adobe Research and Affiliate Faculty at the University of Washington. He is widely recognized for his contributions to computer vision and machine learning, as well as for his theoretical work at the intersection of computer science and visual art. He spent ten years as a professor at the University of Toronto and has worked at Pixar Animation Studios, Microsoft Research, the Mitsubishi Electric Research Laboratories, and Interval Research Corporation.

Coop Himmelb(l)au

COOP HIMMELB(L)AU is an architecture studio founded in 1968 in Vienna by Wolf D. Prix, Helmut Swiczinsky, and Michael Holzer. Under Prix' leadership, the firm became the first in the world to develop an in-house architectural AI, Deep Himmelblau, launched in 2017. Partner and Head of Research Karolin Schmidbaur and computer specialist Daniel Bolojan lead the development of the project.

Anastasis Germanidis

Anastasis Germanidis is Co-Founder and Chief Technology Officer of Runway, one of the world's leading companies applying deep learning to audiovisual content in the arts, creative, and design industries. He is also a machine learning researcher with a background in engineering and interactive art, trained at New York University.

Image Credits

Chapter I

Fig. 1 by the author
Fig. 2 @ AT&T; photographer: Jack St
Fig. 3 @N. Museum of the U.S. Navy
Fig. 4 @DTIC
Fig. 5 @Wikimedia Commons
Fig. 6 @Wikimedia Commons
Fig. 7 @Wikimedia Commons
Fig. 8 by the author
Fig. 9 @B.G. Buchanan and E.H. Shortliffe
Fig. 10 @SERC
Fig. 11 @Wikimedia Commons
Fig. 12 @Krizhevsky et al.
Fig. 13 @ImageNet
Fig. 14 @Wikimedia Commons
Fig. 15 @Kingma et al.
Fig. 16 @MNIST
Fig. 17 @Isola et al.
Fig. 18 @Nvidia Research
Fig. 19 @Ho et al.
Fig. 20 @OpenAI

Chapter II

Fig. 1 by the author
Fig. 2 @Wikimedia Commons
Fig. 3 @Wikimedia Commons
Fig. 4 @Wikimedia Commons
Fig. 5 @Wikimedia Commons
Fig. 6 @Moshe Safdie Architects
Fig. 7 @Electronic edition of Sutherland's Sketchpad dissertation, image adapted to format
Fig. 8 by the author
Fig. 9 @Wikimedia Commons
Fig. 10 @Carol M. Highsmith Archive, Library of Congress
Fig. 11 @Wikimedia Commons
Fig. 12 ACSLM, project 162, f. 3048, 3056, 3055, 3057, Concession #: 1709/2025.
Fig. 13 Kartal Pendik Masterplan Render @ Zaha Hadid Architects.
Fig. 14 @Coop Himmelblau
Fig. 15 by the author
Fig. 16 Negroponte, Nicholas., The Architecture Machine, Figs. p. 80, © 1970 Massachusetts Institute of Technology, by permission of The MIT Press.
Fig. 17 Negroponte, Nicholas., The Architecture Machine, Figs. p. 76, © 1970 Massachusetts Institute of Technology, by permission of The MIT Press.

Fig. 18 @Cedric Price fonds, Canadian Architecture Archives
Fig. 19 @Cedric Price fonds, Canadian Architecture Archives

Chapter III

Fig. 1 by the author
Fig. 2 by the author
Fig. 3 by the author
Fig. 4 by the author
Fig. 5 by the author
Fig. 6 by the author
Fig. 7 by the author
Fig. 8 by the author
Fig. 9 by the author
Fig. 10 by the author
Fig. 11 by the author
Fig. 12 by the author
Fig. 13 by the author
Fig. 14 by the author
Fig. 15 by the author
Fig. 16 by the author
Fig. 17 by the author
Fig. 18 by the author
Fig. 19 by the author
Fig. 20 by the author
Fig. 21 by the author
Fig. 22 by the author
Fig. 23 by the author
Fig. 24 by the author
Fig. 25 @Shabani et al.
Fig. 26 @Galanos
Fig. 27 @Du et al.
Fig. 28 @J. van Lith
Fig. 29 by the author
Fig. 30 by the author
Fig. 31 @Blockade Labs
Fig. 32 @Danhaive et al.
Fig. 33 @Lu et al.
Fig. 34 @Sosnovik et al.
Fig. 35 @Foster + Partners
Fig. 36 @Chronis
Fig. 37 @Autodesk Forma
Fig. 38 @Wu et al
Fig. 39 @Zhuang et al.
Fig. 40 @Hektar
Fig. 41 by the author
Fig. 42 @Xu et al.
Fig. 43 @Runway
Fig. 44 @WorldLabs

Chapter IV

Fig. 1 by the author
Fig. 2 @J. Gips & G.Stiny.
Fig. 2 by the author, after W. J. Mitchell
Fig. 3 by the author, after W. J. Mitchell
Fig. 4 by the author
Fig. 5 after Charles Jencks's "Semantic Map," '69
Fig. 6 by the author

Chapter V

Fig. 1 by the author
Fig. 2 @LAION

Fig. 1 Image courtesy of Hart Howerton
Fig. 2 @Bernstein
Fig. 2-a @Bernstein
Fig. 2-b @Bernstein
Fig. 2-c @Bernstein
Fig. 2-d @Bernstein
Fig. 2-e @Bernstein
Fig. 3 @Bernstein

Fig. 1 Image courtesy of Certain Measures
Fig. 2 Image courtesy of Certain Measure
Fig. 3 Image courtesy of Certain Measures.

Fig. 1 Image courtesy of Runway
Fig. 2 Image courtesy of Runway
Fig. 3 Image courtesy of Runway
Fig. 4 Image courtesy of Runway

Fig. 1 @Koh
Fig. 2 @Koh
Fig. 3 @Koh
Fig. 4 @Koh

Fig. 1 @Hertzmann
Fig. 2 @Hertzmann
Fig. 3 @wikicommons
Fig. 4 @ImageNet

Fig. 1 @Foster + Partners
Fig. 2 @Foster + Partners

Fig. 1 @Coop Himmelb(l)au
Fig. 2 @Coop Himmelb(l)au
Fig. 3 @Coop Himmelb(l)au

References

Chapter I

1. Frank Rosenblatt, "The Design of an Intelligent Automaton," ONR Research Reviews 6, no.2, 1958: 245–260.

2. Warren S. McCullock and Walter Pitts, "A Logical Calculus of the Ideas Immanent in Nervous Activity," Bulletin of Mathematical Biophysics 5 (1943): 115–133.

3. Nokia Bell Labs, "1956 Nobel Prize in Physics," accessed May 8, 2025, https://www.nokia.com/bell-labs/about/awards/1956-nobel-prize-physics/.

4. "New Navy Device Learns by Doing," New York Times, July 8, 1958.

5. John McCarthy, Marvin L. Minsky, Nathaniel Rochester, and Claude E. Shannon, "A Proposal for the Dartmouth Summer Research Project on Artificial Intelligence," AI Magazine 27, no. 4 (2006): 12–14. Originally published on August 31, 1955.

6. Joseph Weizenbaum, "ELIZA — A Computer Program for the Study of Natural Language Communication Between Man and Machine," Communications of the ACM 9, no. 1 (1966): 36–45.

7. Herbert A. Simon and Allen Newell, "Heuristic Problem Solving: The Next Advance Operations Research," Operations Research 6, no. 1 (1958), 1–10.

8. Marvin Minsky & Seymour A. Papert, Perceptrons: An Introduction to Computational Geometry (Cambridge, MA: MIT Press, 1969).

9. James Lighthill, "Artificial Intelligence: A General Survey," in Artificial Intelligence: A Paper Symposium, Science Research Council, 1973.

10. James Lighthill, "Artificial Intelligence: A General Survey," in Artificial Intelligence: A Paper Symposium, Science Research Council, 1973, part 1, 8.

11. Bruce G. Buchanan and Edward H. Shortliffe, Rule-Based Expert Systems: The MYCIN Experiments of the Stanford Heuristic Programming Project (Reading, MA: Addison-Wesley, 1984).

12. Cynthia Matuszek et al., "An Introduction to the Syntax and Content of Cyc," in Proceedings of the AAAI Spring Symposium on Formalizing and Compiling Background Knowledge and Its Applications to Knowledge Representation and Question Answering, 2006.

13. John McCarthy, "Some Expert Systems Need Common Sense," Annals of the New York Academy of Sciences 426, no. 1 (1984): 129–137.

14. Monty Newborn, Deep Blue: An Artificial Intelligence Milestone (New York: Springer, 2002).

15. Sebastian Thrun, et al., "Stanley: The Robot That Won the DARPA Grand Challenge," in The 2005 DARPA Grand Challenge: The Great Robot Race, ed. Martin Buehler, Karl Iagnemma, and Sanjiv Singh (Berlin: Springer, 2006), 1–43.

16. Alex Krizhevsky, Ilya Sutskever, and Geoffrey E. Hinton, "ImageNet Classification with Deep Convolutional Neural Networks," in Advances in Neural Information Processing Systems 25 (2012): 1097–1105.

17. David Silver et al., "Mastering the Game of Go with Deep Neural Networks and Tree Search," Nature 529 (2016): 484–489.

18. Wooseok Hwang et al., "Comprehensive Study on Molecular Supervised Learning with Graph Neural Networks," Journal of Chemical Information and Modeling 60, no. 12 (2020): 5936–5945.

19. Abhishek Rawat, Akshay Sinha, and Suryakant Patil, "A Novel Topology Optimization Approach Using Conditional Deep Learning," in Proceedings of the International Conference on Advances in Computing, Communication and Control, 2019.

20. Diederik P. Kingma and Max Welling, "Auto-Encoding Variational Bayes," arXiv:1312.6114 (2013).

21. Ian Goodfellow et al., "Generative Adversarial Networks," arXiv:1406.2661 (2014).

22. Tero Karras et al., "A Style-Based Generator Architecture for Generative Adversarial Networks," arXiv:1812.04948 (2018).

23. Andrew Brock, Jeff Donahue, and Karen Simonyan, "Large Scale GAN Training for High Fidelity Natural Image Synthesis," arXiv:1809.11096 (2018).

24. Jonathan Ho, Ajay Jain, and Pieter Abbeel, "Denoising Diffusion Probabilistic Models," arXiv:2006.11239 (2020).

25. Ashish Vaswani et al., "Attention Is All You Need," arXiv:1706.03762 (2017).

26. Center for Research on Foundation Models, On the Opportunities and Risks of Foundation Models (Stanford Institute for Human-Centered Artificial Intelligence, 2021), https://crfm.stanford.edu/report.html.

Chapter II

1. A. M. Seelow, "The Construction Kit and the Assembly Line: Walter Gropius' Concepts for Rationalizing Architecture," Arts 7, no. 4 (2018): 95.

2. M. M. Cohen and A. Prosina, "Buckminster Fuller's Dymaxion House as a Paradigm for a Space Habitat," ASCEND (2020): 4048.

3. Le Corbusier, Le Modulor: Essai sur une mesure harmonique à l'échelle humaine applicable universellement à l'architecture et à la mécanique (Boulogne: Éditions de l'Architecture d'Aujourd'hui, 1950).

4. Moshe Safdie, For Everyone a Garden (Cambridge, MA: MIT Press, 1974).

5. Simon Sadler, Architecture Without Architecture (Cambridge, MA: MIT Press, 2005).

6. Wayne E. Carlson, Computer Graphics and Computer Animation: A Retrospective Overview (Columbus: The Ohio State University, 2005), https://ohiostate.pressbooks.pub/graphicshistory/ (accessed May 9, 2025).

7. Ivan Sutherland, "Sketchpad: A Man-Machine Graphical Communication

System," Simulation 2, no. 5 (1964): R-3.

8. Pierre Bézier, "Essai de définition numérique des courbes et des surfaces expérimentales, PhD diss., Université Pierre et Marie Curie, 1977.

9. Pierre Bézier, "Example of an Existing System in the Motor Industry: The Unisurf System," Proceedings of the Royal Society of London. A. Mathematical and Physical Sciences 321, no. 1545 (1971): 207–218.

10. Nicholas Negroponte, The Architecture Machine: Toward a More Human Environment (Cambridge, MA: MIT Press, 1970).

11. Nicholas Negroponte, "Toward a Theory of Architecture Machines," Journal of Architectural Education 23, no. 2 (1969): 9–12.

12. John Haymaker and Martin Fischer, "Challenges and Benefits of 4D Modeling on the Walt Disney Concert Hall Project" CIFE Working Paper no. 64 (Stanford, CA: Center for Integrated Facility Engineering, Stanford University, 2001), https://stacks.stanford.edu/file/druid%3Afw529qc5108/WP064.pdf (accessed May 9, 2025).

13. Deepa Narayanan, "Gehry Technologies: a Case Study,"MIT Media Lab, 2006, http://alumni.media.mit.edu/~tmcleish/arch497_DDF/Research/Narayanan,%20Deepa.%20%20Gehry%20Technologies.pdf (accessed June 1, 2025).

14. Luigi Moretti, "Parametrica Architettura," in Dizionario Enciclopedico di Architettura e Urbanistica (Rome: Istituto Editoriale Romano, 1968), 136–137.

15. Ivan Sutherland, "Sketchpad: A Man-Machine Graphical Communication System," Simulation 2, no. 5 (1964): R-3.

16. John Teresko, "Parametric Technology Corp.: Changing the way Products are Designed," Industry Week, December 20, 1993.

17. Patrik Schumacher, "Parametricism: A New Global Style for Architecture and Urban Design," Architectural Design 79, no. 4 (2009): 14–23.

18. David Rutten, "Computing Architectural Concepts: Grasshopper Stories," lecture, Architectural Association School of Architecture, YouTube video, 1:07:37, March 31, 2010, https://www.youtube.com/watch?v=KaJfUPk1qNs (accessed May 9, 2025).

19. Autodesk, Building Information Modeling: White Paper (San Rafael, CA: Autodesk, 2002).

20. Chuck Eastman, Paul Teicholz, Rafael Sacks, and Kathleen Liston, BIM Handbook: A Guide to Building Information Modeling for Owners, Managers, Designers, Engineers and Contractors (Hoboken, NJ: Wiley, 2011).

21. Nicholas Negroponte, The Architecture Machine: Toward a More Human Environment (Cambridge, MA: MIT Press, 1970).

22. Samantha Hardingham, Price Works 1952–2003, A Forward-Minded Retrospective (London: AA Publications, 2016), 447–470.

23. Francisco Furtado et al., "Cedric Price's Generator and the Frazers' Systems Research," Technoetic Arts: A Journal of Speculative Research 6, no. 1 (2008), 55–72.

24. "Artificial Intelligence and Architecture," Pavillon de l'Arsenal, Paris, 2019, https://www.pavillon-arsenal.com/en/expositions/11466-artificial-intelligence-architecture.html (accessed May 9, 2025).

25. "2025 Venice Architecture Biennale," La Biennale di Venezia, https://www.labiennale.org/en/architecture/2025 (accessed May 9, 2025).

26. Royal Institute of British Architects, "No Turning Back: 41% of Architects Now Using AI," RIBA AI Report (2024).

Chapter III

AI 101

1. Andrew Witt, "Grayboxing," Log 43 (2018): 69–77.

2. Jascha Sohl-Dickstein, Eric A. Weiss, Niru Maheswaranathan, and Surya Ganguli, "Deep Unsupervised Learning Using Nonequilibrium Thermodynamics," arXiv:1503.03585 (2015).

3. Jonathan Ho, Ajay Jain, and Pieter Abbeel, "Denoising Diffusion Probabilistic Models," arXiv:2006.11239 (2020).

4. Ashish Vaswani, Noam Shazeer, Niki Parmar, Jakob Uszkoreit, Llion Jones, Aidan N. Gomez, Lukasz Kaiser, Illia Polosukhin, "Attention Is All You Need," arXiv:1706.03762 (2017).

5. Diederik P. Kingma and Max Welling, "Auto-Encoding Variational Bayes," 2013, arXiv:1312.6114 (2013).

6. Epoch AI, "Compute Trends Across Three Eras of Machine Learning," 2022, https://epochai.org/blog/compute-trends.

7. Rishi Bommasani et al., "On the Opportunities and Risks of Foundation Models," arXiv:2108.07258 (2021).

8. Epoch AI, "Algorithmic Progress in Language Models," 2024, https://epochai.org/blog/algorithmic-progress-in-language-models.

9. Epoch AI, "Trends in Machine Learning Hardware," 2023, https://epochai.org/blog/trends-in-machine-learning-hardware.

Applications

1. Nelson Nauata, Kai-Hung Chang, Chin-Yi Cheng, and Yasutaka Furukawa, "House-GAN: Relational Generative Adversarial Networks for Graph-Constrained House Layout Generation," European Conference on Computer Vision, arXiv:2003.06988 (2020).

2. Stanislas Chaillou, "ArchiGAN: Artificial Intelligence x Architecture," in Architectural Intelligence, ed. Ming Tang and Xiangyu Wang (Singapore: Springer, 2020), 117–127, https://doi.org/10.1007/978-981-15-6568-7_8.

3. Ziniu Luo and Ziniu Luo and Weixin Huang, "FloorplanGAN: Vector Residential Floorplan Adversarial Generation," Automation in Construction 142 (2022): 104470, https://doi.org/10.1016/j.autcon.2022.104470.

4. Kyle Steinfeld, "Imaging Place Using Generative Adversarial Networks (GAN Loci)," paper presented at ACADIA 2019: Ubiquity and Autonomy, University of Texas at Austin, October 24–26, 2019. Also published in Machine Learning and the City: Applications in Architecture and Urban Design, ed. Silvio Carta (Hoboken, NJ: Wiley, 2022), 513–516.

5. Shengyu Meng, "Exploring in the Latent Space of Design: A Method of Plausible Building Facade Images Generation, Properties Control and Model Explanation Based on StyleGAN2," in Proceedings of the 2021 DigitalFUTURES: The 3rd International Conference on Computational Design and Robotic Fabrication (CDRF 2021), 55–68 (Singapore: Springer, 2022), https://doi.org/10.1007/978-981-16-5983-6_6.

6. Mohammad Amin Shabani, Sepidehsadat Hosseini, and Yasutaka Furukawa, "HouseDiffusion: Vector Floorplan Generation via a Diffusion Model with Discrete and Continuous Denoising," November 2022, arXiv:2211.13287.

7. Shibo Hong, Xuhong Zhang, Tianyu Du, Sheng Cheng, Xun Wang, and Jianwei Yin, "Cons2Plan: Vector Floorplan Generation from Various Conditions via a Learning Framework Based on Conditional Diffusion Models," in Proceedings of the 32nd ACM International Conference on Multimedia (MM '24) (New York: Association for Computing Machinery, 2024), 3248–3256, https://doi.org/10.1145/3664647.3680681.

8. Hao Leng, Yuqing Gao, and Ying Zhou, "ArchiDiffusion: A Novel Diffusion Model Connecting Architectural Layout Generation from Sketches to Shear Wall Design," Journal of Building Engineering 98 (2024): 111373, https://doi.org/10.1016/j.jobe.2024.111373.

9. Theodoros Galanos, Antonios Liapis, and Georgios N. Yannakakis, "ArchiText: Language-Driven Generative Architecture Design," arXiv:2303.07519 (2023).

10. Zhi Hao Luo, Luis Lara, Ge Ya Luo, Florian Golemo, Christopher Beckham, Christopher Pal, "DStruct2Design: Data and Benchmarks for Data Structure Driven Generative Floor Plan Design," arXiv:2407.15723 (2024).

11. Changyu Du, Sebastian Esser, Stavros Nousias, and André Borrmann, "Text2BIM: Generating Building Models Using a Large Language Model-Based Multi-Agent Framework," arXiv:2408.08054 (2024).

12. Xinpeng Wang, Xinpeng Wang, Chandan Yeshwanth, Matthias Nießner, "SceneFormer: Indoor Scene Generation with Transformers," arXiv:2012.09793 (2021).

13. Despoina Paschalidou, Amlan Kar, Maria Shugrina, Karsten Kreis, Andreas Geiger, Sanja Fidler "ATISS: Autoregressive Transformers for Indoor Scene Synthesis," arXiv:2110.03675 (2021).

14. Yao Wei, Yao Wei, Martin Renqiang Min, George Vosselman, Li Erran Li, Michael Ying Yang, "Planner3D: LLM-

Enhanced Graph Prior Meets 3D Indoor Scene Explicit Regularization,"arX iv:2403.12848 (2024).

15. EDU-AI: a twofold machine learning model to support classroom layout generation, Karadag et al., 2022

16. Edward J. Hu et al., "LoRA: Low-Rank Adaptation of Large Language Models," arXiv:2106.09685 (2021).

17. Lvmin Zhang, Anyi Rao, and Maneesh Agrawala, "Adding Conditional Control to Text-to-Image Diffusion Models," arXiv:2302.05543 (2023).

18. Renaud Danhaive and Caitlin T. Mueller, "Design Subspace Learning: Structural Design Space Exploration Using Performance-Conditioned Generative Modeling," Automation in Construction 127 (2021): 103664, https://doi.org/10.1016/j.autcon.2021.103664.

19. Some research projects using VAEs for structural analysis; see Gabriele Mirra, Alberto Pugnale,"Comparison Between Human-Defined and AI-Generated Design Spaces for the Optimisation of Shell Structures," Structures 34 (2021): 2950–2961, https://doi.org/10.1016/j.istruc.2021.09.058.

20. Wenjie Liao, Xinzheng Lu, Yuli Huang, Zhe Zheng, Yuanqing Lin, "Automated Structural Design of Shear Wall Residential Buildings Using Generative Adversarial Networks," Automation in Construction 132 (2021): 103931, https://doi.org/10.1016/j.autcon.2021.103931.

21. Bochao Fu, Yuqing Gao, Wei Wang, "Dual Generative Adversarial Networks for Automated Component Layout Design of Steel Frame-Brace Structures," Automation in Construction 146 (2023):104661, https://doi.org/10.1016/j.autcon.2022.104661.

22. Zhenguo Nie, Tong Lin, Haoliang Jiang, Levent Burak Kara, "TopologyGAN: Topology Optimization Using Generative Adversarial Networks Based on Physical Fields Over the Initial Domain," Journal of Mechanical Design 143 (2021):1-13, https://doi.org/10.1115/1.4049533.

23. Zhou et al., "StructDiffusion: End-to-End Intelligent Shear Wall Structure Layout Generation and Analysis Using Diffusion Model," Engineering Structures 309 (2024):118068, https://doi.org/10.1016/j.engstruct.2024.118068.

24. François Mazé and Faez Ahmed, "Diffusion Models Beat GANs on Topology Optimization," Proceedings of the AAAI Conference on Artificial Intelligence 37, no. 8 (2023): 9108–16, https://doi.org/10.1609/aaai.v37i8.26093.

25. TransFrameNet: A transformer-based approach for generalized seismic performance prediction of building structures, Jiangpeng Shu, Jun Li, Hongchuan Yu, Hongmei Zhang, Wuhua Zeng, Journal of Building Engineering 96 (2024): 110628, https://doi.org/10.1016/j.jobe.2024.110628.

26. See the GitHub repository at https://github.com/mitevpi/daylight-gan.

27. Matias Quintana, Stefano Schiavon, Kwok Wai Tham, Clayton Miller, "Balancing Thermal Comfort Datasets: We GAN, but Should We?," arXiv:2009.13154 (2020).

28. Josef Musil, Jakub Knir, Athanasios Vitsas, and Irene Gallou, "Towards Sustainable Architecture: 3D Convolutional Neural Networks for Computational Fluid Dynamics Simulation and Reverse Design Workflow," arxiv:1912.02125 (2019).

29. Jung Min Han and Ali Malkawi, "Airvox: Efficient Computational Fluid Dynamics Prediction Using 3D Convolutional Neural Networks for Building Design," Journal of Building Performance Simulation 18, no. 1 (2024): 1–16, https://doi.org/10.1080/19401493.2024.2410744.

30. We recommend a quick read of Archetype's two-part article "What Is Physical AI?": https://www.archetypeai.io/blog/what-is-physical-ai.

31. Steven Jige Quan, "Urban-GAN: An Artificial Intelligence-Aided Computation System for Plural Urban Design," Environment and Planning B: Urban Analytics and City Science 49, no. 1 (May 2022): 23998083221100550, https://doi.org/10.1177/23998083221100550.

32. Abraham Noah Wu and Filip Biljecki, "GANmapper: Geographical Data Translation," International Journal of Geographical Information Science 36, no. 7 (2022): 1394–1422.

33. Xinyue Ye, Jiaxin Du, and Yu Ye, "MasterplanGAN: Facilitating the Smart Rendering of Urban Master Plans via Generative Adversarial Networks," Environment and Planning B: Urban Analytics and City Science 49, no. 3 (2021): 794–814, https://doi.org/10.1177/23998083211023516.

34. Abraham Noah Wu and Filip Biljecki, "InstantCITY: Synthesising Morphologically Accurate Geospatial Data for Urban Form Analysis, Transfer, and Quality Control," ISPRS Journal of Photogrammetry and Remote Sensing 195 (2023): 90–104, https://doi.org/10.1016/j.isprsjprs.2022.11.005.

35. Wei Gan et al., "UDGAN: A New Urban Design Inspiration Approach Driven by Using Generative Adversarial Networks," Journal of Computational Design and Engineering 11, no. 1 (February 2024): 305–324, https://doi.org/10.1093/jcde/qwae014.

36. Feifeng Jiang et al., "Automated Site Planning Using CAIN-GAN Model," Automation in Construction 159 (2024): 105286, https://doi.org/10.1016/j.autcon.2024.105286.

37. Liangliang Yang et al., "Street Layout Design via Conditional Adversarial Learning," arXiv:2305.08186 (2023).

38. Linning Xu et al., "BlockPlanner: City Block Generation with Vectorized Graph Representation," in Proceedings of the 2021 IEEE/CVF International Conference on Computer Vision (ICCV) (2021), 5057–66, https://doi.org/10.1109/ICCV48922.2021.00503.

39. Junling Zhuang et al., "Text-to-City: Controllable 3D Urban Block Generation with Latent Diffusion Model," Proceedings of the 29th International Conference of the Association for Computer-Aided Architectural Design Research in Asia (CAADRIA) (2024), https://doi.org/10.52842/conf.caadria.2024.2.169.

40. Fangshuo Zhou et al., "ControlCity: A Multimodal Diffusion Model Based Approach for Accurate Geospatial Data Generation and Urban Morphology Analysis," https://arxiv.org/html/2409.17049v1 (2024).

41. Alexander Kamenev, "Aino AI v1: First-Generation LLM for Geospatial Analysis," February 11, 2025, https://medium.com/aino-world/aino-ai-v1-first-generation-llm-for-geospatial-analysis-61e23c54d0c5.

42. Yao Wei, George Vosselman, and Michael Ying Yang, "BuildDiff: 3D Building Shape Generation Using Single-Image Conditional Point Cloud Diffusion Models," in Proceedings of the 2023 IEEE/CVF International Conference on Computer Vision Workshops (ICCVW) (2023), 2902–11, https://doi.org/10.1109/ICCVW60793.2023.00313.

43. Sanghi et al., "Sketch-A-Shape: Zero-Shot Sketch-to-3D Shape Generation," arXiv:2307.03869 (2023).

44. Xu et al., "BrepGen: A B-rep Generative Diffusion Model with Structured Latent Geometry," arXiv:2401.15563 (2024).

45. Jiadong Liang, Ximing Zhong, and Immanuel Koh, "Bridging BIM and AI: A Graph-BIM Encoding Approach for Detailed 3D Layout Generation Using Variational Graph Autoencode," in Proceedings of the 29th International Conference of the Association for Computer-Aided Architectural Design Research in Asia (CAADRIA) (2024), https://doi.org/10.52842/conf.caadria.2024.1.221.

46. Gao et al., "CAT3D: Create Anything in 3D with Multi-View Diffusion Models," arXiv:2405.10314 (2024).

47. Bensadoun et al., "Meta 3D Gen," arXiv:2407.02599 (2024).

48. Anastasis Germanidis, "Introducing General World Models," December 11, 2023, https://runwayml.com/research/introducing-general-world-models.

49. Wang et al., "WorldDreamer: Towards General World Models for Video Generation via Predicting Masked Tokens," arXiv:2401.09985v1 (2024).

50. Zhu et al., "Is Sora a World Simulator? A Comprehensive Survey on General World Models and Beyond," arXiv:2405.03520 (2024).

51. World Labs, "Generating Worlds," 2024, https://www.worldlabs.ai/blog.

52. Agarwal et al., "Cosmos World Foundation Model Platform for Physical AI," arXiv:2501.03575 (2025).

Chapter IV

1. Gottlob Frege, Begriffsschrift: eine der arithmetischen nachgebildete Formelsprache des reinen Denkens (Halle: Louis Nebert, 1879).

2. Alfred North Whitehead and Bertrand Russell, Principia Mathematica, Alfred North Whitehead and Bertrand Russell, 3

vols. (Cambridge: Cambridge University Press, 1910–1913).

3. Ferdinand de Saussure, Cours de linguistique générale, ed. Charles Bally and Albert Sechehaye (Lausanne and Paris: Payot, 1916).

4. Noam Chomsky, Syntactic Structures (The Hague: Mouton, 1957).

5. Tim Berners-Lee, "The Semantic Web," World Wide Web Consortium, September 2000, Tim Berners-Lee, 2000, https://www.w3.org/2000/Talks/0906-xmlweb-tbl/text.htm.

6. George Stiny and James Gips, Shape Grammars and the Generative Specification of Painting and Sculpture," in Information Processing '71, ed. C. V. Freiman (Amsterdam: North-Holland, 1972).

7. Patrik Schumacher, "Parametricism as Style: Parametricist Manifesto," paper presented at the 11th Venice Architecture Biennale, 2008, https://patrikschumacher.com/parametricism-as-style-parametricist-manifesto/.

8. Christopher Alexander, Sara Ishikawa, and Murray Silverstein, A Pattern Language: Towns, Buildings, Construction (New York: Oxford University Press, 1977).

9. Bill Hillier and Julienne Hanson, The Social Logic of Space (Cambridge: Cambridge University Press, 1984).

10. Charles Jencks, The Language of Post-Modern Architecture (New York: Rizzoli, 1977).

11. Umberto Eco, "Function and Sign: The Semiotics of Architecture," in The City and the Sign: An Introduction to Urban Semiotics, ed. Mark Gottdiener and Alexandros Ph. Lagopoulos (New York: Columbia University Press, 1986), 55–86.

12. Charles Jencks, "Semiology and Architecture," in Meaning in Architecture, ed. Charles Jencks and George Baird (London: Barrie & Jenkins, 1969), 10–25.

13. William J. Mitchell, "The Logic of Architecture," William J. Mitchell: Design, Computation, and Cognition (Cambridge, MA: MIT Press, 1990).

14. Andrew Witt, "Grayboxing," Log 43 (2018): 69–77.

Chapter V

P. Bernstein

1. Andrew Witt, Formulations: Architecture, Mathematics, Culture, Writing Architecture Series (Cambridge, MA: MIT Press, 2021), 36.

2. See references to the "Data Interstice" in Phil Bernstein, Machine Learning: Architecture in the Age of Artificial Intelligence (London: RIBA Publishing, 2022), 11ff.

3. Mario Carpo, Beyond Digital : Design and Automation at the End of Modernity (Cambridge, MA: MIT Press, 2023), 130.

4. The negligent management and control of the supply and delivery chain was the cause of the disastrous Grenfell Tower fire in 2017. For a phased report of the resulting investigation, see Grenfell Tower Inquiry, https://www.grenfelltowerinquiry.org.uk/ (accessed November 15, 2024).

5. Allison Nathan, "Gen AI: Too Much Spend, Too Little Benefit?," Top of Mind (New York: Goldman Sachs Group, Inc., 2024), 12.

6. The website "AI in AEC" purports to follow every AI-based tool for the building industry market. It currently lists almost 1,500 such applications. See https://stjepanmikulic.notion.site/AI-in-AEC-AEC-AI-Hub-b6e6eebe88094e0e9b4995da38e96768 (accessed 15 November 2024).

7. The construction industry has a longstanding reputation for diminishing productivity. For an interesting study of the underlying statistics, see Austan Goolsbee and Chad Syverson, "The Strange and Awful Path of Productivity in the U.S. Construction Sector" (National Bureau of Economic Research, 2023).

8. As described by MIT's Daron Acemoglu in Nathan, "Gen AI: Too Much Spend, Too Little Benefit?," Top of Mind (New York: Goldman Sachs Group, Inc., 2024), 4.

9. In the CAD era, AutoCAD's DWG file format served this role. Today, the Industry Foundation Classes (IFCs) move geometry and limited metadata between various applications. See "Industry Foundation Classes," buildingSMART, https://www.buildingsmart.org/standards/bsi-standards/industry-foundation-classes/ (accessed November 15, 2024).

A. Witt

1. Noam Chomsky, Syntactic Structures (The Hague: Mouton, 1957).

2. Ray Brassier, foreword to An Epistemology of Noise, by Michel Serres (Los Angeles: Errant Bodies Press, 2013), 7–12.

3. A. Aldo Faisal, Luc P. J. Selen, and Daniel M. Wolpert, "Noise in the Nervous System," Nature Reviews Neuroscience 9, no. 4 (April 2008): 292–303, https://doi.org/10.1038/nrn2258.

A. Germanidis

1. Anastasis Germanidis, "Introducing Gen-3 Alpha: A New Frontier for Video Generation," Runway Research, June 21, 2024, https://runwayml.com/research/introducing-gen-3-alpha (accessed May 9, 2025).

2. For a brief presentation of Runway's Gen-1 model, see: Runway, "Introducing Gen-1: The Next Step Forward for Generative AI," YouTube video, 1:49, February 6, 2023, https://www.youtube.com/watch?v=I4OeYcYf0Sc.

3. On the notion of scaling law, see "Neural Scaling Law," Wikipedia, last modified March 2025, https://en.wikipedia.org/wiki/Neural_scaling_law (accessed May 9, 2025).

4. On general world models, see Anastasis Germanidis, "Introducing General World Models," Runway Research, December 11, 2023, https://runwayml.com/research/introducing-general-world-models (accessed May 9, 2025).

5. Since our interview with Anastasis, Runway has released Gen-4. See "Introducing Runway Gen-4," Runway Research, March 31, 2025, https://runwayml.com/research/introducing-runway-gen-4 (accessed May 9, 2025).

A. Hertzmann

1. Aaron Hertzmann, Algorithms for Rendering in Artistic Styles (PhD diss, New York University, 2001).

2. Aaron Hertzmann, Charles E. Jacobs, Nuria Oliver, Brian Curless, and David H. Salesin, "Image Analogies," in Proceedings of the 28th Annual Conference on Computer Graphics and Interactive Techniques (SIGGRAPH 2001), 327–340.

3. Alumit Ishai, Sharon L. Fairhall, and Robert Pepperell, "Perception, Memory and Aesthetics of Indeterminate Art," Brain Research Bulletin 73, no. 1 (2007): 283–292.

4. Alexander Mordvintsev, Christopher Olah, and Mike Tyka, "DeepDream – A Code Example for Visualizing Neural Networks, Google Research Blog, July 1, 2015.

I. Koh

1. "Encode," Oxford Learner's Dictionaries, https://www.oxfordlearnersdictionaries.com/definition/english/encode (accessed May 7, 2025).

2. "Digitize," Oxford Learner's Dictionaries, https://www.oxfordlearnersdictionaries.com/definition/english/digitize (accessed May 7, 2025).

Coop Himmelb(l)au

1. See Deep Himmelblau presentation, Coop Himmelb(l)au, https://coop-himmelblau.at/method/deep-himmelblau/ (accessed May 6, 2025).

2. Jeff Hawkins, A Thousand Brains: A New Theory of Intelligence (New York: Basic Books, 2021).

3. Daniel Kahneman, Thinking, Fast and Slow (New York: Farrar, Straus and Giroux, 2011).